Danger and Vulnerability in Nineteenth-Century American Literature

Danger and Vulnerability in Nineteenth-Century American Literature

Crash and Burn

Jennifer Travis

LEXINGTON BOOKS
Lanham • Boulder • New York • London

Published by Lexington Books
An imprint of The Rowman & Littlefield Publishing Group, Inc.
4501 Forbes Boulevard, Suite 200, Lanham, Maryland 20706
www.rowman.com

Unit A, Whitacre Mews, 26-34 Stannary Street, London SE11 4AB

Copyright © 2018 by The Rowman & Littlefield Publishing Group, Inc.

All rights reserved. No part of this book may be reproduced in any form or by any electronic or mechanical means, including information storage and retrieval systems, without written permission from the publisher, except by a reviewer who may quote passages in a review.

British Library Cataloguing in Publication Information Available

Library of Congress Cataloging-in-Publication Data

Names: Travis, Jennifer, 1967- author.
Danger and vulnerability in the American imagination : crash and burn / Jennifer Travis.
Description: Lanham : Lexington Books, 2018. | Includes bibliographical references and index.
Identifiers: LCCN 2017058432 (print) | LCCN 2018021467 (ebook) | ISBN 9781498563420 (Electronic) | ISBN 9781498563413 (cloth : alk. paper) | ISBN 9781498563437 (paper : alk. paper)
Subjects: LCSH: American fiction--19th century--History and criticism. | Disasters in literature. | Risk in literature. | Vulnerability (Personality trait) in literature.
Classification: LLCC PS374.D53 (ebook) | LCC PS374.D53 T73 2018 (print) | DDC 810.9/003--dc23
LC record available at https://lccn.loc.gov/2017058432

For Mike, Miles, and Stuart, always

Table of Contents

List of Figures		ix
Acknowledgments		xi
Introduction: Crash and Burn		1
1	A "damsel-errant in quest of adventures": E. D. E. N. Southworth, Sensation, and the Law	19
2	Crash Lit: Trains, Pains, and Automobiles	43
3	"Hurts That Will Not Heal": Theodore Dreiser, Masculinity, and Railroad Labor	67
4	Burning Down the House: Comets, Hurricanes, and the Fire to Come	91
5	The Tremblor: Disaster and Vulnerability, San Francisco, 1906	117
Bibliography		135
Index		151
About the Author		161

List of Figures

Cover Art Collision on the Housatonic Railroad near Bridgeport, August 14, 1865, photographed by Jurgan Frederick Huge, wood engraved print on wove paper, museum purchase, 1979.46.16, the Connecticut Historical Society.

Figure 2.1 Art and Picture Collection, The New York Public Library. "In the Wake of a Cable Car." Edward Windsor Kemble, Artist (1894). Date Issued: 1895. New York Public Library Digital Collections. Accessed October 27, 2017. http://digitalcollections.nypl.org/items/510d47e1–05ea-a3d9-e040-e00a18064a99

Figure 4.1 Art and Picture Collection, The New York Public Library. "Saving lives at a tenement-house fire [(a]n actual scene)." Andrew Varick Stout, Artist (1899). New York Public Library Digital Collections. Accessed October 24, 2017. http://digitalcollections.nypl.org/items/510d47e0-cdd2-a3d9-e040-e00a18064a99

Figure 4.2 The Miriam and Ira D. Wallach Division of Art, Prints and Photographs: Print Collection, The New York Public Library. "The Life of a Fireman: The Metropolitan System." Currier & Ives, Lithographer. Date Issued: 1866. New York Public Library Digital Collections. Accessed October 24, 2017. http://digitalcollections.nypl.org/items/8f4d2673–795a-28c1-e040-e00a18061ade

Acknowledgments

I started this project at a time of hope and finished at a time of danger and vulnerability. It has been impossible to write about these topics in the long nineteenth century and not be consumed with their currency in our contemporary political climate, where misogyny, racism, nativism, anti-environmentalism, anti-intellectualism, ignorance, and profound malevolence have taken hold of our political institutions and, by extension, our nation. Writing this book has been a source of some solace; reading literature, a reminder that art, at its best, can awaken its audience and animate activism. I am grateful for the good cheer (even in dark times) of my friends and colleagues at St. John's: Dohra Ahmad, Steven Alvarez, Lee Anne Brown, Gabe Brownstein, Raj Chetty, Scott Combs, Bob Fanuzzi, Bob Forman, G. Ganter, Anne Geller, Rachel Hollander, Amy King, Brian Lockey, John Lowney, Kathy Lubey, Greg Maertz, Steve Mentz, Stephen Paul Miller, Melissa Mowry, Derek Owens, Nicole Rice, LaToya Sawyer, Steve Sicari, Shanté Paradigm Smalls, Elda Tsou, and Lana Umali. I always look forward to catching up with Anne Geller at Acquista Trattoria. Lana Umali has been my savior on numerous occasions. I am grateful for the guidance of Steve Sicari, a wise and kind department chair.

This book was made possible with the assistance of a fellowship from the Humanities Institute at the University of Connecticut and with research support from St. John's University. Caroline Fuchs in the library at St. John's has been an important resource throughout my research. I also have benefitted from the insight and enthusiasm of Alyse Hennig, one of the archivists at the Kathryn and Shelby Cullom Davis Library, St. John's University; and the library's director, Ismael Rivera-Sierra. Inspiration for the final chapter on the San Francisco earthquake comes from a collaborative project that art historian Dr. Susan Rosenberg and I began at the Davis Library (one of the few remaining insurance archives), and now that both our monographs are published, to which we plan to return.

Over several years, my writing group has generously read various iterations of this work and offered brilliant advice for which I am grateful. They include: Jeff Allred, Sophie Bell, Sarah Chinn, Anna Mae Duane, Joseph Entin, Hildegard Hoeller, and Meg Toth. I appreciate the valuable questions, critique, and feedback on chapter drafts, conference papers, and early pieces of this work by Dale M. Bauer, the late Stephen C. Brennan, Ashley Cross, Jean Lutes, Keith Newlin, and Paul Sorrentino.

My work also has benefitted from the friendship and support of Wayne K. Bodle, Harry Denny, Jessica DeSpain (with whom I co-edited a collection on digital humanities pedagogy and American literature), Barbara Koziak, and Susan Rosenberg. My graduate research assistants, Scott Koski, Amity Nathaniel, and Catherine Saunders, helped me to correct and polish the final manuscript. I am especially grateful for my undergraduate and graduate students at St. Johns, including Donya Nasser, Patricia Milanes, Erin Ponton Fiero, and Kathleen Mulligan; their rigor and insight about gender, race, sexuality, trauma, and literature has made teaching a delight.

Portions of this book have appeared elsewhere, and I thank the original publishers for their permission to reprint. A shorter version of chapter 3 on Theodore Dreiser originally appeared in 2008 as "Injury's Accountant: Theodore Dreiser and the Railroad" in *Studies in American Naturalism* published by the University of Nebraska Press. Portions of chapter 2 were first published as "Accidents, Agency, and American Literary Naturalism" in *The Cambridge History of American Women's Literature* (2012), edited by Dale M. Bauer and published by Cambridge University Press. I also want to thank my editor Lindsey Falk and Nick Johns at Lexington Books. Lindsey saw promise in this project and helped me envision a path to its completion quicker and more efficiently than I had thought possible.

Over the lifetime of this project and beyond, the love and support of my family has remained constant. My children, Miles and Stuart, have grown up along with this book and are now teenagers with passions of their own. Their gentle ribbing about my ability to turn almost anything into a lesson about American literature helps to keep things real. Barbara and Frank Malone are caring and generous in-laws, parents, and grandparents. My mother, Gail Travis, remains my biggest cheerleader, and I am proud—and I know my father Stuart would be too—of how she has turned vulnerability into resilience and strength. Mike Malone started this journey with me over three decades ago and his companionship and love fills me with gratitude.

Introduction

Crash and Burn

> The earth revolves, men are born, live their time, and die; communities are formed and are dissolved; dynasties appear and disappear; good contends with evil, and evil still has its day; the whole, however, advancing slowly but unerringly . . . to arrive in the end. (James Fenimore Cooper, *The Crater*)[1]

The philosopher king, military strategist, and former governor-for-life, Mark Woolston in James Fenimore Cooper's *The Crater: or Vulcan's Peak, A Tale of the Pacific* (1847), isn't particularly vengeful against the colonists who voted him off "paradise" island (461). He knows their end will come. After all, he surmises that his former countrymen of the crater are just "mites amid millions of other mites," their "temporary possessions" aboard a "globe that floats . . . in space," waiting at any moment to be "suddenly struck out of its orbit" (461). Woolston has reason to think apocalyptically. The novel begins with a naval disaster in which Cooper's hero and his shipmate, Bob Betts, wash up on a crater of a volcano in the middle of the Pacific Ocean. Woolston and Betts, trapped on what appears to be an inhospitable reef, believe themselves the sole survivors of the wreck. Partners toward their mutual survival, they learn to cultivate the soil, build an escape vessel, and bridge their class differences. Thus begins a social, political, and ecological experiment born out of catastrophe.

Cooper's *The Crater* is seafaring fiction, political philosophy, and disaster narrative rolled into one. Perhaps Mark Woolston puts the novel's plot best when he reflects at the end of the novel about his life's adventures:

> He would thus recall his shipwreck and desolate condition when suffered first to reach the rocks; the manner in which he was the instrument in causing vegetation to spring up in the barren places; the earthquake, and the upheaving of the islands from out of the waters: the arrival of his wife and other friends: the commencement and progress of the colony; its blessings, so long as it pursued the right, and its curses, when it began to pursue the wrong; his departure, leaving it still a settlement surrounded with a sort of earthly paradise, and his return to find all buried beneath the ocean. (461)

Although they are not struck out of orbit as Woolston first fancies, the colonists, it turns out, do meet an "awful" end: they are swallowed whole in the wake of a second earthquake, with only Woolston, Betts, their families, and a few additional original colonists—those who became disillusioned with their new world once they lost the power to rule it— returning to America as the sole survivors. "Of the colony of the crater and its fortunes, little was ever said among its survivors. It came into existence in a manner that was most extraordinary, and went out of it in one that was awful" (460). The survivors are content to bury the colony and their former compatriots deep in the Pacific.

The Crater is filled from beginning to end with environmental and societal danger. In addition to a shipwreck and two earthquakes, a hurricane drags Betts away from the island and leaves Woolston to survive on his own for the better part of a year. Woolston continues agricultural experiments with great success—"the progress of vegetation in such a climate" transformed "wilderness into a garden"—and after the first earthquake raises portions of the reef from the sea, Woolston's territory for exploration and cultivation expand (264). "His limits were so much enlarged as to offer something like a new world to his enterprise and curiosity" (163). A colony is born when Betts miraculously returns to the Reef with Woolston's wife and a few others who decide to remain and build a new "new world." Despite agricultural success and a "settlement surrounded with a sort of earthly paradise," insecurity is fundamental to political order on the crater; the colonists are mobilized and largely motivated by their sense of endangerment (461).

The colony of the crater defines itself not in relation to the environmental threats and incipient achievements that have marked its brief existence, but rather in terms of military conflict, particularly against what the colonists see as the danger posed by "savages" who populate nearby islands. The colonial council, trusted advisors to Woolston the newly elected "governor-for-life," determines that "sound policy required such an exhibition of force on the part of the colony, as should make a lasting impression on their turbulent neighbours" (224, 102). The perceived "impetuosity of [the] savages" and the feared "weakness" of the colony posed great "dangers to its existence" (23). The tactics to combat this threat are gravely debated and become subjects of great interest among the colonists, "as ever banks, or abolitionism, or antimasonry, or free-trade, or any other of the crotchets of the day, could possibly be in America" (23). As the colony increasingly embraces violence and racial terror, Cooper's novel expresses "no contradiction between [the] egalitarian principles" it espouses in the first half, as Paul Lyon notes in *American Pacificism: Oceania in the U.S. Imagination* (2006), and the "exploitative racial hierarchy" it expounds in the second (Lyons 70).[2] Although the colony promotes itself as an exemplary society built on egalitarian principles—even the women of the colony take up arms against the "savages":

"At the first alarm everybody rushed to arms, and every post was manned, or *womaned*, in a minute"—the colonists' relations with their neighbors are characterized by battle cries and bigotry (45 my emphasis).

Rather than acknowledge frailty in the face of an unstable environment, the colonists of the crater seek security through force. They perceive vulnerability as a condition they must overcome, and their desire for invulnerability is used to justify their violence. Contrary to this model of community, which calls its citizens to arms and cultivates the political value of danger, *Danger and Vulnerability in Nineteenth-Century American Literature: Crash and Burn* examines how a vocabulary of vulnerability in the American imaginary recognized the causes of the structurally disempowered and animated progressive insight. Against the emerging rhetoric of danger in evidence in narratives like Cooper's *The Crater* and, as I will show, throughout the long nineteenth century, *Danger and Vulnerability* reads a variety of texts by writers such as Kate Chopin, Stephen Crane, Rebecca Harding Davis, Theodore Dreiser, W. E. B. Du Bois, Ellen Glasgow, Jack London, Nell Nelson, and E. D. E. N. Southworth, as well as legal, medical, and public policy debates, to demonstrate how emergent discourses about universal vulnerability in the face of technological and environmental peril challenged hegemonic notions of individual autonomy, white masculine citizenship, and sovereign political agency. In reimagining how vulnerability and vulnerable subjects were represented, *Danger and Vulnerability* argues that literary texts helped to narrate a crucial shift in America's cultural ethos: from lauding autonomy and privileging mastery to cultivating a sympathetic state and encouraging new forms of cultural recompense.[3]

For James Fenimore Cooper, writing his novel in the United States at a time of intense social and political conflict, particularly about the nation's most vulnerable, slaves, environmental eruptions like earthquakes were ready metaphors for social and political volatility. In his preface to *The Crater*, Cooper urges his readers "who now live in this [American] republic" to read the novel as a "timely warning" (5). He positions *The Crater* as a fundamental American allegory, from the colony's founding and flourishing to its projected destruction (5). Cooper insists that "whatever may be thought of the authenticity of its incidents," the book is "not . . . totally without a moral" (5). Yet, what moral does Cooper wish *The Crater*—a novel that builds upon alternate registers of colonial triumphalism, misplaced vulnerability, and racial fear—to illustrate? In Cooper's novel, his interconnected fantasies of environmental disaster, race war, and political conflict breed little more than insecurity and violence. In fact, *The Crater* may be the culmination of Cooper's national prophesies of insecurity; as Russ Castronovo notes, Cooper's early fictions of the frontier and Leatherstocking tales such as *The Pioneers* (1823) are warnings of an "impending devolution back to the state of nature."[4] Cooper's early work, like his late novel, *The Crater*, expresses anxiety about the security of property and persons and postulates "justification enough for surveillance and other security measures to operate" (Castronovo 678).

If concerns about danger and insecurity characterize Cooper's fiction, the principle illustrated in *The Crater* may well be how Woolston and his compatriots dangerously misconstrue their own vulnerabilities. One earthquake may have produced the conditions for life to flourish on the crater, yet another swiftly takes it away. Cooper's hero flees the colony for the United States only to return to the crater's annihilation: "the crust of the earth had again been broken; and this time it was to destroy, instead of to create" (224). It is no wonder that Mark Woolston is consumed with catastrophic thinking. In building a society that seeks to defy its vulnerability to the ebb and flow of the natural world, the colonists displace the recognition of their own fragility in their built environment, joining together to destroy their neighbors. The colonists of the crater willfully ignore their settlement's unsettling of the ecosystem and expose the fragility of a political system defined by a belief in dangerous "Others." In fact, the crater's survivors stifle the mutual recognition that the colony's "End of Days" was not characterized by the violent encounter with their neighbors for which they endlessly prepare. "The End" is marked by the incontrovertible hubris of their very enterprise itself.[5] Woolston and his compatriots pull the strings of their own catastrophe; it is their blind desire to build a colony on a fragile and inhospitable reef and to ignore the warning signs in the sea and air that ultimately seals their fate.[6] In the end, *The Crater* is a story much as Woolston fantasized: about the ways humans dangerously colonize a "globe" that "floats in space" and the manifold opportunities for humans to become inadvertent authors of their own distress (461).

At what price, Cooper's readers must ask, and at whose expense do they gain purchase on security? This is a question that the surviving colonists of the crater refuse to ask, preferring to return stateside in a silent pact; however, this question and others like it invite readers to examine the emerging nineteenth-century disaster-security state and to question its foundation in our more recent terror-security state.[7] Environmental dangers like those imagined in *The Crater* were representative of the shifting nature of state power, argued Nathan Shaler, a popularizer of earthquake science in the mid- to late nineteenth century. In magazines like *The Atlantic Monthly* and *Harper's*, Shaler warned that governments would "stand or fall *not* by their feats of warfare" but rather by their "power to combat the elemental enemies": the earthquakes, volcanoes, fires, and floods that endanger human communities (Shaler 647 my emphasis). The military might that once characterized a nation's prowess, cautioned Shaler, offers little comfort in the new "age we are entering."[8] By contrast, the actions of the colonists on the crater are a ready example of Shaler's critique: they believe that their "feats of warfare" will secure their community; yet, their ongoing conflict with their "savage" neighbors produces a mere chimera of safety (Shaler 647). The colonists adopt measures that erode their own freedoms, promote forced labor, and, in the end, the colonists quickly perish at the whim of nature rather than at the hands of their supposed enemies. Although Cooper promoted this narrative as a unique and faithful account of a fledgling society, the polis as it ultimately is practiced in *The Crater* is anything but unique: it proves to be another instance in a long history of human collectivity predicated on fear, danger, and the belief that violence is justified to forestall it.

Close to two hundred years later, collective vulnerability continues to be deployed as a rationale for state-sponsored acts of violence. Critical theorists, perhaps most notably Judith Butler's groundbreaking work on precarity in the years following September 11, 2001, have critiqued how communities' efforts to secure safety and to deny human vulnerability often result in violence. In her celebrated work *Precarious Life* (2004), Butler examines how the American state-subject has used force in the years following September 11 to deny vulnerability to harm, and she asks what it would take to "produce another public culture and another public policy in which suffering unexpected violence and loss and reactive aggression are not accepted as the norm of public life" (Butler xvi). Why is vulnerability often a trigger for violence? How has insecurity and catastrophic reasoning come to define our actions? Can we rethink conditions of vulnerability so that their associations are productive of human potential rather than stigmatizing? Against reactive responses to danger, not only demonstrated by the crater's colonists but also by so many other communities before and since, can we imagine an engagement in the world anchored in and arising from an acknowledgment rather than disavowal of human fragility?[9]

Cooper's novel illustrates that the process of refusal—to acknowledge the humanity of our neighbors and to respect the environment in which we live—ultimately is self-defeating. In Cooper's novel, Woolston espouses alarm about dangerous "Others," ignores environmental risks, rejects progressive social reorganization, and envisions a world spinning off its axis and out of control. In many ways, his vision is prescient. Today we speak of similar insecurities: financial, informational, environmental, and political, and we obsessively express our worry and fear for the future. Cultural theorist Paul Virilio refers to these feelings as the "threat horizon," one that endlessly identifies and produces new dangers.[10] Why, he asks, does it seem easier for humanity to imagine a future shaped by ever-deadlier accidents than a decent future? Rather than envision a path to overcome the plagues of human suffering, humanity is gripped by a "catastrophic imaginary"; we seem only to be able to see a landscape "littered with corpses" of the disasters to come.[11] As the Enlightenment project of rationalization and its faith in scientific progress has proven illusory, our comportment toward the future also has transformed. Today we live in fear of "trans-spatial and trans-temporal" threats, threats that impact not just a singular island in the Pacific, to recall *The Crater*, or one nation-state, but dangers that encompass the entire globe.[12]

Danger and Vulnerability in Nineteenth-Century American Literature: Crash and Burn invites readers to examine the "threat horizon" through its nascent expression in literary and cultural history. The earthquakes, shipwrecks, and deadly storms of *The Crater* were among a host of real and imagined perils—social, political, military, technological, and environmental—animating the nineteenth-century literary imagination. Americans saw danger lurking everywhere: in railway cars and trolleys, fireplaces and floods, and amid social and political movements, from the abolition of slavery to suffrage. After the Civil War, Americans were shaken by financial panic and a volatile post-slave economy. They were awestruck and progressively alarmed by technological innovations that promised speed and commercial growth but also posed unprecedented physical hazard. Most of all, Americans were uncertain, particularly in light of environmental disasters like hurricanes and wildfires, about their own city on a hill and the once indisputable and protective hand of a beneficent God. Dramatic environmental events like Cooper's earthquakes and, as we shall see, the fires, accidents, and collisions pervading nineteenth-century industrial culture, had enormous explanatory power, metaphoric and real.

As Mark Woolston's vengeful fantasies about his fellow "mites" suggest, catastrophic thinking is not new. The growing sense of contingency, insecurity, and danger engulfing the long nineteenth century has been linked by scholars to the concept of risk and the rise of modernity. Sociologist Anthony Giddens often is noted for his observation that what characterizes the modern age is the acknowledgment and acceptance of risk, which replaced older paradigms of fate and providence. To understand risk, argues Giddens, is to recognize not just "the possibility that things might go wrong, but that this possibility cannot be eliminated" (Giddens 30). Ulrich Beck suggests that what exemplifies modernity and our contemporary "risk culture" is how we live in the face of it, and, particularly, the mechanisms we construct to assuage and accommodate it. The damage wrought by fire to a metropolitan cityscape, or the violence of machines on the human body, inspired new forms of social organization—what would become known as risk management—in order to contain, supplement, control, and compensate for the perils of a modern industrial and technological society. According to risk society theorists like Giddens and Beck, the most pressing aspects of "modern societies is that they invest huge quantities of resources, human and economic, in managing risk."[13] Through institutions like insurance and methods of statistical analysis, societies quantify and seek to counterbalance the crashes, fires, and environmental catastrophes that distinguish the modern age.[14] As risk management fed the growth of the regulatory state, the development of safety movements, and industries like insurance, it also facilitated what Kevin Rozario has called the "catastrophic logic of modernity."[15] This logic recognizes not only the omnipresence of risk and its management, but also how cataclysms like earthquakes, with which this study begins and concludes, were cultivated as opportunities for urban development and commercial growth. In other words, accidents, disasters, and their regulation fueled capitalism's narratives of progress, while Americans' faith in these narratives often led states and industries to minimize known risks in favor of expansion and consumption. This dangerous model of economic development has escalated environmental crises like climate change that we face today.

Among the voluminous accounts of the technologies of risk and the institutions that define and manage it, literary critics also argue that its vocabulary and attendant meanings have transformed the landscape of American cultural history and the mood and tone of its storytellers.[16] For example, Joseph Fichtelberg has read perceptions of risk in early America, examining how performance functioned across literary texts and cultural histories to imagine and resist a dangerous new world. Eric Weirtheimer has analyzed the intimate relationship between the developing business of insurance, the commercial discourse that tries to tame, stabilize, and accommodate risk, and literary texts, demonstrating their mutually constitutive language. New methods of statistics and probability, argues Maurice S. Lee, changed the perception and function of chance in nineteenth-century American culture, shaping not only how literary writers conveyed belief and doubt, but also the way these changes impacted diverse fields and professions, from economics and sociology to insurance and the arts. Reading chance in the context of nineteenth-century accidents, Jason Puskar argues that literary texts produced a concept of chance that encouraged new modes of collectivity against the competitive individualism of the Gilded Age. Societies work to imagine and to manage risk, chance, and accident in a variety of ways, as these critics amply describe: they write novels, stories, plays, and poems, sell insurance policies, create financial regulations, bolster the military industrial complex, and celebrate capitalism's slogan to "make it new," often in an effort to explore, abate, confront, or deny exposure to harm.[17] To this discourse on risk, chance, and accident, we must add more nuanced examinations of the language of vulnerability, from its epistemic foundations to its expression in certain power dynamics. Vulnerability complicates the vocabulary of risk by continuing to challenge cultural fantasies of control, self-reliance, and security.[18]

If risk is the structure of feeling animating modernity, as so many scholars across multiple disciplines have proposed, vulnerability may well inhabit its interiors.[19] Like risk, the concept of vulnerability has inspired cross-disciplinary debate, especially among feminist scholars in philosophy, political theory, and the law. Many have endeavored to "re-signify vulnerability" by emphasizing, much as risk theorists do, its universality and "our shared condition of precariousness as human beings" (Cole 262; Butler, Gambetti, and Sabsay 36). Vulnerability theorists ask us to embrace the recognition of our constitutive vulnerability—an effect of our common human embodiment—and argue that re-examining vulnerability may inspire changes in the social institutions we build to address it. By challenging the more conventional associations of vulnerability with weakness, regulation, stigmatization, and dependence, these theorists ask whether and how vulnerability can be understood apart from discourses of paternalism and victimization and reanimated as forms of political agency and modes of resistance. Indeed, vulnerability has become a keyword with a vast array of meanings, as Alyson Cole amply describes: "The term readily accepts all variety of adjectival modifiers" (Cole 263). Scholars have theorized "social vulnerability," "ontological vulnerability," "racial vulnerability," "economic vulnerability," "embodied vulnerability," "environmental vulnerability," and more (Cole 263).[20] Human vulnerability is universal and particular, constant and changing, unique and collective, and dependent upon circumstance and subject position. Given the manifold conditions through which one might experience forms of vulnerability, recognizing its constitutive capacity, argues legal scholar Martha Albertson Fineman, "must be at the heart of our ideas of social and state responsibility" and fundamental in visions of social justice ("Vulnerable Subject" 9).

Despite its many modifiers, the term "vulnerability" continues to be burdened with negative associations. Against a range of derogatory connotations, including helplessness, dependency, poverty, violation, susceptibility, and abjection, feminist philosophers like Erin Gilson cast vulnerability as a "condition of openness" (Gilson 310). Gilson writes in the *Ethics of Vulnerability* (2014) that it is "pervasive, fundamental, shared . . . unsettling. It presents us with the reality of fallibility, mutability, unpredictability, and uncontrollability" (Gilson 310). In contrast to these attributes, Americans have famously prized *invulnerability*, autonomous selfhood, and, to recall the lauded nineteenth-century American image of the self-made man, the ability to pull oneself up from one's bootstraps.[21] If vulnerability suggests fallibility, dependency, and uncontrollability, it is everything that self-made manhood rejects. When the disavowal of vulnerability turns deadly in Cooper's *The Crater*, it is an example of what Richard Slotkin identified in American frontier literature as "regeneration through violence." Although feminist theorists and vulnerability scholars have advanced critiques of liberalist notions of invulnerability as representative of a privileged white "masculinist ideology or affect, one that disavows weakness and dependence in any form," the binary of vulnerability/invulnerability remains not only operational (if false) but also deeply gendered (Cole 262).

Against American myths like self-made autonomous manhood, myths that often impede the establishment of a more responsive state, the challenge is to think "beyond current ideological constraints," argues scholars like Fineman, and to imagine "responsive" state structures that might empower the vulnerable by addressing "existing inequalities of circumstances" ("Vulnerable State" 40). As an alternative to the autonomous, inviolable individual championed by liberal individualism, Fineman calls for the recognition of the vulnerable subject as a model for social action.[22] Such a recognition requires that we expand our vocabulary, rethink diverse modes of vulnerability, and, especially, question how this work may inform resistance to institutions that privilege mastery, as scholars advocate in the recent collection, *Vulnerability in Resistance* (2016) (Butler, Gambetti, and Sabsay 6). For Judith Butler, one of the editors and a contributor to the book, "undoing" the binary opposition between vulnerability and agency is a start in this effort as well as a paramount "feminist task" (Butler 25).

Inspired by these conversations, as well as work in the environmental humanities, the history of technology, and feminist, gender, and critical race theories, this study turns to imaginative fiction and non-fiction of the nineteenth and early twentieth centuries to explore how literature's capacity for narrating vulnerability brings its complexities and nuances into fuller view, imagining new ways to express and embrace vulnerability, embodiment, interdependency, and agency. Unlike the work of many of the critics I cite here, *Danger and Vulnerability in Nineteenth-Century American Literature* is not a sustained theorization of vulnerability as a concept; rather, I read an array of texts and literary genres—and I am more exploratory than exhaustive—from sensation serials and autobiographies of neurasthenic anxiety to "felt reports" written in the grip of catastrophe, as invitations to dispute normative cultural constructions of invulnerability and vulnerability and to show how conditions of vulnerability may be mobilized toward empathy, compassion, community, and social change (Gilson 360). I begin in chapter 1 with E. D. E. N. Southworth's sensation fiction, which I analyze in the context of emerging tort law to show how Southworth imagines and advocates for the recognition of women's wounds. Chapter 2 argues that crash lit by Rebecca Harding Davis, Kate Chopin, and Harriet P. Spofford, among several others, employs cultural anxieties about accident in the industrial age to make visible forms of vulnerability, especially gendered violence, which often remained unrecognized. Chapter 3 focuses on the work of Theodore Dreiser, a successful journalist and author, and his efforts at self-examination and healing in the face of depression and anxiety, arguing that these efforts inspired his turn toward progressive social thought and a challenge to binary thinking: vulnerability/invulnerability, female/male, and body/mind. Through readings of Stephen Crane's "The Monster" and W. E. B. Du Bois's "The Comet," chapter 4 shows how discourses about environmental hazard animate critiques of precarity, vulnerability, and racial violence. Finally, like Cooper's *The Crater*, this study begins and ends with an earthquake. Chapter 5 concludes with the San Francisco earthquake of 1906, demonstrating how literary, scientific, and technocratic vocabularies worked to understand disaster while recognizing and adapting their own disciplinary limitations. The texts at the heart of this study, from mid-nineteenth-century sensation novels to turn-of-the-twentieth-century journalistic fiction, imagine spectacular collisions, terrifying conflagrations, and all manner of catastrophe, social, political, and environmental. Together they write against illusions of inviolability in a growing technological and managerial culture, and they imagine how the recognition of universal vulnerability may challenge normative representations of social, political, and economic marginality.

Danger and Vulnerability is mindful about the different ways that vulnerability may be expressed and experienced depending on subject and context and is especially attentive to how gendered and raced bodies are made vulnerable by structural violence in post–Civil War America. The following chapters analyze the narrative techniques that writers use to resist and expose what Rob Nixon has called in another context, "slow violence." Slow violence, in Nixon's work, describes violence that "occurs gradually and out of sight" (Nixon 2). Because violence is often experienced as explosive and immediate, he argues that the "insidious threats" and social afflictions that affect the quality of life of women, people of color, and the poor often remain invisible (Nixon 3). Moreover, "bloodless, slow motion violence . . . is more likely to be buried, particularly if it's relayed by people whose witnessing authority is culturally discounted" (Nixon 16). Nixon asks how, in an age that "venerates instant spectacle," we can draw "public attention to catastrophic acts that are low in instant spectacle but high in long-term effects" (Nixon 6, 10). While this continues to be a pressing question, particularly for our contemporary moment in which "slowly unfolding environmental catastrophes represent formidable representational obstacles," this study examines how accidents, conflagrations, and cataclysms that were growing in visibility in the nineteenth and early twentieth centuries and affecting the powerful and the dispossessed alike provoked the literary imagination. The texts examined here represent meaningful "aesthetic encounters," which as Marianne Hirsch writes, may "move us toward an ethics and politics of . . . openness, interconnection, and imagination," and possibly too, the recognition or acknowledgement of our own complicity in violence (Hirsch 82).[23] By representing and often spectacularizing collective vulnerability and risk in an emerging era of mechanization, *Danger and Vulnerability* explores how literary texts remade the politics of victimhood, national responsibility, and discourses of debility for underrepresented groups.

Danger and Vulnerability begins by juxtaposing vulnerable bodies with seemingly invulnerable machines, particularly railways and automobiles, new vehicles of technological acceleration in the nineteenth and early twentieth centuries. Inventions like the railroad transformed people's consciousness about their environment, their embodiment, and their movement through time and space, offering both an "optimistic sense of security, of being in control of events, and a sense of insecurity, a sense of a world speeding out of control," argues Judy Wajcman in *Pressed for Time* (2016).[24] These two sensibilities ran in tandem. On the one hand, the railroad symbolized speed and human progress and the ability for technological innovation to improve material prosperity (if only selectively). On the other hand, technological innovation led to forms of insecurity and endangerment in the form of increased accidents, collisions, and deaths. Chapters on E. D. E. N. Southworth and the laws of fright (chapter 1), periodical literature on railway collisions (chapter 2), and Theodore Dreiser and traumatic neurasthenia, or railway brain (chapter 3), describe how universal human vulnerability in the face of machine culture—and the body's very real capacity for harm—became an opportunity to explore more complex social and political forms of vulnerability and agency. The narrative of human progress that was closely aligned with a new machine mediated society inspired many writers to critique the acceleration or lack thereof of social progress.[25]

No other literary genre captured the relationship between the culture of speed and the pace of social change more acutely than the sensation novel. Chapter 1 parallels shock and injury cases in the law with E. D. E. N. Southworth's fiction to show how Southworth used new perceptions of universal risk and susceptibility to harm to challenge American myths of autonomy and self-sufficiency and to advocate for the recognition and compensation of women's wounds. The sensation novel not only capitalized on the risks and thrills of a newly emerging technological society but also imagined and cultivated expressions of human vulnerability that could be read as examples of and occasions for what Martha Albertson Fineman calls a "responsive state" ("Vulnerable State" 40). Examining the genre of the sensation novel through one of its most prolific practitioners, this chapter reads two of Southworth's novels: her most well-known serialization, *The Hidden Hand* (1886), and her novel of legal heroism, *Ishmael* (1889), both preoccupied with accidents and injuries and the laws put in place to mitigate them. Law, like literature, began to inhabit a culture of harm and to examine how compensatory mechanisms may recognize the physical injuries of a growing technological society. While enjoying the relative safety and security of the printed page, the sensation novel invited readers to experience the frights and shocks that lurked beyond its covers.

Southworth is particularly interested in legal plots and narratives; yet, most critics who have read Southworth and her preoccupation with the law tend to look at marriage law and married women's property rights. Southworth's well-known biography, including spousal abandonment, lends itself to the reading of women as victims of patriarchal legal structures. If readers turn to another growing arena of law in the nineteenth century, tort law, and the way such laws began to frame notions of harm and responsibility, we see how Southworth's novels engage emergent perceptions of danger and vulnerability and challenge the masculinized myth of autonomy. Southworth's heroine Capitola Black is a risk taker and a caretaker; she is vulnerable and inviolable, mobile and fixed, black and white, boy and girl, and her adventures invite alternative readings of these many facets of her character and her embodiment. She is also a model for how conditions of vulnerability may lead to avenues that address concrete injustices. Chapter 1 describes how Capitola's popularity and her appearance and reappearance in print over thirty years in the mid- to late nineteenth century correspond with the flourishing of legal discourse about the physical and psychological impact of technological violence and the social responsibility to acknowledge, compensate, and repair traumatic injuries. Through claims by women plaintiffs, law courts came to recognize a right to recover for injuries resulting from fright and shock. Southworth's fiction critiques legal paternalism and also imagines a model of female agency that surmounts it.

Chapter 2 turns to a subgenre of women's writing in the nineteenth and early twentieth centuries that I call crash lit. Crash lit imagines accidents and collisions and uses growing social concerns about safety in the industrial age to expose forms of vulnerability disregarded and dismissed by patriarchal society, particularly forms of cultural violence against women. In a new risk society, epitomized by the high-speed crash, mobility often meant freedom, but it also indicated susceptibility to forces beyond one's control. The effects of technological modernity affected the stories men and women narrated about gender and bodies in motion and at rest/home. With readings of several canonical and noncanonical writers like Rebecca Harding Davis, M. Sheffy Peters, Harriet P. Spofford, and Nell Nelson, I argue that American women writers seized and shaped the tropes that became critical to the cultural vocabulary of the crash, a vocabulary that embraced the speed, energy, sensations, and chaos of modern transport, but also exposed its vulnerabilities, its webs of interconnection, and its demands of interdependence. In Rebecca Harding Davis's story "Anne," for example, railway mobility offers the story's protagonist the promise of escape from stultifying social norms, while the railway crash unsettles Anne's sense of identity, security, and freedom. Crash lit confirmed that Americans were universally vulnerable to technological violence, and this chapter shows how women writers adapted this recognition as a heuristic tool through which to critique core social institutions like marriage and motherhood and to challenge the cultural meanings of vulnerability and victimhood.

Living in the railroad age transformed the way nineteenth-century Americans thought about danger and vulnerability, gender and mobility, and injuries to body and mind. Theodore Dreiser, the subject of chapter 3, may seem an unlikely voice of vulnerability; however, his multiple bouts of depression, nervous anxiety, and writer's block, and his manifold efforts to find a cure encouraged Dreiser to think progressively about gender and economic vulnerabilities, particularly white working-class manhood in America. This is a topic to which he returned repeatedly, writing about railroad labor and the railroad's part in the explosion of physical and psychological injuries in American culture. Like Southworth, whose novels about accidents and injuries were serialized and reissued throughout the second half of the nineteenth century, Dreiser turned to the railroad as ritual refrain through which he tackled the fragility of the masculine mind and body and through which he questioned the presumption that mobility and bodily autonomy was the exclusive right and privilege of manhood. Dreiser began his career as a journalist reporting on accidents, disasters, and irruptions of social violence, and these topics highlighted the importance of the written word as a form of cultural accounting. For Dreiser, the injuries, physical and psychological, pervading turn-of-the-century culture required treatment, especially as they were suffered by so many: from society's most valued writers to the nation's most invisible workers. Indeed, the characteristics that excluded some injured subjects from the full rights of citizenship were adapted by others as the surest signs of their humanity: the masculine psychic wound often could transcend his broken body, making him that much more a man. Injury claims, especially within the law, appeared to support a compensatory model in which disability, as Rosemarie Garland Thompson argues, connotes not "physiological variation, but the violation of a primary state of putative wholeness" (Thomson 49). Economic compensation, in other words, seeks to repair physical loss; yet, this compensatory model often fails to recognize those who by virtue of gender, race, sexuality, or ability are excluded from the ideals of liberal individualism and its able-bodied standards of independence, strength, and self-mastery. This chapter examines a significant challenge to this ethos, casting emotional injury rather than bodily autonomy as the basis for new claims of cultural authority.

The final two chapters turn from technological violence in the machine age to ecological hazard, arguing that literary responses to and imagination of environmental danger at the turn of the twentieth century were efforts to critique social injustice and to challenge the cultural compulsion toward mastery and control, whether of the environment or persons and groups made vulnerable because of race, class, gender, or sexual orientation.[26] For example, Stephen Crane's "The Monster," one of the texts central to chapter 4, is a story about self-proclaimed white fragility and the cultivation of racial violence that takes as its central motif a house fire. For Crane, systemic disruptions brought on by unforeseeable events like a building fire allow stories of precariousness to emerge in sharper focus. In this chapter, I argue that the state of ecological risk imagined in Crane's fiction and, later, W. E. B. Du Bois's writings reflect deep trepidations about social injustice, racial vulnerability, and political and structural methods of recompense. Using Americans' cultural fascination with "demons of the flame," Crane likens it to another national obsession, the perception of dangerous Otherness that draws attention away from potential real threats, whether environmental, social, or political. In the late nineteenth and early twentieth centuries, fires and other ecological dangers became mechanisms for a nation, at once socially volatile and increasingly vulnerable to widespread hazards given rapid urban growth, to embrace industrial capitalism's promise of a more glorious future and to narrate social cohesion and security in the face of universal vulnerability and social divisiveness. Crane, Du Bois, and, more recently, Ta-Nehisi Coates use metaphors of environmental catastrophe to critique the cultural politics of race. White America, Coates concludes in *Between the World and Me* (2015), has plundered "not just the bodies of humans but the body of the Earth itself," and its "vengeance," he writes, is "not the fire in the cities but the fire in the sky" (Coates 150). In both associating and challenging racial and ecological hegemony, these writers anticipate critiques that emerge in the twenty-first century in disaster studies and ecocriticism: namely, that the dream of mastery—whether over nature or the dispossessed—leads to unpredictable and uncontrollable irruptions.

The book ends where it begins, with an earthquake. If Cooper's quake cultivated a story of alarming Otherness to displace real ecological insecurity and fragility, the San Francisco earthquake, with which the book concludes, ushered in what historian Eric Hobsbawm has called the "age of catastrophe," an era of human conflict and environmental risk that soon came to characterize the twentieth century.[27] The San Francisco disaster often is read as a triumph of economist Joseph Schumpeter's vision of "creative destruction," the idea that catastrophe facilitates human fecundity and the march of economic progress. Against this master narrative and the "anthropocentric hierarchy of reason over nature," this chapter examines pieces of short narrative non-fiction that describe, in immediate and personal terms, experiences of the quake (Garrard 464). These narratives by literary writers, insurance adjusters, philosophers, and scientists alike are imaginative examples of "felt reports," citizen-scientist records of earthquake phenomena, impressions, and reflections.[28] The flourishing of "felt reports" after the San Francisco earthquake showed environmental catastrophe as beyond human control and intimately human made.

In the aftermath of the San Francisco earthquake literary narratives and statistical sciences converged around questions of ecological agency and environmental justice, anticipating the concerns and interventions of contemporary movements like the environmental humanities. As an emerging interdisciplinary field of study, the environmental humanities illuminate how ecological challenges are inseparable from society, culture, and politics (Garrard 462). Work by scholars in this field such as Ursula Heise and Stephanie LeManger describe the field's emergence at a moment, in Heise's words, "when the humanities and qualitative social sciences are reinventing what being human means—and by extension what it means to study human cultures and societies" (Heise 4). The final chapter of this book describes another such moment of convergence and critique around environmental catastrophe, as science relied on storytellers, insurance technocrats turned to narrative arts, and citizen observers became collectors and nascent archivists of disaster. Against an expert dominated risk culture, *Danger and Vulnerability* concludes by demonstrating how disciplinary vulnerabilities in the aftermath of catastrophe may challenge notions of mastery and how literary narrative appeals to a shared sense of vulnerability in ways that may cultivate cultural responsiveness and change.

NOTES

1. James Fenimore Cooper, *The Crater, or Vulcan's Peak*, 446. All page numbers refer to the two-volume 1847 edition.

2. Warren Motely also writes that "just as the activities of the writer and hero are closely bound in *The Crater's* first half, so in the second Cooper's writing, instead of dedicating itself to the evocation of an ideal world, more aggressively asserts its claim to authority over the world as found," *The American Abraham: James Fenimore Cooper and The Frontier Patriarch*, 163. The promise of a new world is destroyed by the colonists' desire to dominate the natural world as well as their neighbors.

3. I draw on the idea of the "sympathetic state" from Michelle Landis Dauber and her study of disaster and the American welfare system, *The Sympathetic State: Disaster Relief and the Origins of the American Welfare State*.

4. See Russ Castronovo, "James Fenimore Cooper and the NSA: Security, Property, Liberalism," *American Literary History*, 680. Cooper's frontier fiction, Castronovo argues, expresses "worry that property is always capable of being seized, alienated, or left to rot," and that it is "essentially never secure"; fictions of the frontier and its "culture of liberalism and the notion of property that it upholds" requires us to examine the "consolidation of the security state that was pioneered in the eighteenth and nineteenth centuries," 690.

5. See Sheila Hones, "Distant Disasters, Local Fears: Volcanoes, Earthquakes, Revolution, and Passion in *The Atlantic Monthly*, 1880–84," in *American Disasters*, 170–96. By the nineteenth century, scientists and social scientists began dismantling the rigid distinctions between the natural and the cultural, insisting that disasters like earthquakes, hurricanes, and volcanoes always have social dimensions. In novels and magazines, descriptions of catastrophes near and distant not only "reassure[d]" the public of "present safety through controlling narrative," argues Hones, but also employed catastrophe as "safe theater" through which "to explore areas of immediate cultural or social concern," 171.

6. In *Living in the End Times* Slavoj Žižek argues that "the limitation on our freedom that becomes palpable with ecological disturbances is the paradoxical outcome of the exponential growth of our freedom and power: our increasing ability to transform nature around us can destabilize the basic geological conditions of human life," 423.

7. See *American Literary History* 28, no. 4 (Winter 2016): 663–858, for several insightful essays on security studies and American literary history.

8. N. S. Shaler, "The Floods of the Mississippi Valley," *Atlantic Monthly*, May 1883, 647. For more on Shaler, see Sheila Hones, "Distant Disasters," 170–96. Kimberly K. Smith's *African American Environmental Thought* also discusses Shaler in the context of his scientific racism, 106–16.

9. As long as humans have grappled with danger, cultural texts have represented it. Much like the polis in *The Crater*, political theory evolved from a sense of danger, argues George Shulman in "On Vulnerability," 227. From Plato, who once dreamed about a republic safe for philosophers, to Thomas Hobbes, who cultivated the public's dread of unchecked violence in order to rally support for sovereign state power, fear, danger, and the promise of safety have animated centuries of political and social organization. See Shulman, "On Vulnerability as Judith Butler's Language of Politics: From *Excitable Speech* to *Precarious Life*," 232. See also Giorgio Agamben's *Homo Sacer*, which has been highly influential in the discussion of security and the politics of fear after 9/11.

10. Quoted in Lacey, *Security, Technology and Global Politics*, 4.

11. For more on catastrophic thinking, see Brad Evans and Julian Reid, *Resilient Life: The Art of Living Dangerously*, Kindle edition, loc. 350, 388. All future references are to this edition.

12. Jane Arthurs and Iain Grant, "Introduction," in *Crash Cultures: Modernity, Mediation and the Material*, 7. Global warming and nuclear weapons are examples of trans-spatial and trans-temporal threats.

13. See Arwen P. Mohun, *Risk: Negotiating Safety in American Society*, for a discussion of how Americans understand and manage risk, 7.

14. Writing about life insurance, Lorraine Daston notes that the ability to "calculate risk, even to control it, has not tipped the balance in favor of hope." On the contrary, she argues, "even the most secure societies seem by and large to be the most timorous, the most cowed by the prospect of future danger, whether probable or improbable." Daston, "Life, Chance & Life Chances," *Deadalus*, Winter 2008, 14.

15. This phrase recognizes "modernization as a quest to make the world more secure (modernity as anti-disaster) through development patterns that move through cycles of ruin and renewal, bust and boom, destruction and construction, producing as their collateral damage myriad social conflicts as well as technological and environmental hazards (modernity as disaster)." See Rozario, *The Culture of Calamity*, 10. Steven Biel writes in *American Disasters* that "perhaps nothing marks a disaster as 'American' more than this ability to transform death and destruction into good news," 7.

16. For literary discussions of risk and accident outside the United States, see Elaine Freedgood, *Victorian Writing about Risk*; Paul Fyfe, *By Accident or Design*; and Ian Baucom, *Specters of the Atlantic*. See also Ross Hamilton's *Accident: A Philosophical and Literary History* for an intellectual history of accident.

17. See Joseph Fichtelberg, *Risk Culture: Performance and Danger in Early America*; Eric Wertheimer, *Underwriting: The Poetics of Insurance in America, 1722–1872*; Maurice S. Lee, *Uncertain Chances: Skepticism and Belief in Nineteenth-Century American Literature*; and Jason Puskar, *Accident Society: Fiction, Collectivity, and the Production of Chance*. See also David Zimmerman, *Panic: Markets, Crises, and Crowds in American Fiction*, for his discussion of the relationship between novel reading and economic panic.

18. Literature has imagined vulnerable subjects for centuries, if not since the origins of storytelling itself. Marina Berzins McCoy, for example, shows how Greek drama and philosophy privileged "vulnerability as a virtue" in *Wounded Heroes: Vulnerability as a Virtue in Ancient Greek Literature and Philosophy*. In modern times, vulnerability often has been stigmatized. Like McCoy and other scholars mentioned here, I am interested to see where and how vulnerability becomes a model for social action.

19. "Structure of feeling" is Raymond Williams's phrase for the "conscious and critical" vocabulary that inspires and aggregates "social and cultural discussion," Raymond Williams, *Keywords: Vocabulary of Culture and Society*, 24.

20. See Alyson Cole's instructive critique: "All of Us Are Vulnerable, But Some Are More Vulnerable Than Others," 263. My understanding of vulnerability is especially indebted to the work of Cole, Fineman, Butler, and Gilson.

21. See Martha Fineman's *The Autonomy Myth*, and "The Vulnerable Subject": "The importance of the idea of independence to the construction of an autonomous and equal individual may be traced to the fact that the very existence of the United States begins with a document entitled—The Declaration of Independence," "The Vulnerable Subject," 14.

22. See Fineman and Grear, "Introduction," in *Vulnerability: Reflections*; and Fineman, "Equality, Autonomy." In contrast to Fineman, Alyson Cole urges caution about reclaiming vulnerability as an alternative language to conceptualize injustice, arguing that the notion of universal vulnerability may mask important distinctions among vulnerable subjects and groups; vulnerability scholars, she argues, "have yet to elaborate the path from acknowledging constitutive vulnerability to addressing concrete injustices." Cole, "All of Us Are Vulnerable," 260.

23. Stephanie Foote and Stephanie LeMenager use a similar description to unpack the concept of resilience. Stories of resilience offer "adaptable points of view, ways of seeing the world that can be picked up, pieced apart, borrowed and brocolage-ed into modes of resistance and response." "Editors' Column," *Resilience: A Journal of the Environmental Humanities*.

24. Wajcman, *Pressed for Time*, 43. For more on how we have become a machine-mediated society, see Bauman, *Liquid Times*; Urry, *Mobilities*; Wajcman, *Pressed for Time*; and Cassedy, *Connected: How Trains, Genes, Pineapples, Piano Keys, and a Few Disasters Transformed Americans at the Dawn of the Twentieth Century*.

25. To be certain, the growth of technology was not only about speed and progress but also about territorial expansion, commerce, and capitalism. Americans have a very complicated relationship with notions of mobility, as chapter 2 describes. The railroads brought ravenous development of the landscape, the damaging displacement of people, and the destruction of the environment; but, they also encouraged social and political mobility, contests over human rights, and visions of freedom (the underground railroad).

26. I am indebted to studies like Rob Nixon's *Slow Violence*, Kimberly K. Smith's *African American Environmental Thought*, and Jeffrey Myers's *Converging Stories*. Myers argues that "the ethnocentric outlook that constructed 'whiteness' over and against the alterity of other racial categories is the same perspective that constructed the anthropocentric paradigm at the root of environmental destruction," 5.

27. See Hobsbawm, "The Age of Catastrophe," in *The Age of Extremes: The Short Twentieth Century 1914–1991*, 21–199.

28. In the final chapter, I improvise on a practice discussed at length in Deborah R. Coen's *The Earthquake Observers*.

ONE

A "damsel-errant in quest of adventures"

E. D. E. N. Southworth, Sensation, and the Law

Capitola Black in E. D. E. N. Southworth's *The Hidden Hand* (1888) isn't "sentimental" (155).¹ In fact, this is her guardian, Old Hurricane's, most vociferous complaint. He consults with doctors aghast that Capitola fails to submit to his authority, especially his entreaty that she must embrace domesticity and the "safe" confines of Hurricane Hall. Capitola, however, not only snubs "proper" feminine sentiment, she willfully courts danger: she vows to catch the novel's villains, save her sisters in distress, and have a little "merriment" too (299). Despite the sentimental tag that often attends Southworth's work, *The Hidden Hand* embraces its protagonist's refusal of this label; it routinely eschews sentiment in favor of the sensational, the adventurous, and the melodramatic: characters escape sinking ships, live on mean city streets, roam wild across rural landscapes, and fight on bloody battlefields. Southworth encourages her audience to shun tears and, along with her heroine, to experience the intense shocks, outrages, and exploits her adventures invite. Capitola is a self-described "damsel-errant in quest of adventures"; and indeed, her escapades have long electrified Southworth's readers (242).

Although nineteenth-century women's fiction in the United States often is read through the vocabulary of sentiment, sympathy, and domesticity, these genres fail to represent Southworth's range as a writer, as Melissa J. Homestead and Pamela T. Washington rightly note in their recent essay collection on Southworth (Homestead and Washington xx). Southworth especially capitalizes on the characteristics of sensation fiction, which has been linked by Victorian literary scholars to the growing energy and speed of nineteenth-century industrial technology. Writing about the English sensation genre, Nicholas Daley argues that the novel "aclimatized its readers to railway time and space," offering "new aesthetic pleasures in the form of suspense" (Daley 7). The growing industrial and metropolitan landscape exposed its inhabitants to what sociologist George Simmel would describe as "sharp discontinuit[ies]" and the "unexpectedness of onrushing impressions" (Simmel 175). Walter Benjamin famously called this the "human sensorium," the busy city streets with their crowds, streetcars, and advertisements subjected their inhabitants to a "complex kind of training" (Benjamin 171). Rather than promoting an escape from a "hostile machine culture" into books, sensation fiction prepared its readers for the accidents, anxieties, and nervous energies associated with the rapid pace of modern technology.

Adapting Benjamin's depiction of the human sensorium, literary critic Shelley Streeby has argued that a similar reaction to "onrushing impressions" is at the heart of nineteenth-century American literature. As "capitalist modernity altered the human 'sensorium' and inaugurated new modes of perception," sensation fiction, she argues, reflects and is shaped by "all of its shocks, thrills and sensational intensities" (Streeby 180). American sensation fiction, however, has inspired less critical attention than its Victorian counterparts or other genres of nineteenth-century prose, particularly those associated with women writers such as sentiment or sympathy. Novelists like Southworth, Mary Denison, and Louisa May Alcott were among the most successful sensation writers, a designation, as Streeby notes, that for reviewers "then, as now . . . was by no means a compliment" (Streeby 187).[2] With its ties to the dime novel, penny paper, and melodrama, women writers in the United States were criticized for adopting sensation fiction's conventions and addressing "topics that were beyond the pale of middle-class white womanhood," including representations of sexual and domestic violence (Streeby 187). Southworth's contemporary reviewers regularly condemned her fiction as intemperate, wild, and "unsuppressed" (Homestead and Washington xvi). It comes as little surprise, therefore, that a writer like Louisa May Alcott wrote sensation fiction under the pseudonym A. M. Barnard, or that her most famous heroine, Jo March, sees herself as a "damsel-errant" with regard to her own authorship: as Jo matures chronologically and, presumably, emotionally and intellectually, she abandons sensation fiction and pokes fun at her original inspiration, E. D. E. N. Southworth (S. L. A. N. G. Northbury). Whereas literary critics have noted that sentimental literature written by women in the nineteenth century often cultivated tears as an alternative path to participatory democracy, its "uncanny double," sensation literature, emphasized a wider range of embodied responses, also working, as Dana Luciano argues, against the "putative disembodiment of the rational bourgeois public sphere" (316–17).

This chapter reads Southworth's fiction, particularly *The Hidden Hand*—her most popular serialization and the work best familiar to Southworth readers today—as well as its "uncanny double," *Ishmael* (1876), as instances of the "human sensorium"; they embrace "shocks, thrills, and sensational intensities" and domesticate their dangers (Streeby 180). Southworth's novels entertain readers with startling accidents while shielding them from their very real capacity to injure. Southworth's fiction expands literary expressions of embodiment and illuminates a crucial shift in the national imaginary away from a masculined myth of disembodied and unencumbered independence toward a different manner of person, one that acknowledges mutual dependence and, crucially, the modern subject's susceptibility to harm. In *The Hidden Hand*, Southworth's heroine Capitola Black is neither the individualistic idol of national fantasy nor is she a sentimentalized victim. Her exhibition of vulnerability along with measured displays of fearlessness and strength reflects a shifting cultural ethos for women and men alike. This chapter describes *The Hidden Hand*'s preoccupation with the language of safety and danger and examines the ways that these discourses encourage readers to imagine and to vicariously experience imminent perils while also seasoning them in a nascent language of physical and emotional security. Like many of Southworth's novels, both *The Hidden Hand* and *Ishmael* enact encounters with numerous hazards—fires, collisions, and frequent accidents—hallmark conventions of the sensation genre, but they also elicit feelings of care; they prepare their audience for precisely the qualities of personhood, thriving on risk and freedom but also dependent upon others and vulnerable to new harms, which marked a new manner of person in a rapidly changing nation.

Since the centennial reissue of the novel in 1988, much of the critical conversation about *The Hidden Hand* has centered on Capitola as a feminist protagonist who subverts gender ideology while remaining palatable to popular audiences. *The Hidden Hand* is Southworth's most widely read and studied novel. First serialized on the eve of the Civil War, contemporary critics have looked with renewed interest at race and gender politics in the novel; Capitola Black is sold into slavery, and she passes, first as Grewell's kin and, later, as a boy. The novel also ventures to the front of the Mexican American War and has occasioned debate about the novel's attitudes toward U.S. imperialism.[3] True to the "sensorium" that inspired sensation fiction, the novel's characters encounter numerous dangers as they navigate across the continent and its increasingly complex physical and social terrain. It is notable, therefore, that full as the novel is with sensational adventures and, often, the "mad cap," it is also heavily administered by the more somber hand of the law.

The novel is framed at the beginning and end and punctuated throughout with court scenes and legal queries. In step with the novel's embrace of danger is its preoccupation with how law courts punish crimes, settle disputes, manage trusts and estates, assign guardianship, recognize inheritance, and sanction romantic unions. *The Hidden Hand*, like several other Southworth serials, is chock-full of legal proceedings. Recent criticism on Southworth and the law such as Elizabeth Stockton's "Southworth's Reimagining of the Married Women's Property Reforms" have noted Southworth's particular attentiveness to married women's property rights. Abandoned by her husband, Southworth wrote about women's legal status and the difficulties of marriage in serials and novels like *The Deserted Wife* (1850), *The Discarded Daughter* (1852), and *The Lost Heiress* (1854). Literary critics have drawn ample attention to Southworth's biography in their readings of her work, noting that Southworth often fictionalized what she experienced first-hand (Homestead xxii). Given her personal history, it is not surprising that in many of Southworth's novels the law is shown to privilege men's interests over women's welfare, patriarchal law over women's legal rights, the property entitlements of men, and the sanctioning of women's literal bondage.

Studying Victorian women writers and the law, Kristin Kalsem has characterized nineteenth-century women's fiction and its preoccupation with legal issues as a form of feminist jurisprudence, calling these narratives "outlaw" texts. Outlaw texts fall outside the "purview of much legal inquiry" because they are not official legal documents; however, they constitute an "integral signifying system" that provides narrative resistance to unjust laws and imagines new possibilities for systems of justice (Kalsem 5). The idea of *The Hidden Hand* as an outlaw text is especially fitting not only with Capitola's self-description as a desperado but also in light of the novel's exposure of unjust laws and the legal disregard of women and children. Demonstrating the power of the law to dictate the patriarchal rules that its heroine works stubbornly to resist, Southworth populates her novels with numerous court scenes and legal disputes. For example, early in *The Hidden Hand* we see Capitola hauled into court for cross-dressing; in the subplot, Clara Day (Capitola's alter-ego and damsel in distress) finds herself at the mercy of the orphan's court after the accidental death of her father Doctor Day. Black Donald is tried in criminal court; Traverse Rocke, Old Hurricane's son, is court-martialed in military court. Despite the numerous trial scenes throughout the novel, the only legal domain that the novel does *not* literally enter is the tort court; yet, it is precisely the language of this growing arena, injury law—the legal response to a world of dangers—that spirits the novel and inspires its refashioning of juridical subjecthood, the novel's hidden hand.

Given Southworth's interest in the law in several of her novels and the preponderance of legal discourse in *The Hidden Hand*, the law of torts figures like something of a determining absence, especially in view of the novel's repeated invocation of torts' central vocabulary: safety, danger, negligence, and care. Indeed, tort law adjudicates many of the dangers that the sensation novel voluminously describes, particularly the collisions, falls, accidents, and frights that are caused by startling hairbreadth escapes. The "shocks and collisions" that Benjamin hailed as the very foundation of modern selfhood were inseparable in the nineteenth century from the legal questions about personhood that such shocks inspired. As legal doctrine responded to the cultural upheavals wrought by technology and mechanization, litigiousness became a part of modern life. The industrial accident crisis awakened a new cultural vocabulary around notions of safety and danger. Historian John Fabian Witt has argued that "the industrial accident crisis" of the mid- to late nineteenth century in the United States introduced "new ideas and institutions organized around risk, security, and . . . insurance—ideas and institutions that to this day remain at the heart of much of our law" (Witt 5). Southworth's novels are veritable catalogues for the shocks and thrills of the human sensorium as well as the ideas and institutions that sprang up to address it; the novels feature innumerable accidents, railway and carriage crashes, and they critique ideas of security and peril throughout. It is these scenes of accident and injury that tort law began to address with rigor. In the nineteenth-century "sensorium," nervous shock, legal narrative, and sensation fiction collide.

Like *The Hidden Hand*, collisions, catastrophes, and accidents animate virtually all of the major plot points in Southworth's novel of legal heroism, *Ishmael*. When a train collision early in the novel is reported to have killed Herman Brudenell's estranged wife the Countess of Hurstmonceux, he believes he is free to marry Nora Worth and to make their impending child Ishmael his legitimate heir. Brudenell soon learns, however, that the Countess survived the crash, leaving Nora single, pregnant, and the "victim of a false marriage" (378).[4] Once born, Ishmael is left with no "legal right" to his father's name (377). "Ishmael had neither father, mother, name, nor place in the world. He had no legal right to be in it at all; no legal right to the air he breathed or to the sunshine that warmed him into life" (175). Vowing to avenge his mother's sullied reputation (she dies in childbirth) and "prove it to the world" (384), he studies, apprentices, and ultimately masters the law.

Long before Ishmael delves deep into the law, he also finds himself combating danger outside the courtroom: he physically rescues women and children on several occasions prior to becoming a legal advocate on their behalf. This risk taking begins early, when the young Ishmael saves his social betters, the Burghe boys, during a fire at Brudenell Hall. Despite the offer of "freedom to any slave who will save the Burghe boys" (303), only Ishmael is willing to take the risk—a risk for which he is told he is "mad" and will most certainly perish. "Horrors of horrors! What a scene met his appalled gaze! One portion of the floor of the room had fallen in, and the flames were rushing up through the aperture from the gulf of fire beneath. The two boys, standing in the open door, were spellbound in a sort of panic" (306). Although "fire raged with the utmost fury," Ishmael leads the boys to safety, "scorched, singed, blackened, choked, breathless, but safe!" (306). His heroism earns him an education, paid for by the elder Burghe, and this puts him on his early path to the law. Another act of fearless valor a few years later begets his apprenticeship with Judge Merlin. Ishmael is trampled by horses when he boldly averts a carriage accident, saving the Judge's daughter Claudia from certain death: "Plunging madly towards the brink of the high bank were the horses of Claudia's returning carriage . . . Ishmael saw and hurled himself furiously forward between the two rushing horses and the edge of the precipice," turning them from "the brink of destruction" (451). Ishmael is nearly "crushed to death" in the effort: "The severe injuries that must have caused the death of a less highly vitalized human creature really confined Ishmael for weeks to his bed and for months to the house" (451, 490). During his extended convalescence, Ishmael assists the Judge and commences an apprenticeship in the law. While Ishmael's physical bravery is indicative of his strength of character, it also sets the foundation for his position as a legal mediator and defender of women and children. The fires, carriage crashes, and other dangers that Ishmael confronts on his path toward the legal profession are brought safely under control once he becomes a heroic legal voice, a defender of the voiceless.

Southworth's novels narrate in some detail the legal decisions that portray the law as a domain of inequity; yet, her novels do not merely reflect women's legal disabilities nor do they characterize women's empowerment as solely extra-legal, as possible only in rejection or defiance of the law. Both *Ishmael* and *The Hidden Hand* cast the law as paternalistic and as ignorant of and disinterested in the threats and outrages suffered by women; however, *The Hidden Hand* also anticipates another legal frame of mind. The novel uses the literary conventions of sensation, including shock, fright, and a novel sensibility, collective human vulnerability in the face of new technologies, as a challenge to legal corruption and to women's disempowerment and erasure. In its narration of women's safety and danger, which tort law commenced to adjudicate with rigor in the nineteenth century, *The Hidden Hand* imagines and embraces a new vision of the juridical subject, one that challenges conventional notions of gendered subjectivity, community, and responsibility.

A brief look at two of *The Hidden Hand*'s court scenes demonstrates the novel's depiction of the law's fundamental biases and sets the scene for Southworth's more expansive revisioning of juridical subjecthood. Early in the novel, Capitola is arrested in New York City for cross-dressing. "What," the court clerk inquires, "caused this young girl to dress in boy's clothing?" "'Want, sir—and—and—*danger*, sir' crie[s] the little prisoner, putting her hands to a face crimson with blushes, and for the first time since her arrest on the eve of sobbing" (36). The implication here is that Capitola, unable to find work because she is a girl, not only experiences hunger, but also because she is homeless and sleeps on the streets at night is especially vulnerable to sexual violence:

> I couldn't get a job or work for love nor money, when my last penny was spent for my last roll—and my last roll was eaten up—and I was dreading the gnawing hunger by day, and the horrid perils of the night, I thought to myself if I were only a boy, I might carry packages, and shovel in coal . . . and sleep without terror by night! And then I felt bitter against fate for not making me a boy! . . . And then, all of a sudden, a bright thought struck me: and I made up my mind to be a boy! . . . And from that day forth I was happy and prosperous. (40–41)

The court is indifferent at best to Capitola's narrative, and the judge and clerks quickly prepare to send her to prison, when Old Hurricane, who happens to be at the police station and in attendance at the proceedings, declares himself her legal guardian: "I will enter into a recognizance for any sum to appear and prove my right if it should be disputed" (42). But the court finds no reason to dispute Old Hurricane's claim to the girl he now calls Capitola Black, and the court quickly "assume[s] the fact of [his] responsibility and delivers up the young girl to [his] charge" (42). This exchange, while initially welcome to Capitola, further underscores the utter disregard the court has for Capitola's security. Even after her testimony about facing threats of sexual violence, the court readily hands her over to an anonymous male bystander without any inquiry at all. The clerks and crowds even "wink" and "jibe" and call Old Hurricane "a hoary-headed sinner" (43). Unaware of the court's salacious assessment of Old Hurricane's claim, Capitola, at first, is delighted to acquiesce to this "gentleman," whom she mistakenly believes to be the father she has never known. "To find herself blest with wealth, leisure, and safety" is all she thinks she needs (45). This scene pivots on perceptions of safety and danger: the court willfully ignores Capitola's endangerment and believes her to be jeopardizing the safety of society by disregarding gender rules.[5] The court does not acknowledge society's failure to provide Capitola and young women like her recourse against sexual violence; in fact, the novel shows that Capitola's search for safety is not only unrealized on the streets but also in a court of law and in the privacy of home. All Capitola sees in this moment, however, is that the legal protection of Old Hurricane must be far superior to a workhouse prison.

The same cannot be said of a parallel court scene imagined later in the novel in which readers witness how Clara Day is assigned her wardship. Again, the novel's secondary plot reminds us of the grave dangers women face at the hands of a legal system that historically has failed to recognize their rights. Clara, who also finds herself at the mercy of the court, is far less fortunate with her appointed guardian. She is in court to dispute Colonel Le Noir's decision to remove her from her father's home and to ensconce her at Hidden House. Despite testimony that corroborates her father's deathbed wish that Clara remain in her ancestral home until old enough to marry Traverse Rocke (which was not written in his will because he suffers a chance accident that prematurely ends his life), the court denies her plea. Here too, Clara is encouraged to speak, yet her voice is quickly dismissed. Unlike Capitola's narrative, Clara's address employs vocabulary more familiar to the court:

> Your honor . . . while I bend to your honor's decision, and yield myself to the custody of my legal guardian for the period of my minority, I here declare to all who may be interested, that I hold my hand and heart irrevocably pledged to Doctor Rocke, and that, as his betrothed wife, I shall consider myself bound to correspond with him regularly . . . until my majority, when I and all that I possess will become his own. (227)

Even as Clara speaks firmly of her intent to obey the court's decision and marital convention, the sheriff turns to the colonel and declares him "likely to have a troublesome charge in [his] ward" (228). Le Noir, however, merely "shrug[s] his shoulders by way of reply" (228). In comparable instances, the court is indifferent to women's testimony and incapable of recognizing their perspectives. All that is of interest to the court is that Clara's "person and property are legally" at a man's immediate "disposal," regardless of who the man is or his intentions (211). In the guise of Clara's best interests, the court hands her over to the novel's ultimate villain. Again, the law court dispenses danger for women rather than relief or protection.

Despite his humble birth, Ishmael navigates the halls of justice and injustice far more fluidly. As Southworth's legal idol on behalf of women's safety and protection, the "self-made barrister" is the sole legal voice for downtrodden women (642). His first case, recommended to him by Judge Merlin, promises to build his client base and propel his career; however, Ishmael learns that the prominent client is a husband who abandoned his wife and children and now wishes to deny her any access to their children. Ishmael not only refuses to represent the man, he commences to defend the man's wife without remuneration. Although everyone scolds Ishmael that his case is doomed and his legal career in jeopardy before it has even begun, his two-hour oratory in the courtroom on the wrongs suffered by women helps to "wake . . . up the world" and inspires a change in the "laws of the nations in regard to woman" (623). Southworth devotes several pages to Ishmael's address to the jury, casting the husband as the pillager rather than the protector: "If the court did not protect her home against his invasion, he would again bring ruin and desolation within its walls" (615). Ishmael is Southworth's fictional antidote to the reality of women's legal status, status evidenced in *The Hidden Hand* and scores of Southworth's other novels, many of which envision a legal system that frequently fails to take into account women's lives, experiences, and testimony, particularly with regard to marriage laws and women's property rights. Ishmael, who becomes an advocate and official voice of the voiceless, also, perhaps unwittingly, reinforces the very legal paternalism that he seeks to undo. Writing about Southworth and married women's property rights, Elizabeth Stockton argues that "[Ishmael] becomes the hero by bringing the story of his mother—and the countless number of wronged women just like her—into the masculine space of the courtroom and asserting the rightful place of sympathy within its walls while keeping women hidden in its benevolent shadows" (259). Ishmael's role is as the protector of women rather than as the facilitator of their agency, and as such, he is a sentimental legal mediator. However, in the more haphazard romp through the legal sphere in *The Hidden Hand* readers see that there are alternative forms of legal recognition in which women's voices may be heard rather than solely mediated by men. Given Ishmael's legal heroism and his reinforcement of the "masculine space of the courtroom," it is all the more notable that Capitola, Southworth's most widely embraced adventurer and advocate on behalf of women, speaks her mind and raises her voice both in legal courtrooms and private domiciles. Capitola rejects juridical and domestic paternalism alike.

FAILURE OF THE LAW AND FAITH IN THE FIRESIDE

As Southworth well knew, the legal disregard of women's rights is a far older story than the novel itself.[6] For Southworth's female protagonists, as for many women, the laws that failed to recognize their interests often succeeded in confining them to domestic spaces like Hidden House and Hurricane Hall supposedly for their safety and protection. Southworth's use of gothic conventions is evident in the mortal danger she ascribes to the domestic sphere.[7] In *The Hidden Hand*, the public court of law *and* the private home are sites of potential danger rather than self-evident safety. In fact, the novel encourages its readers to ask just what it means to be or to feel safe. It demonstrates the ways in which insecurity is normalized for the women in the novel and, by extension, for vulnerable subjects in nineteenth-century America.[8] By using sensation tropes and by adapting forms of the domestic gothic, Southworth systematically exposes the protection of conventional "safe" spaces like the hearth and home as illusory.

For instance, the momentary comfort that Capitola embraces in her fantasy of domestic security at Hurricane Hall is quickly usurped. When she returns with Old Hurricane to Virginia, dressed in fine silk and, at long last, a proper girl, she realizes quickly she is nothing short of a prisoner in Hurricane Hall: "the absence of thinking and caring for herself, left a dull void in her heart and brain" (154). She is no longer physically hungry as she was on the streets of New York City, but she is mentally and emotionally starved: "bored half to death with the monotony of her life at Hurricane Hall" (190). Soon Capitola is wishing for the dangers from which she sought refuge: "Praying not *against* but wishing *for*—fire, floods, or thieves, anything to stir [her] stagnant blood" (190 my emphasis). Her mind-numbing domestic safety soon has her praying for all forms of peril. Capitola seeks solace in her horse, which Old Hurricane incessantly implores is both "impudent and unsafe" (155). Cap repeatedly refuses his counsel: "the restriction of her liberty is too heavy a price to pay for protection and support" (155). Characteristic of their conflict, Capitola confronts Old Hurricane and tells him that she will not suffer domestic imprisonment; she is "not a cur to be fed with roast-beef and beaten with a stick" (109). "Freedom and peace," she tells him, "are even sweeter than wealth and honor" (109). Capitola ultimately threatens to return Old Hurricane to court if he dares to detain her: "I will have you up before the nearest Magistrate, to show by what *right* you detained me! I wasn't brought up in New York for nothing" (109). Cap's "pluck" and self-representation is a notable contrast to Old Hurricane's true legal relation, Marah Rocke, the wife whom he abandons on mistaken pretenses and who lives secluded for over two decades "starving," we are told, in "mind, body, and soul" (94). Clara Day, moreover, is legally imprisoned at Hidden House.

The *domestic insecurity* the women in the novel confront is in notable contrast to the men in the novel who cultivate the comforts of home. For example, when we first meet Warfield, a.k.a. Old Hurricane, at the start of Southworth's novel, he is settling in for an evening at home on his Virginia estate, while his slaves prepare to go "off to a banjo break-down, held in the negro quarters of their next neighbor" (6). Old Hurricane scoffs at their merriment and wonders to himself "if there is anything on the face of the earth that would tempt [him] to leave [his] cozy fireside and go abroad to-night" (7). This question is significant. It anticipates an event that will demand Old Hurricane abandon his "cozy fireside" and brave the evening's winter storm. Old Hurricane is summoned to perform a legal duty, one that will set in motion the novel's action. His reluctance to leave the safety of his home, about which he argues with the Reverend Goodwin who calls upon him with a matter of "life and death," posits home as a refuge and the world beyond its walls as fraught with hazards.

Only when the Reverend Goodwin insists that Old Hurricane fulfill his legal duty as a "commission of the peace," reasoning that he is "bound to get up and go" to a dying woman's bedside to take her final deposition, does Old Hurricane relent (11). As it turns out, Hurricane's reluctance is fairly well founded. As he and the Reverend "lumber" over "rough roads" toward "the bowels of the earth," otherwise known as the "Devil's Punch Bowl," Old Hurricane asks the Reverend to chant the church litany that "prays to be delivered from 'battle, murder, and sudden death;' for if [they] should be so lucky as to escape Black Donald and his gang, [they] shall have at least an equal chance of being upset in the darkness of ... dreadful mountains" (12). The danger that lurks outdoors, whether malicious gangs or menacing mountain passes, are in sharp contrast to the comforts of home. While we have good reason to distrust Old Hurricane's meteorology, the deposition he takes from Nancy (Granny) Grewell, the mixed-race midwife who had "vanished from sight so mysteriously some thirteen years ago," emphasizes the immediate dangers that lurk beyond the safety of Hurricane Hall (14). In her deposition, Grewell relays to Old Hurricane how she was kidnapped by bandits on the very same roads that he lately traveled; she was forced to deliver the twin babies of an imprisoned and masked woman, and at this woman's request, secret the surviving child (one of the twins was stillborn) away to safety. Before Grewell and the infant girl make it to New York City, where she raises the child, Capitola, as her own, she and the infant are sold into slavery, survive a shipwreck on their journey south, and escape to the north with the help of Old Hurricane's nephew, Herbert Greyson.[9]

"What would it take to leave the safety of the fireside?" The question that Old Hurricane muses upon self-referentially at the start of the novel is not only heightened by the novel's focus on safety and danger, but it is also reimagined as we follow Southworth's serial and the adventures of its protagonist. For the women of the novel, home is hardly a "safe" place and venturing beyond it is the only hope for a measure of personal freedom and, ironically, safety. Domestic boredom turns out to be the mildest discomfort that the women in the novel experience. Clara is threatened with sexual violence at Hidden House, and virtually every time Capitola's life is in jeopardy it is *within* the supposed safety of Hurricane Hall. In a chapter titled "The Peril and Pluck of Cap," readers find three "stalwart ruffians armed to the teeth, lurking in ambush under her bed" (171). "Black Donald," the racialized bandit who skulks in the shadows and corridors of Devil's Alley, sends his gang to abduct Capitola on behalf of Gabriel Le Noir. Although readers learn "the danger was extreme," Capitola is able to lock her room, send for help, and secure the prisoners (172). Nonetheless, "no one thought of retiring to bed at Hurricane Hall that night" (177).

On other occasions, Black Donald is readily invited through the front door of the house. He dresses as a sailor selling "foreign goods" and is welcomed inside by domestic servants who are likened to curious consumers (135). Subsequently, disguised as the minister, Father Gray, Black Donald gains the confidence of Mrs. Condiment, Hurricane Hall's housekeeper: no one "admired Father Gray more than did the little old housekeeper of Hurricane Hall ... she often invited and pressed good Father Gray to rest and refresh himself ... until at length he seemed to live there altogether" (192). When Black Donald's disguises fail to propel his plans to abduct Capitola, he risks, so he says, his own "personal safety" in order to enter Capitola's bedroom and carry her off himself. Several chapter titles underscore Capitola's domestic endangerment. "The Awful Peril of Capitola" begins by citing a Shakespearean couplet: "Out of this nettle, danger/I'll pluck the flower, safety!" (344). Capitola is the flower, who is described by Black Donald as abundant in "charmed safety" (339). His plan, of course, is to disrupt her safety and, possibly, to deflower his prize: "to gain access to her chamber, secret himself anywhere in the room, and when the household should be buried in repose, steal out upon her, overpower, gag, and carry her off, in the silence of the night, leaving no trace of his own presence behind" (340). Again, Capitola foils his plans, plunging him through a trap door in her bedroom and down into a hidden cave, "One shuddering glance at the awful void, and then Capitola turned and threw herself, face downwards, upon the bed, not daring to rejoice in the safety that had been purchased by such a dreadful deed, feeling that it was an awful, though a complete victory!" (353).

Despite her "victory" and the "safety" she secures against Black Donald's planned attack—and the narrative's invocations of racial fear are intended to amplify the assault—Capitola cries herself to sleep distraught and unheard. However, once she and women like her step beyond the supposed safety of their uncle's, father's, and husband's homes, which Capitola constantly reminds readers is purchased at too great a price, their cries are more readily heard. Like Capitola, they may even turn out to be protagonists in their own sensation thrillers. In Louisa May Alcott's story "Honor's Fortune," the protagonist becomes a "runaway" rather than conform to convention: "Gliding like a shadow past the curtained windows looking on the balcony, she crossed the garden unseen, leaped the low wall, and hastened down the deserted street toward the open country. *Once in the park she felt safe*" (96 my emphasis). Her bold escape leads to a chance meeting with a stranger who helps her to restore both her fortune and her happiness.[10] Similarly, once untethered from the fireside, Capitola secures her own safety, while her physical mobility also saves other women's lives. She rescues Clara Day, defends her honor against Le Noir, and assists in the final capture of Black Donald and his gang. By countering the subplot of Marah Rocke's abandonment (and silence) and Clara Day's imprisonment (and silence) with Capitola's adventures and agency, we see the importance of spatial mobility beyond the domestic sphere. To Capitola, mobility is freedom; yet, Old Hurricane perceives only danger beyond the supposed comforts of home, especially for his young charge. He echoes some of the popular advice literature of the day that cautioned women travelers and readers against a world of anonymity and potential accident.[11]

Perhaps the success of Southworth's serials, dime novel authors like Laura Jean Libbey, and women writers of sensation and adventure fiction has much to do with these exploits, particularly how they envision women's mobility beyond the domestic sphere, a topic I will address in more detail in relation to late nineteenth-century women's fiction and crash literature in the following chapter. Like Capitola, women by the mid- to late nineteenth century were in "quest of adventures," traveling in larger numbers, lured by employment opportunities, cheaper transport, and faster machines. The mid- to late nineteenth century was nothing short of a revolution in mobility. By the second half of the century, numerous published etiquette and guidebooks counseled women on the rules, risks, and potential rewards of the open road. Although travel by railroad often appeared to stand in opposition to female respectability, Amy G. Richter writes in *Home on the Rails* (2006) that women's entry into the "public life of the railroads" led to a new sensibility, a form of "public domesticity," which helped to blur the boundaries of the public and private spheres and "stood at the very center of the transition from Victorian to modern American culture" (7).

The railroad often symbolized technological promise and national progress, and although it frequently was masculinized in its force and efficiency, it was also hailed as a harbinger of freedom, especially for women. In the summer of 1869 *Godey's Lady's Book* celebrated the completion of the transcontinental railroad by emphasizing its feminine reach: "The great works of modern civilization, the Pacific Railway . . . are chiefly made in the interest of those humane and peaceful employments in which the feminine element is so prominent; for the advancement of trade, the intercourse of friends, the binding together of the nation" (qtd. in Richter 14). However, *Godey's Lady's Book*'s praise of women's ability to "bind the nation" together through travel was countered by a storm of nineteenth-century advice literature that confirmed the cautions of Old Hurricane, emphasizing the dangers and manifold risks associated with increased mobility. Women were urged to use extreme vigilance with the strangers they might meet during their travels; they were unknowable, used disguises, and often preyed on the social confusion of public spaces. If "trains were new and enticing, an attractive lure for a naïve girl, and seemingly safe," writes Patricia Cline Cohen, they also "posed great dangers: fast moving trains, this literature cautioned, teemed with 'fast-moving men'" (Cohen 2). Etiquette books advised women to closely observe their fellow passengers and act with caution.

Railway travel was thought to pose risks to women's physical safety and respectability. The railroad was not only the vehicle binding the nation together it also was a potential harbinger of individual as well as collective hazard. For Southworth, the ubiquitous warnings about travel helped to create suspense in her serialized fiction, while it simultaneously exposed the excessive fearmongering in the growing trade of advice literature. Against the fear of proximity to strangers in train travel, Southworth reminds readers how little the inhabitants of the Virginia community in *The Hidden Hand*—characters who are all in some way related—actually know each other, despite their blood ties. Southworth imagines the most fruitful and compassionate relationships in the novel as those developing between complete strangers: Nancy Grewell saves Capitola's life, Old Hurricane gains Capitola's trust when they believe each other to be total strangers, Marah Rocke embraces the Greysons, the Days help the Rockes, and Capitola plots the rescue of the hidden guest of Hidden House, Clara Day, all supposed strangers—potential threats according to advice literature—who come to the aid of one another.

FICTIONAL FRIGHTS, FEARSOME ACCIDENTS, THE DEVELOPMENT OF TORT LAW

Sensation fiction imagined new challenges for privileged white women: they must rely on their own "pluck," like Capitola, and face dangers from which they were heretofore seemingly protected by the safety of the fireside.[12] Beyond the fireside sprang a sea of suspicious strangers and a tide of potential accidents.[13] The barrage of cautions about women's safety and security amid strangers on a train, cautions that filled etiquette books and often dictated the behavior of women in public, was surpassed by the growing literature documenting the physical risks of railroad travel and the dangers of work on the railroad itself. Mark Aldrich writes in *Death Rode the Rails* (2006) that by 1900 railroads were the "largest single American industry . . . dwarfing other dangerous trades" (4). Accident and death statistics show that "from 1882 to 1912, 48 percent of all deaths were from railroad accidents, in comparison to 7 percent from typhoid fever, the next largest cause" (4). Thus, one of the most substantial dangers women and men faced as they moved in larger numbers beyond the fireside was the risk of injury; the revolution in mobility led to an explosion of industrial and mechanical accidents, and the resulting physical and emotional wounds were suffered by men and women alike. In *Ishmael*, for example, the action is propelled forward by one such previously noted collision "on the London and Brighton Railway" that mistakenly reports the Countess of Hurstmonceux "instantly killed" (87). "Railroads . . . killed passengers by the hundreds each year," writes Aldrich, their dangers "amplified by the popular press" (2–3). By the early twentieth century, passenger fatality rates reached 110 times those of modern airlines (Aldrich 2).

The railroad, streetcars, and horses and buggies that provided the catalyst for mobility and freedom of movement for men and women also transformed accidental injury—so much of it associated with the new technology of the railroad—from discrete "individual events into a shared American experience" (Welke 80).[14] With increasing technological violence, the discourse on injury, suffering, and human vulnerability in the face of machine culture became a shared idiom. The law was certainly a formative voice in this discourse, but so too was literature. Here and in subsequent chapters, I describe the literary preoccupation with the dangers of machine culture and its collisions. Literature animated a changing cultural ethos: from the valorization of self-sufficiency to the recognition of forms of dependency and from privileged inviolability to universal vulnerability. This cognitive shift is manifest in unexpected places: through Theodore Dreiser's loosely fictionalized autobiographical character, Teddy, who becomes injury's accountant (chapter 3), and through Stephen Crane's use of urban conflagrations to critique racial discrimination (chapter 4).

In sensation fiction like *The Hidden Hand,* accidents and collisions illustrate our collective endangerment. Southworth's novel courts danger, and as readers follow Capitola's adventures, they are encouraged to experience its risks. In Southworth's serial, a ferry boat sinks at start of novel; Dr. Day dies in a riding accident; and Capitola is thrown from her horse at the feet of one of the novel's most dangerous villains. Such accidents were far less sensational than commonplace in the nineteenth century, and they indicate the large degree to which personal safety was often beyond individual control: on a ferry, railway, or streetcar people needed to rely on the judgment and expertise of others, to trust strangers with their own welfare. Indeed, tort law began to articulate the legal obligation that persons had to one another, even complete strangers, calling it "duty of care." The responsibilities for reasonable standards of care were considered legally binding between individuals whether or not there was a direct relationship (familial, contractual, or otherwise) to unite them. Strangers of the sort that Southworth imagines in her novel were abstractly joined not only by undetected blood ties, but more importantly, through a delicate legal web. While patriarchal laws of coverture and kinship recognized men's property interests in women and little else, with women's increased mobility and, subsequently, with their growing role as plaintiffs/protagonists in accident suits, tort law began to acknowledge, however reluctantly, something quite different from its institutionalized patriarchal conventions. Tort law began to recognize women's accounts of pain and injury.[15]

The stories of nineteenth-century women plaintiffs, while often veiled from history, provide crucial counter-narratives to contemporary conjectures about nineteenth-century women's lives. Joyce Warren's *Women, Money, and The Law: Nineteenth-Century Fiction, Gender, and the Courts* (2005) examines the legal records of New York Supreme Court cases from 1845–1875 and finds surprising clarity of voice among female plaintiffs. While the Supreme Court of New York retained the history of its legal decisions, it discarded most of the accompanying case materials, which often included women's testimony. Some of the records that were expunged from the official court documents were saved from destruction and now are part of the New York Supreme Court archive. Warren calls these documents the "stories behind the decisions" (9). In analyzing these narratives and the cases involving women whose accounts of injury "exist nowhere," who were, in fact, "erased from history," Warren finds hundreds of actions involving female litigants: "The court cases tell the compelling stories of individual and nonpublic women, some of whom were defeated and others of whom struggled against and triumphed over overwhelming legal obstacles and social pressures. Their actions run counter to the official narrative, which scripted women as economically dependent and financially uninvolved" (11). Novelists like Southworth played important roles in representing these "outlaw" voices—voices that often were counter to convention—by introducing them to mainstream readers. For women writers and women plaintiffs, growing anxiety about technological violence prompted debates about women's physical and emotional security. Although human vulnerability is a shared condition and physical injury a common experience, women's narratives of vulnerability helped to shape and define modern sensibilities.

Tort or injury law emerged in the nineteenth century in response to industrialization and the growing dangers of a crowded and mechanized public sphere. On the one hand, tort law demanded accountability; it marked the recognition of community and the duty of care to prevent harm to others, even utter strangers. The courts, seeking to promote innovation and technology, also tried to limit the web of responsibility with specific rules that closely articulated the relationship and duty one human being (or business) had to another. What dangers were acceptable to the community and when have they grown too threatening? Approximately midway through Southworth's novel, an accident mirrors the sort of cases that tort law was beginning to adjudicate. The facts of the case go something like this: riding his horse to Staunton on personal business, Dr. Day encounters a traveling circus company whose caravan charging toward town "frightens" Day's horse; the horse throws Day, tramples him, and runs away, leaving him fatally wounded and alone on a country road (201). When the horse reappears at Day's stables "frothing" at the mouth, Traverse Rocke follows its path to find the "fallen figure" of Dr. Day "doubled up helplessly" on the road (201). Numerous pages are devoted to the doctor's pain, injury, and suffering. He is transported back to his home, near death, where Day relates the story of his fatal wounds to family and friends: "my horse ran away, stumbled and fell upon me, and rolled over me in getting up; the viscera is crushed within me, breathing is difficult, speech painful; motion agonizing;—but you may examine and satisfy yourselves" (202). Despite "speaking cheerfully, though with great suffering," this accident presents readers with a detailed account of accidental injury (202). It is a scene, moreover, that reverses the supposed reluctance of men to express sensations (if white men were impervious to pain, white women were acutely sensitive to it). In addition to the caricatures of excessive male emotions in Old Hurricane and Le Noir—Hurricane is tempestuous and Le Noir filled with sinister ire—men in Southworth's novel teem with sensation and feeling rather than the want of it. Dr. Day's example shows us that men too are vulnerable to injury. As Day himself recounts, he is fragile, breakable, and, like women in the novel, susceptible to the risks associated with the human sensorium.

Were Southworth to turn to the law, as she does in so many other crucial moments in the novel, to adjudicate Dr. Day's injury and subsequent death, a court might have found the caravan to be negligent of other riders and vehicles in the road upon its entry into town. It might even reward Day's survivor, Clara, with a monetary settlement to offset her pecuniary loss.[16] In a notable absence, Southworth does not pursue this potential court scene amid the numerous other legal proceedings that she writes about in her novel. However, Southworth does use the accident to scrutinize physical as well as psychological shock and to dwell on its traumatic effects. Dr. Day is "helpless," "crushed," "pained," and "agonized," and Southworth devotes several pages to Day's collision and its aftermath (202). Compare, for instance, Dr. Day's fictional accident to the similar case of Alexander Hanlon, whose horse took fright after a locomotive engineer discharged steam quite close to Hanlon and his wagon. Like Dr. Day's scene in Southworth's novel, the horse throws Hanlon and he is gravely injured. The court described the engineer of the Philadelphia and West Chester Turnpike Road Company as "reckless" and found that the plaintiff had "a right to safe passage" (*Hanlon v. Philadelphia and West Chester Turnpike Road Company*, 1897). Hanlon's injuries resulted in lost work and pay, and the courts required the railroad to compensate him the sum of his lost wages. With the death of Dr. Day, Southworth's novel additionally imagines what the law declares it cannot value: the consequent non-material pain, especially the emotional loss that comes with the death of a family member. For many years, law courts believed they could not calculate, nor did they want to, any redress for emotional injuries.

Tort law sought to establish, as best it could, a law of equivalents, and it resisted what it saw as areas of indeterminacy; it sought to eschew the nuance of narrative, despite the need for detailed description in understanding injury's scope. The reluctance to recognize the potential extent of traumatic injury, especially its frights and shocks, led feminist legal scholars to criticize what they saw as tort law's historic privileging of physical and property interests over elements like emotional and psychological security.[17] In their landmark article "Women, Mothers, and the Law of Fright" (1990), legal scholar Martha Chamallas and historian Linda Kerber argued that rigid distinctions between "physical and emotional harm [have] obscured how courts and commentators used injuries associated with men as the dominant standard" for assessing legal value (21). The early cultural and gendered prohibitions against women's narratives of pain and injury meant that what became known as the "reasonable man standard" set the stage for how courts interpreted harm and had the effect of "devaluing emotional or psychological injuries which then became associated with women" (Chamallas and Kerber 21). Unmaking these dichotomies—reason/emotion, material/immaterial, and male/female—became an urgent focus of feminist legal scholarship.[18]

More recently, feminist and gender theorists have extended this critique, looking at the language of vulnerability to understand and theorize individual and structural harms and to critique the cultural value attached to autonomy over interdependence. For example, legal scholar Martha Albertson Fineman suggests that in order to rethink vulnerability and its unilateral association with victimization we must think beyond American myths that privilege individualism and self-sufficiency above all else. As Southworth's novels demonstrate, susceptibility to suffering and liability to harm does not discriminate by gender; we see this in characters like Clara Day, Marah Rocke, Old Hurricane, Ishmael, and Dr. Day. Southworth shows how the capacity to suffer is inherent in human embodiment; it is, as Judith Butler argues, an ontological condition of humanity. Butler proposes that the "apprehension of common human vulnerability" should yield to "the principle of protecting others" from violence rather than masking vulnerability by resorting to violence (*Precarious* 30). Capitola models this ethics in her many relationships and interpersonal encounters in the novel. Like her beloved character, Southworth's *The Hidden Hand* embraces human interdependence and fragility not as weakness or powerlessness but as a condition of modern personhood.

While enjoying the relative safety and security of the printed page, the sensation novel brought to the reading public many of the frights and shocks that lurked beyond its covers. It is notable that Capitola's popularity and the narrative's serialization for over thirty years corresponds with the flourishing of legal discourse about the physical and psychological impact of sensations like fright and shock as well as the social responsibility to acknowledge, compensate, and repair these injuries. In 1859, the year that *The Hidden Hand* was first serialized, fright cases were only a small subset of the accident cases emerging in tort law. By the 1870s and 80s, when Southworth's fiction was re-serialized and subsequently published in novel form, "accident figures and suits began their precipitous climb. More and more women were among those suffering injuries and more and more cases involving injured women reached state appellate courts" (Welke 93). Legal narratives in *The Hidden Hand* represent an occasion to rethink the gendering of independence, interdependence, vulnerability, and security alike. The nineteenth-century fright case is a small but important piece in the literary history of the sensation novel as well as in the development of tort law precisely because it begins to address how the dangers and harms of modern life demanded redress. Legal historian Barbara Welke argues that it was especially "through the minds and bodies of women" that law courts came to "recognize a right to recover for injury resulting from fright and shock" (202). Between 1870 and 1920, American courts decided hundreds of fright and shock cases, and women were plaintiffs in the overwhelming majority of them (195–96). The "original precedent established by the highest court" in many states involved injuries to women (Welke 196). It is notable that the repetitive reprinting and retelling of Capitola's story in serialized and novel form subtended the growing attention to these legal cases. Women's narratives, literary and legal, were remaking the meaning of autonomy, dependency, and legal personhood.

In a typical fright case, *Oliver and WIFE vs. The Town of La Valle Wisconsin* (1875), the court records include detailed testimony from the female plaintiff in a joint action with her husband to recover from injuries caused by fright after a bridge collapse in La Valle Wisconsin. Although some states were quicker than others to recognize women as plaintiffs in their own right, the case builds on Mrs. Oliver's testimony: "I got out of the wagon, very much frightened, and felt safer on the ground. [My brother] told me to unhitch the cross lines. I was so frightened, I could not. I didn't seem to have any use of my right hand. I was all of a tremble. He told me to keep cool; if I was frightened, I couldn't do any good." While Mrs. Oliver and her brother were able to get the horses to safety, she tells the court that "within about an hour after reaching her father's house, [she] had a miscarriage." The medical testimony "sworn upon the trial" was that "sudden emotions, fright, and violent exertions after fright are exciting causes of miscarriage" (*Oliver and Wife v. The Town of La Valle*). The Olivers won their case and were awarded $750 in damages.

Cases of fright could encompass circumstances as varied as the fall from a horse due to the animal's fright to, later, the nervous shock of an accident victim where no visible physical injuries were immediately sustained.[19] Physicians provided expert appraisal that women could suffer grave physical and emotional harm even several days after an initial shock or impact (*Benjamin v. Holyoke Street Railway Company*, 1893). "Modern medical science declares in the plainest language that physical injuries may result from acts through mental shock where there is no physical impact. This has become a matter of common [medical] knowledge . . . Is it not flying in the face of reason for a law court to decide otherwise?" (qtd. in Meighen 349). Annie Benjamin, who in 1893 was the sole plaintiff in her lawsuit against the railroad, suffered a miscarriage twelve days after she was thrown from her carriage by a frightened horse. She filed a legal action against the railway company seeking to recover damages for the injuries she sustained due to its negligence. Benjamin won her suit. Juries were returning verdicts in favor of plaintiffs in fright cases despite the courts' suspicion of false narratives, judges' fear of a flood of cases, and charges of immeasurability for proximate injuries. In what became typical of some of these cases featuring female plaintiffs, fright often involved miscarriage and relational loss. The compromise of physical integrity, especially the loss of a fetus, precipitated the recognition of emotional integrity.[20] "Courts and juries found women justified in their fright, and drew a connection between a woman's mental state and her health and well-being. Thus, generalizing from cases involving women, sometimes pregnant women, appellate courts and treatise writers fashioned a new law of negligence," writes legal scholar Felice Batlan (9). Even "remote injuries," injuries that emerge significantly after a near accident, expanded in scope. In *Purcell v. St. Paul City R. Co.* (1892) a female plaintiff was a passenger on a streetcar line that came close to a collision with a cable train. "The passenger was riding on the horse car railway when a collision between the two lines seemed imminent. As a result of her fright, the passenger suffered a miscarriage and was confined to her bed for three months" (*Purcell v. St. Paul City R. Co*). The opinion in the case reasoned that the plaintiff's fright surely was "as serious as the breaking of an arm or leg" and held the defendant liable for damages.[21]

Fright actions were at once deeply normative: a woman's physical vulnerability and her reproductive body provoked state intervention; but, striking too, she became emblematic. The connections the courts made between a woman's mental state and her physical symptoms would surpass paternalism and come to apply to all injured persons. Characteristics and feelings attributed to her, her vulnerability as well as her demand for legal recognition, became standard in the law. In place of the fetus, in other words, grew several new sensations recognized by law. Her pains and injuries bore fruit, and her vulnerability became a model for legal action. In chapter 3 on women's crash literature, Ellen Glasgow's novel *Barren Ground* (1925) imagines a traffic accident that results in a miscarriage, leaving the protagonist physically "barren" in the most literal sense; however, the collision also precipitates the protagonist's emotional and spiritual growth and, ultimately, the fecundity of her farm. The power of accident challenged "masculine fantasies of power, self-sufficiency, and control, but also opened the door to important progressive reforms implemented by and for women" (Puskar 27). Tort law and its burgeoning recognition of women's physical and emotional injuries echoes the promise that Southworth's character Ishmael makes: women's wrongs will be recognized.

If the law is a site of sentimental negotiation and paternalistic protection in *Ishmael*, in *The Hidden Hand* it is a vehicle for the recognition and expansion of women's personhood. In contrast to how marriage laws often are imagined in Southworth's novels and critiqued by literary critics, the power of accident and the law of torts is far more capacious in envisioning women's potential agency. Capitola is a model of a triumphant plaintiff/protagonist. While quite literally born of fright (readers might recall the shock that lead to her birth) and facing it repeatedly in the novel, her experiences are not confined by the polite conventions of her gender. She is a woman who because of her ability to withstand peril and danger, we are told, "deserve[s] to be a man" (285). When we first meet her, she is a boy discovered to be a girl. In fact, Capitola's gender trouble serves to remind readers of another mistaken divide that Capitola gleefully undermines: she reminds readers of the inseparability of physical and emotional integrity throughout *The Hidden Hand*.

Readers see this inseparability not only in her stand against Old Hurricane, whom she threatens with legal action should he fail in the recognition of her "rights," but also in her response to a small accident that she herself suffers in which, again, the subplot and main plot parallel each other. While the circumstances of this accident do not mirror the emerging legal cases as closely as Dr. Day's accidental death, and while Capitola's physical safety from her fall is only momentarily in doubt (she quickly casts off any concern with bruises and, with equal speed, thwarts the threat of sexual violence), Capitola's riding accident underscores her ability to recognize her vulnerability and not become a victim. Southworth shows readers that physical and emotional integrity go hand in hand. As the narrative tells us, "It happened this way: she had come to a steep rise in the road, and urged her pony into a hard gallop, intending, as she said to herself, to 'storm the height,' when suddenly, under the violent strain, the girth, ill-fastened, flew apart, and Miss Cap was on the ground, buried under the fallen saddle" (318). Because of the negligence of "those wretches in uncle's stable [who] did not half buckle the girth," Capitola grumbles, she is found by Le Noir, the notoriously "dangerous individual" who has vowed to Capitola's destruction by any means necessary (318). Le Noir uses her accident and the question of Capitola's physical safety as an occasion to launch an assault through an insidious sentimental appeal. He abandons plans to overcome Capitola with physical violence (which he threatens in an earlier encounter and for which he hires Black Donald) and believes the best path to victory over her mind and body is through her heart; thus, he tries to persuade Capitola to marry him. Like an earlier encounter with Le Noir in which Capitola plays up her gentile femininity in order to elicit protection from him, a performance that disrupts his intent to overtake her on horseback and sexually violate her, Capitola again flirts with gender expectations only to overturn them. To Le Noir's emotional appeal she ultimately replies, "It is downright sentimental, I suppose, if I had only the sense to appreciate it (319). She lures Le Noir by feigning her susceptibility to his appeal, and she undermines him by mocking her misunderstanding of the self-same terms. She employs then destabilizes the presumption of her vulnerability and defenselessness and she triumphs.

Numerous characters in *The Hidden Hand* critique Capitola because she adopts what they see as a masculine model of invincibility and emotional detachment; yet, she ultimately succeeds as the novel's unabashed hero when she secures her own and others' physical and emotional integrity; this is her valued currency and it is fundamental to her own personal sensibility. Against the dominant script of nineteenth-century liberal individualism, which privileges self-protection and independence above all, Capitola prizes interdependence and she embraces care. True to the sensation plot, she is often vulnerable to harm; yet, she still takes risks. Capitola may be a model for a new form of sociability; her narratives of danger and her embrace of responsibility, her physical daring and her demand for emotional integrity, are all part of her appeal. Not only does she stretch the possibilities for the modern subject in literary narrative, but she also urges its reexamination before the law.

NOTES

1. All citations are from the 1997 Oxford University Press edition of the novel. The novel was first serialized in the *New York Ledger* in 1859 and published in novel form in 1888.

2. For more on women writers and the sensation genre, see Shelley Streeby, "The Dime Novel, the Civil War, and Empire," in *American Sensations*, 227–47.

3. Criticism on Southworth and these topics includes: Abate, "Launching a Gender B(l)acklash"; Habegger, "A Well-Hidden Hand"; Huddock, "Challenging the Definition of Heroism"; Ings, "Blackness and The Literary Imagination"; Jones, "'This Dainty Woman's Hand'"; Landry, "Of Tricks, Tropes, and Trollops"; Looby, "Southworth and Seriality"; and Okker, "Reassuring Sounds."

4. *Ishmael: Or, in the Depths* (Grosset & Dunlap, 1884). All further citations are from this edition.

5. For more on cross-dressing and the space of the courtroom, see Clare Sears, *Arresting Dress: Cross-dressing, Law, and Fascination in Nineteenth-Century San Francisco*.

6. See the discussion on rights in Deborah L. Rhode's "Natural Rights and Natural Roles," in *Justice and Gender*, 9–28.

7. For more on the domestic gothic, see Evie Shockley, "The Haunted Houses of New Orleans: Gothic Homelessness and African American Experience," in *Katrina's Imprint: Race and Vulnerability in America*: "The genre's fundamental characteristic is that it is designed to communicate to readers or viewers feelings of intense terror or horror. Far from being purely punitive, this goal recognizes the pleasure that such feelings can bring when safely contained within the pages of a book or the frames of a movie . . . the gothic is intended to produce a catharsis in its audience: to articulate its readers' fears in a form that allows them to be resolved—in narrative, if not in life," 99.

8. For more discussion of safety as a "rhetoric, and as a practice of power relations," see the special edition of *WSQ, Safe* (Spring/Summer 2011) and particularly the introduction by Alyson M. Cole and Kyoo Lee, "Introduction: Safe," 15–27.

9. The plot features hairbreadth escapes, hidden identities revealed, and numerous confrontations between the forces of good and evil. Recognizing Capitola's identity from Grewell's story, Old Hurricane embarks on a journey to New York, finds the young girl (who is disguised as a boy in order to survive on the city streets), and returns with her to Hurricane Hall to begin her domestication. After a series of adventures, including Capitola's capture of the outlaw Black Donald and her escape from her Uncle and premier villain Gabriel Le Noir, who wants to finish the deed he failed to do over thirteen years ago, Capitola is reunited with the biological mother she never knew (her mother was imprisoned in Hidden House and later a madhouse for thirteen years). Capitola is restored to her rightful place as heir of the estate, Hidden House, and, in the end, she is united in marriage to Old Hurricane's nephew and her oldest

friend, Herbert Greyson. If this were not sensational enough, a secondary plot involves Old Hurricane's estranged wife and son and the restoration of their families and fortunes.

10. Also significant is Alcott's posthumously published novel, *A Long Fatal Love Chase* (1866). It is the story of a young woman who is willing to sell her soul to the devil in order to win her freedom. Joyce Warren notes, "because of the controversial subject matter, Alcott could not find a publisher for this novel during her lifetime, and it was not published until 1995," *Women, Money, and the Law,* 288.

11. See Patricia Cline Cohen, "Women at Large: Travel in Antebellum America"; Sidonie Smith, "By Rail: Trains, Tracks, and the Derailments of Identity," in *Moving Lives,* 121–65; and Amy Richter, "When Spheres Collide: Women Travelers, Respectability, and Life in the Cars," in *Home on the Rails,* 32–58.

12. As Nancy Grewell's story makes plain, women of color rarely had such luxuries.

13. For a fuller legal analysis of women's injuries before the law, see Margot Schlanger, "Injured Women before Common Law Courts, 1860–1930," 79–140.

14. See Barbara Welke, *Recasting American Liberty*: "From thousands of individual sufferers of accidental injury, the experience of injury radiated outward to those who witnessed accidents, to those who cared for the injured, to those who read about accidents and the courtroom contests that followed, and to those who determined legal responsibility," 80.

15. Accidents have played a crucial role in the fiction of some of the most celebrated American authors, as Nan Goodman argues in *Shifting the Blame: Law, Literature, and the Theory of Accidents in Nineteenth-Century America.* Women writers also imagined and critiqued accidental injuries and their impact.

16. "Litigation moved away from an eighteenth-century model of masters suing for the loss of service of a servant, slave, wife, or child, toward the now more familiar model of suits for loss of wages and support." See John Fabian Witt, "From Loss of Services to Loss of Support": these cases often "embodied and reproduced a new nineteenth-century conception of the family in which men worked as free laborers and women were . . . removed from the market and dependent for their support on the wages of their husbands" 717.

17. "While 'justice' is typically associated with universal rules, consistency, reason, rights, the public sphere, and, hence, masculine virtues," writes Robin West in *Narrative, Authority, and Law,* "care is typically associated with particularity, context, affect, relationship, the private sphere and, of course, femininity," 23. West argues against the supposedly incompatible opposition between the law's interest in justice and notions care, maintaining that the two are necessary preconditions of each other. Legal scholar Susan Bandes takes to task what she calls "law's devotion to an emotionless cognitive sphere" and suggests that at its core emotion may "threaten . . . much of what law hopes to be," *The Passions of Law,* 7.

18. See collections like *The Passions of Law.* More recently, Judith Butler has argued that the unmaking of the binary opposition between vulnerability and agency must be a priority for feminism. "Rethinking Vulnerability and Resistance," 25

19. See Roger Luckhurst, "The Genealogy of a Concept," in *The Trauma Question,* 20–49; and Reichman, "Woolf and the Lessons of Tort," in *The Affective Life of Law,* 15–26.

20. See J. F. D. Meighen, "May Damages be Recovered from Physical Injuries Resulting from Fright?" for a more in-depth discussion of remote injuries.

21. The judge continued, "Fright was the cause of the injury, and the defendant's wrong caused the fright. . . . That a mental condition (such as fright) comes between the negligence and the injury does not break the required sequence of immediate causes" (*Purcell v. St. Paul City R. Co.*). See also *Gulf, C. & S. F. R. Co. v. Hayter* (1900) for a discussion of men suffering from fright.

TWO
Crash Lit

Trains, Pains, and Automobiles

The Young Housewife

At ten A.M. the young housewife
moves about in negligee behind
the wooden walls of her husband's house.
I pass solitary in my car.

Then again she comes to the curb
to call the ice-man, fish-man, and stands
shy, uncorseted, tucking in
stray ends of hair, and I compare her
to a fallen leaf.

The noiseless wheels of my car
rush with a crackling sound over
dried leaves as I bow and pass smiling.
—William Carlos Williams, 1917

William Carlos Williams's poem "The Young Housewife" envisions a landscape from the view of a car; it is a proto-suburban scene: a young woman, the "housewife," observed and imagined at moments during her day. Morning, as the narrator passes in a car, she moves in her "negligee" within the "wooden walls of her husband's house." In the next stanza of the poem, she reaches the "curb," fetches provisions, calls "the ice-man, fish-man," and the narrator, who presumably sees her more clearly from the car as she moves from "behind" the walls of her husband's house, imagines her as "shy" and compares her "to a fallen leaf." In the final stanza of the poem, the narrator and the housewife "meet"; they share a glance, illusory or otherwise: she from the curb, the narrator from the car; he mobile; she a fallen leaf that the narrator's wheels "rush with a crackling sound over." Voiceless, faceless, and nameless, the narrator bows and smiles at the "young housewife" as he rolls "noiselessly over" and drives on.[1] In its expression of desire and destruction, metonymic violence (likened to a falling leaf she is crushed) and neighborly courtesy (he smiles, bows, and passes on), the poem is enigmatic. Are these brief encounters cautionary? Sympathetic? Hostile? The crush of car tires forecasts the young housewife's figurative death; constrained in her husband's house, she, like the leaf, will wither, fall, and crumble. The narrator's self-evident freedom in the poem is juxtaposed with the housewife's relative stasis—yet, both are ensnared in a kind of solitude that is symbolized by the enclosure of the automobile, their singular encounter emblematic of social death, and, through the promise of automobility, also the very precipice of social change.

The poem encapsulates with stunning simplicity the critical dilemma that women, and, presumably, in the case of the young housewife, privileged white middle-class women, often faced in the late nineteenth and early twentieth centuries, when new technologies and changing social mores made mobility, moving from "behind the walls" of their homes, seductive and dangerous. The promise and the violence played out repeatedly in women's fiction in the heyday of passenger transportation, when riding the rails and, later, automobility were subjects of extensive cultural fascination. Williams's poem demonstrates the "masculine logic of mobility," which Sidonie Smith in *Moving Lives* (2001) has described as the freedom of movement and travel that was associated predominantly with men and "masculine prerogatives"; by contrast, women often were imagined as immobile, static, and tethered to the home.[2]

The notion of mobility was itself gendered, and women often occupied a troubled place in male narratives of discovery and adventure. Williams's poem joins a long legacy of literary accounts of masculine mobility, its privileges passed down from iconic figures like James Fenimore Cooper and Henry David Thoreau to Jack London and Stephen Crane, writers for whom geographic mobility spelled independence and self-making and the belief in which exacted extraordinary power in the American imaginary. Yet, the high-speed mobility that seemed to marshal masculine confidence and control was also vexed by anxiety that the world was speeding out of control. The fantasies of sovereign self-sufficiency and freedom of movement that were constitutive of masculine agency collided in the late nineteenth and early twentieth centuries with the realities of industrial and technological violence; the danger that accompanied new methods of high-speed travel threatened the very idea of masculine autonomy and bodily integrity. Although Williams's poem "The Young Housewife" does not climax with a startling automobile crash so much as a disquieting quotidian landscape—fallen leaves crushed beneath car tires—it is the threat of collision, literal and symbolic, physical and social, that gripped the late nineteenth- and early twentieth-century literary imagination for men and women alike.

In magazines and periodicals, fiction and non-fiction, stunt reporting and academic scholarship, poetry, short stories, and novels, the violent encounter, the collision of machines and bodies became a ubiquitous symbol for the adventures, risks, and potential harms of modern culture, its seductions and dangers narrated across cultural texts. New technologies for travel became the subject of much social commentary, and it was commonplace to worry about these inventions moving faster than the ability of human societies to cope (Wajcman 21). Scholars have called the preoccupation with technological disaster "crash culture" and argue that in it we can see "the subjection of men [and women] to the inhuman machinery of industrialization and technological rationalism."[3] In imaginative fiction in the late nineteenth and early twentieth centuries the theme of the "disastrous wreck" became a way of "redirecting risk, of displacing, exaggerating, or transforming a sense of threat," as Nancy Bentley argues in *Frantic Panoramas* (2008) (Bentley 231).[4] The thrills and sensations of crash culture spawned a whole entertainment industry, literary and extra-literary, dedicated to replicating its sensations, as literary criticism from Bill Brown's readings of amusement parks and disaster spectacles in *The Material Unconscious* (1996) to Katherine Biers's readings of new media technologies in *Virtual Modernism* (2013) amply document.[5] Consumers were eager to experience the physical risks of technological innovation in relative safety, and the growth of risk-seeking entertainment, from sensation novels and amusement parks to scripted conflagrations on the theater stage, satisfied this need. At the turn of the twentieth century an array of new "amusements greatly increased the emphasis placed on spectacle, sensationalism, and astonishment" (Singer 88). The culture of spectacle and its "commerce in sensory shocks" influenced lowbrow recreation as well as highbrow art (Singer 88). Real and virtual catastrophe had entertainment value, and its absorption by the public appeared indefatigable.

The simulation of danger and the commercialization of excitement were symptoms as well as reflections of a new technological modernity, a curious feature of what Ulrich Beck notably labeled a "risk society." Modern methods of mobility like the railroad and automobile brought substantial increases in bodily peril and nervous stimulation. From Beck and Giddens to Robert Wiebe and François Ewald, scholars have addressed how the juridical, economic, political, and epistemological dimensions of risk became the very principle of a new world order.[6] At the turn of the twentieth century, President Theodore Roosevelt warned that easing a culture of escalating risk was the single greatest challenge facing the United States, and he urged leaders nationwide to find statistical, quantifiable, administrative, and technological solutions (Rozario 104).

While a search for order was one response to the risks, threats, and chaos of late nineteenth-century accident, as Robert Wiebe described in his renowned study by that name, it also anticipated "a cult of chaos or a search for *disorder*" (Rozario 105 my emphasis). Against the social, political, and technocratic efforts to manage risk and to increase security came a cultural fascination with spectacles of violence, sensational thrills, and the contours of crash culture.

The friction between simulating danger and seeking safety was particularly pronounced in a new genre of women's crash lit, in which scenes of collision were immediate and visceral and the pervasive symbol of technological violence also underscored the promise of a new era of social relations. Despite the image of Williams's "shy" housewife, not only men but also women on the move gained new agency as the logic of mobility allowed them to challenge the idea of their "cultural construction in difference" (Smith 23). Technological modernity affected the stories men and women narrated about gender and bodies at rest as well as in motion. This chapter describes how American women writers seized and shaped the tropes that became critical to the cultural vocabulary of the crash, a vocabulary that embraced the speed, energy, sensations, and chaos of modern transport, but also exposed its vulnerabilities and its webs of interdependence. Literature in concert with developments in industry, technology, law, and medicine imagined socially vital and shared feelings, prominent among them, a collective sense of risk and vulnerability. This chapter argues that narratives by women inhabited these sensibilities and, in turn, deployed cultural anxieties about collective vulnerability in the face of technological change toward a wider recognition of social injuries.

ENGINE TROUBLE

The figurative evocation of the trodden housewife in Williams's poem is startlingly literal in Harriet P. Spofford's "The Black Bess."[7] Published just a few short years after the end the American Civil War, far before automobility would prevail as the reigning symbol of crash culture, the powerful but dangerous train engine became a metaphor for the complexities of post–Civil War culture, as the customs of race and gender were quite literally transformed aboard fast-moving trains.[8] Spofford's railroad engineer is haunted by the fear that he will crush his fiancée beneath the wheels of his beloved train engine, Black Bess. Spofford's story is an alarming allegory for the imagined threats black womanhood posed to white womanhood in the post–Civil War years (in the engineer's nightly hallucinations, Black Bess crushes the lady in white), and, like Williams's poem, it enacts male fantasies of violence against women, expresses masculine anxieties of impotence, and betrays male fears of

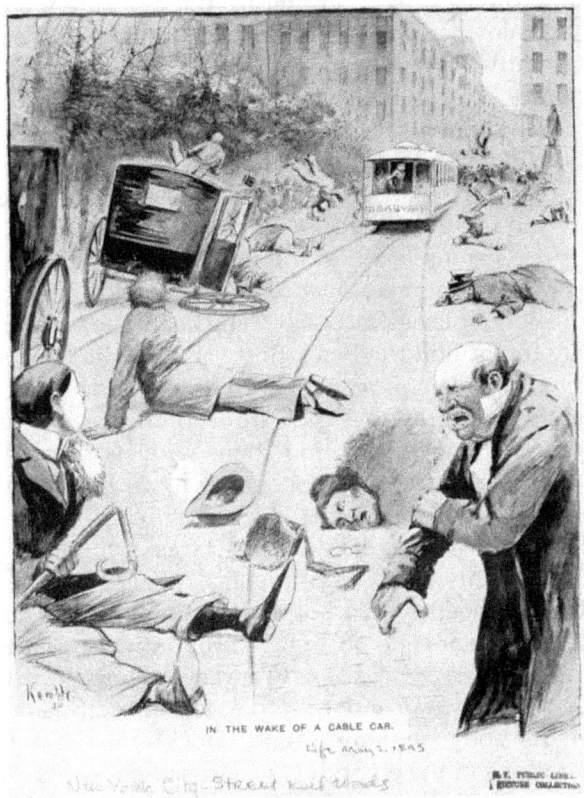

Figure 2.1. Art and Picture Collection, The New York Public Library. "In the Wake of a Cable Car." *New York Public Library Digital Collections.*

and about women. In "The Black Bess," the railroad and its vocabulary of real and indeterminate injury invite readers to grapple with the impact of less habitually visible forms of cultural violence.

The nameless narrator in Spofford's story is "the master of an engine on the Great Interior Railway, running a night train across the State, and earning [his] living by the sweat of [his] brow, in soot, and grime and smoke, and all in the midst of a wild relish of danger" (517). The narrator loves his "iron steed" for the "dangers she had passed," and he notes, "there are few whose affections are not drawn to their companion in peril" (518). Although he is engaged to Margaret, the admiration of his "companion in peril" Black Bess far outpaces his loving descriptions of his fiancée at the start of the story. The engineer's "affections" for Bess and Margaret are soon put to the test, as a train collision and derailment trigger the engineer's delusion that his beloved Bess flattens Margaret beneath her wheels. "One second the face, the face of that sleeping man, branded on my brain as if by a searing-iron; the next, a wild thought of Margaret, a great blow, and dumb darkness. The man and his load were dust together, the Black Bess was off the track and above her wheels in meadow mud, and I lay stunned and senseless" (518). In the engineer's mind, the original accident, the collision that crushes a nameless "man and his load" to "dust," is replaced by a repetitive fantasy in which Margaret, the engineer's fiancée, is herself flattened into the "meadow mud." Although the "shock he received" by the initial crash and its unsettling misapprehensions leads to a long and protracted "concussion" and "depression," the engineer eventually returns to Bess and the violence of the collision fantasies increase: "The beating of my heart and the breathing of my lungs, and the Black Bess ran as if the fires of hell were blazing beneath her boilers. It was the face of Margaret that I had seen!" (520). "Margaret's great gray eyes gaze up from the tracks, "as the belching monster pounded down to blind them with its fierce and blazing head-light, to crush them from their sockets with its remorseless wheels" (521). The engineer is powerless to stop a "blazing" Black Bess from crushing "gray eye[d]" Margaret beneath her tracks.

Black Bess is not only an agent of physical hazard and, like the automobile in Williams's poem, a symbol of desire and destruction, fear and fantasy, but also the engineer's post-crash traumatic reenactments underscore the railroad's role in a host of new and bewildering disorders. With the swift pace of industrial and technological growth came vast new pathologies of the body and mind, and shock and nervousness were common exhortations in the emerging sciences of psychophysiology and psychology (Schnapp 7). While much has been written about the transportation revolution and the fundamental psychic and physiological changes it occasioned, the railroad collision and the new and surprising face of some of its victims—writers like Theodore Dreiser, whose neurasthenia and work cure on the railroad I discuss in the next chapter, or heroic engineers like the narrator of "The Black Bess"—inspired an innovative vocabulary through which to understand physical and psychological vulnerability, particularly the psyche and its capacity for harm.[9] It is notable that in Spofford's story it is not the uncontrolled train engine but rather its engineer, not the machine but the man, who truly inflicts injury; it turns out that the only way to rid himself of his violent fantasies about Margaret's death is to physically assault her himself.

In "The Black Bess" the violent illusions and psychoses of the narrator sharply contrast with the dominant cultural image of the railroad engineer as a heroic figure. According to *Scribner's Magazine*, he was the "hero of the rail," powerful and fearless, taking "charge of a steam boiler that may explode and blow him to atoms, and of machinery that may break and kill him, and to try to keep up a vigilance which only a being more than human could successfully maintain" (qtd. in Richter 149). The engineer's strength and nerve was hailed across periodical literature in the late nineteenth century as an example of a new social class of mobile men, and as Amy G. Richter notes in *Home on the Rails* (2005), he "was frequently portrayed as the most heroic of all" especially because he was entrusted with the public's safety. "Engineers must not only look out for themselves," offers one account, but for "hundreds who are back of them in the passenger coaches" (qtd. in Richter 150).

The danger and delight of riding with the heroic engineer in his engine cab became a conventional feature of railroad narratives, with women's presence often part of the adventure. In these narratives, the central focus is the experience of mobility itself. If celebrated accounts of railway travel like Wolfgang Schivelbusch's *The Railway Journey* (1977) see the railway voyage in "instrumental terms: as movement within a network of departure and destination between which extends only vacant, useless space"—space, in other words, to be collapsed—the growing number of stories and reports of riding in the engine cab embrace the thrill of speed and the vastness of the American landscape (Schnapp 7). It is hard to overstate the cognitive transformation brought on by railways and steam engines, argues Judy Wajcman in *Pressed for Time* (2014): "The traveler's view of landscape as a multitude of swiftly moving visual impressions was unprecedented" (Wajcman 38).

Women often welcomed this transformation in the tempo of their everyday lives. In H. G. Prout's "Safety in Railroad Travel" (*Scribner's* 1889), readers follow the experience of a "Lady" who joins the engineer in "the cab of locomotive hauling a fast express train over a mountain road." Watching the "bright line of the rails and the slender point of the switches, she heard the thunder of the bridges and saw the track shut in by rocky bluffs, and new perils suddenly revealed as the engine swept around sharp curves. The experience was to her magnificent, but the sense of danger was almost appalling" (Prout 327–28). The article marvels at the Lady's relative safety in light of the "magnificent" and "appalling" hazards she recounts. Ultimately, the article contends, she is in strong hands: "When one reflects upon the destructive energy which is contained in a swiftly moving train, and sees its effects in a wreck; when he understands how many minute mechanical details, and how many minds and hands must work together in harmony to insure its safe arrival at its destination, he must marvel at the safety of railroad travel" (Prout 328). In these railway narratives, women face the dangers of train travel and embrace the intensity of the engine cab with aplomb, and they emerge relatively unscathed (and in many fictional accounts with rings on their fingers). Novels like Francis Lynde's *A Romance in Transit* (1897) and Frank Spearman's *The Daughter of a Magnate* (1903) tell a vehicular variation of the marriage plot in which the female passenger and the male engineer unite in the face of the dangers of train travel (Richter 135–48). Richter argues that women's narratives of railroad travel are representative of new forms of "public domesticity," an interstitial realm in which masculine publicity and feminine domesticity meet.

The decorative domesticity that women often brought to the engine cars turns dangerous and deadly in M. Sheffy Peters story "Danger Ahead!" Published in *Godey's Lady's Book* (1884), it begins as one more in a long line of narratives told from the engine cab; however, in this story, the passenger in the "black veil" who appears to haunt the train is not a decorative accessory but rather the embodiment of danger, the precursor to accident, the executioner, and simultaneously a casualty. A male reporter who rides the New Jellico rail route and dispatches news stories about his adventures for a newspaper, the *Interior*, narrates the short story. Like the "Lady" in Prout's report, the narrator describes the railway route as "a chain of fascinating, if awe-inspiring dangers," as they pass "the towering precipices and bottomless rogers of the Tennessee and Kentucky mountains" (469).[10] When a woman in a black veil enters the reporter's car, the attending porter succumbs to a terrible fright. He tells the reporter that this very same woman forecast an earlier collision with her haunting cry, "danger ahead." The porter recommends that the reporter de-board the train at the next station, which the porter himself does, effectively quitting his job on the spot, but the reporter dismisses the warning and joins the engineer in his cab, eager to capture his scoop. At the casual mention of his recent sighting of the woman in black (meant to invoke the engineer's gregariousness rather than horror), the engineer falls into a frenzy of nerves, abandons control of the engine, and the "runaway" train roars toward its doom. The collision is "a crunching of iron ribs; a mangling and grinding of quivering human flesh and bones; a hell of sulphurous misery—of cries, and groans, and shrieks of pain" (475). Instead of publishing his electrifying ride in an engine cab, the newspaper reporter's byline becomes his own obituary: he and the engineer are found among the mangled bodies, their deaths reported by his newspaper the *Interior*. Readers learn in the final paragraphs of the story that the enigmatic woman in black who forecasts the collision is the engineer's widow, and she dies not on impact but subsequently of her loss. Like Margaret in Spofford's story, "The Black Bess," the woman in black haunts the train and the engineer's imagination; she embodies danger, and she becomes a victim of crash violence.[11]

It is no surprise given the volume of crash lit circulating in periodical literature that the female stunt reporter Nell Nelson became front-page news when she set out on a "Midnight Ride" in an engine car and lived to tell the tale. Her story, published in *The World*'s Sunday Edition, January 5, 1890, begins with Nelson's dramatic relinquishing of her rights to sue the railroad should she encounter harm: "Nell Nelson Signs a Document Releasing the Pennsylvania Railroad from All Claims of Damages" reads one of the leads to the story. Nelson, who writes that she had "signed her own death warrant" to accept the assignment, dresses in anticipation of a violent collision: she forgoes "skirts" in favor of the "security" of "leather leggings and Turkish trousers."[12] Nelson's stunt capitalizes on the danger of train travel from the New Woman's point of view (her trip does not end with a marriage proposal); however, it does continue to emphasize the heroism of the train's engineer. "My head reeled, my knees quaked, my teeth chattered, my heart was in my throat and every nerve in my body stung," writes Nelson as she describes the sensations of the engine cab. Covered in showers of cinder and ash, "soot clung to her face and eyelashes, feet swelling with heat." Nelson emphasizes the speed of the journey, the volumes of fire feeding the engine, the precarious rails that are being set by technicians moments before they hurtle toward them: "I could see nothing but the advancing tracks and heed nothing but their product and prospect. Now and then we shot past a night patrol, lantern in hand and pockets full of tools, going over the track in search of broken rails." The engine is a "chamber of torment" always on the brink of disaster, and she "expect[s] every moment [will] be [her] last." Like Spofford's engineer, Nelson personifies the engine, calling it a "pretty creature as ever ploughed the track and as sensitive as a baby." This image of the engine as "pretty," "sensitive," and a "baby" contrasts with Nelson's use of military analogies to describe the engineer, who is "as brave as any soldiers that ever drew swords or muskets on the battlefield." In Nelson's report, the engineer's "devotion to duty" and "heroism" is analogous to her own bravery in taking this scoop. Nelson declares that she is terrified by the train's speed across the treacherous terrain, and she describes herself as barely able to put on a courageous face in order to complete the ride and bring the story to the public. Sadly, Nelson's narrative ultimately collapses into convention, as the potential transgression of women's mobility and authorship emphasized at the start of the report is overshadowed by her sycophancy about male heroism at the article's conclusion.

Given the engineer's privileged place in the culture of safety and danger, it is notable that the engineer/narrator in Spofford's story "The Black Bess" does not merely confound the danger on the road, he embodies it. Although the engineer/narrator seeks out medical help for his violent fantasies, he cannot be cured by medical science alone. Indeed, only when the nightmare is made real, when the fiction of accident and injury becomes a literal domestic assault, is the narrator healed. Dismayed by the inability of heroic masculine force or medical science to heal her fiancée, Margaret invites him to act out his brutal vision against the woman in white; she brings him a "toy knife" and "lifts the sleeve from the bare ivory of her rounded arms," which he sees as a tacit summons for him to stab her (528). He scans the "fair, feint veinery" and, relishing the invitation, slices into her wrists (528). Margaret, bloody, collapses, and the engineer is cured. Over the severed female body cultural normalcy is restored: "And all is well indeed. From that hour, I am myself" (528).

Emerging from "his whitewashed prison room"—whether literal or figurative remains ambiguous in the story—the engineer and Margaret marry, procreate, and, according to the engineer/narrator, finally live happily ever after.

Using the dangers of the rail, the ubiquity of the train crash, and the new and emerging science of the mind, Spofford's story envisions not only the male's capacity for psychological damage—a controversial topic in the post–Civil War years when malingering and other forms of neurasthenia were suspect—but also his capacity to injure, not by accident, mechanical or otherwise, but by sheer will.[13] The dangers of the rail are a window into other acute, if briefly narrated, forms of domestic violence and racial fear. Indeed, this story and others like it published in the periodical press in the late nineteenth and early twentieth centuries might be said to domesticate danger not as readers might suppose, by sanitizing it between the pages of a book or magazine, mitigating its power to harm by making its shocks safe for sedentary readers, or by appropriating, redirecting, or expelling danger from the domestic scene, although they sometimes did that too, but rather by shifting focus on the very nature of the harms it imagines: the shock and awe of the train crash, in other words, heightens a domestic, less spectacular scene of violence/violation. Spofford's story inhabits multiple dangers, from the technological to the corporeal, and from the fragility of the masculine mind and its capacity for injury to his ability to injure others. Through the psychological vulnerability of one of the culture's most celebrated heroes, the story reveals the deep structural inequalities of material social relations. The cultural fascination with the threat of imminent destruction and the loss of control that it symbolizes is a potent reminder of the kinds of social, political, and personal vulnerabilities that women, black and white, routinely endure.

The growth of technological modernity and the threat of technological violence were vehicles through which women writers reimagined the gendering of injury, assembling an etiology of wounds less visible to the naked eye. Women writers saw "collective precariousness," what Judith Butler has described as our "fundamental dependency on" and "primary vulnerability to" others, as opportunities for reflection and invention; in imagining the threat of injury, the potential crash, they implored their characters as well as their readers to reexamine the thresholds of physical as well as psychic harm (*Precarious* xxi). In a new risk society, epitomized at the turn of the twentieth century by the high-speed crash, mobility often meant freedom, but it also indicated susceptibility to forces beyond one's control. The crash scene demonstrated that Americans were universally vulnerable, and women writers adapted this sensibility as a strategy by which to critique social conventions and institutions like marriage, motherhood, and widowhood, and to challenge the cultural meanings of vulnerability and victimhood. In the *Cult of True Victimhood* (2007), Alyson Cole analyzes how anxieties about discourses of victimhood have underscored contemporary American politics, warping the language we use to talk about suffering and collective responsibility. Being a victim, writes Cole, is no longer a matter of harms or injustices suffered, but a disparaging verdict about individual character. Those who claim to be victims are shamed, portrayed as passive, or cynically manipulative (Cole 47). Crash lit written by women remade the instrumentality of technology toward a wider social critique, complicating the meaning of vulnerability and victimhood. They imagine heroic engineers who were not impervious to claims of injury, for example; in these stories vulnerability is experienced as a multivalent condition that often connects each to other, implicating the nation's most heroic guardians of safety as readily as its seemingly stereotypical victims.

Like so many other texts in the period, Kate Chopin's "The Story of an Hour," published in *Vogue* magazine in 1894, pivots on a report of a railroad accident. Concerned that Brently Mallard's wife may be critically wounded by the news of her husband's death (like the widow in "Danger Ahead!"), the victim's friend Richards rushes to Louise Mallard's home to protect her from accident reports by "less careful" acquaintances.[14] Readers learn from the first sentence of the story that Mrs. Mallard is "afflicted with heart trouble." Could news of the fatal accident inflict another mortal blow? At once, the story links physical vulnerability with a psychological counterpart, both corporeal and emotional trauma can kill. Mrs. Mallard does not experience the deleterious shock that her friend and family fear, however, at least not initially. After a brief "storm of grief" over the loss, Louise Mallard is far from "paralyzed with inability"; in fact, her troubled heart awakens. The report of her husband's accidental death does cause a shock. Yet, what overcomes and overwhelms Louise Mallard is not grief and loss, but rather the startling recognition as she gazes out the window at the burgeoning spring that with her husband's death comes new life. Anticipating Chopin's most well-known heroine, Edna Pontellier, Louise realizes that for the first time in the wake of her husband's death "she would live for herself." Aware too that this recognition and the joy that it brings might seem "monstrous" to some, she tries in vain to suppress this revelation, to "beat it back with her will," but against its force she is "powerless." While Josephine pounds on the bedroom door, certain that her sister is dangerously ill with grief, Louise, it turns out, is "drinking in a very elixir of life."

The railroad accident and the unexpected loss of her husband shocks Louise Mallard into an awareness of her loss of self: her life has been defined by her husband's "right" to impose his "private will" on her. The accident that reportedly takes Brently Mallard's life reveals to Louise Mallard the sustained and pervasive injury of her own social station as a woman and a wife; indeed, it is the accident of her birth and her gender that has sealed her own social death. It is little wonder that her heart is "troubled." For Louise, however, the industrial accident incites new ways of thinking about subjectivity and identity and presses her to reject earlier and injurious gender constructions. As the shock of the accident jolts her from a personal and social stupor, her weak heart gains strength. When she reaches the height of her felicity, she opens the door to her room and stands at the top of the stairs, "feverish triumph in her eyes," as if she has just conquered death; she is the "goddess of Victory." Almost.

In this story, feminist subjectivity is fashioned through a wounding event and, in the brief space of an hour, destroyed. At the moment Louise emerges from her room, in effect reborn, her newfound life is quickly extinguished. Her husband, who missed his train and therefore escapes the accident that would have taken his life, walks in the front door, very much alive. For less than one hour, Louise grasps the "possession of self-assertion," but her revelations merely lead to a literal dead end. Her husband's turn of the key and with it the shock of a return to her former life swiftly kills Louise Mallard. Family, friends, and the medical community report that staggering surprise at her husband's unexpected appearance cause Mrs. Mallard's death; hers is a "joy that kills." With the death of the story's protagonist, however, the narrative replicates the painful shock that it portends. Against the public event of the railroad accident, the trauma in the official lexicon, readers are left with an invisible victim. Chopin's readers know that Louise's injuries are not simply physical or mechanical, her shock not "joy" but rather a very different kind of mental blow. With her husband's arrival home, Louise Mallard's heart stops, unable to accept the painful knowledge of a return to her former condition and the eradication of subjectivity that such a confinement entails.

Through the industrial accident, "The Story of an Hour" brings together the potentially deadly consequences of technological expansion in the late nineteenth and early twentieth centuries—the explosion of accidental injuries and deaths—with the psychological trauma of gendered social relations. Like Spofford, Chopin evokes technological violence and the public trauma of the railroad accident in order to illuminate another genus of wounds, wounds that often proliferate in private. Chopin's use of the trope of the high-speed accident implores readers to ask just what constitutes a traumatic event—the accident, her awakening, the reversal of circumstance, the fatality—and articulates another way of framing human vulnerability in the face of technological change. Although the wound that Louise suffers remains misread by family, friends, and physicians, her story, and others told by writers like Rebecca Harding Davis, Willa Cather, and Ellen Glasgow, illustrates a more capacious terrain of danger and vulnerability. The strategic use of the railway crash introduced a new representational logic. If the crash was a metaphor for social ruptures, it also was an occasion to rethink the politics of injury, suffering, vulnerability, and victimhood.

In Chopin's story, the idea of the crash inspires visions of personal freedom that are abruptly foreclosed, in Rebecca Harding Davis's story "Anne" (1889) it also inspires fantasies of egalitarian community, suggesting that various forms of mobility can annihilate or liberate women from stultifying social bonds. The rapidity of the railroad in "Anne" offers the story's protagonist Nancy Palmer a quick escape from a life of "uneasy" domestic safety. Bound by routine, Nancy has lost her former self, Anne, along with a once glorious voice that "could sing at heaven's gate"; moreover, her dreams of youth and romance are of little interest to her grown children who consider her "childish." She resolves to "go away" and "live out her own life" amid "music and art and the companionship of thinkers and scholars" rather than in domestic and financial drudgery. She buys a one-way rail ticket to Boston and boards a train.

The train's parlor cars welcome her into the "company" of "Immortals," the romanticized title she gives the famous painter and female reformer who happen to take seats nearby. She imagines herself part of a railway public, what Benedict Anderson has famously called an "imagined community," a genteel traveler experiencing the human connectedness as well as the social distinctions characterized by train travel. The train journey occasions a chance meeting with a former paramour with whom the young Anne once dreamed of a more vibrant life. Tucked anonymously away in a seat, the ignoble conversation she overhears between the "Immortals" in the parlor car begins to unsettle her ideals, and the connections she imagines become more invisible and elusive as her journey continues. Her restive fantasy comes to a crash, quite literally, as the parlor car goes black and she is pinned between "two beams" listening to the "shrieks of women in mortal agony" (Davis 749). "Cut out and laid on the bank, wet and half frozen," Mrs. Palmer survives the crash, but "every joint ached," "her gown was in tatters, the mud was deep under her, and the rain pelted down." In Davis's story the railroad journey encapsulates manifold risks, from her rejection of social convention to her breach of the threshold of physical danger.

Like Kate Chopin's "The Story of an Hour," Davis's "Anne" seizes the mechanical accident in its exploration of the technology of injury as well as its expression of a unique female economy of pain. The accident defines the social limits of mobility and self-determination for Davis's character; it becomes an allegory for the impermanence of identity, autonomy, and social privilege. The railroad is at once a dangerous and an uninhibited social and textual space, an emblem of modernity, and a vehicle that disrupts gender and class norms.[15] Although Nancy Palmer never reaches her destination, her experience in the train car and the shock of the crash lead her to a place of unsettling insight: her brief experience of mobility irreparably crushes her rich fantasy of Anne's freedom. Women's mobility, its adventures and dangers, often rejected domestic safety as oppressive; yet, Davis's story ends with Mrs. Palmer once again safely ensconced at home among her children. She has physically survived the crash, although she is left with a recurrent and still haunting wound: if Anne is "dead" in this domestic space, she wonders, will "she ever live again?" (Davis 750). The survival of her body portends the death of her spirit; as if prophesying Williams's young housewife, she is literally crushed and defeated. Willa Cather's Paul, in her story by that title, would rather die than return to a life of enforced gender norms. His answer to the nagging question that Anne asks is to throw himself in front of an oncoming train.

The cultural upheaval wrought by technological violence and the nascent discourse on wounds, physical and psychic, inspired new possibilities in women's writing for narrating what may once have been inexpressible. The specter of the local accident, to recall Paul Virilio, invited women writers to unsettle established hierarchies and to retrace the contours of social vulnerability and the social contract.[16] Indeed, technological innovations and their impact on mobility must be understood alongside revolutions in consciousness and agency. The deployment of accidents and the language of injury and vulnerability in the work of these writers traces a version of a "countertradition" that Sandra Macpherson describes *In Harm's Way* (2009). Focusing on literary depictions of injury, Macpherson narrates a counter-tradition of the English novel, one that focuses on "harms rather than rights, accident rather than will and its analogues (intention, consciousness, sovereignty, freedom)" (Macpherson 4). Both Macpherson and Ravit Reichman in *The Affective Life of Law* (2009) ask how literature embraces an alternative language of injury and agency against a seemingly axiomatic sense that modernity progresses from "'status to contract' [and] from a feudal to a liberal-democratic society organized around the freedom of persons to choose their associations" (Macpherson 4). Recognizing the vulnerability of the subject in light of technological danger was a way for women writers to question and re-theorize subjectivity and agency. By pitting public shock against private wounds, and technological dangers and physical injuries against other forms of cultural violence, their literary narratives recognized that the meaning of pain, injury, freedom, and agency was pliable, their values often culturally fashioned. Engaging with an emergent "risk society" and its culture of harm, women writers showed that these designations were not arbitrary but rather culturally patterned. As women's literature made the crash, with its accidents and injuries, a central feature, they demonstrated how the speed and energy of modern culture collided with the changing contours of gender and sexuality in the cultural imaginary.

THE YOUNG ORPHAN

In the early years of automobility, Eleanor Porter created one of America's most famous crash victims: a young orphan named Pollyanna. The children's literature classic, serialized in 1912–1913 and published in book form in 1913, became an instant bestseller, translated into numerous languages and spawning sequels, board games, theatrical productions, films, and much more. Perhaps it is no surprise that Pollyanna, the character who would ultimately enter the cultural vocabulary as an eponymous label for naïve optimism, culminates with a car accident. Pollyanna, naturally sunny, sees the bright side of everything, even after she is orphaned and sent to live with her Aunt Polly, who feels obligated by duty to care for Pollyanna and shows little warmth toward her niece. Like Ellen in Susan Warner's *The Wide Wide World* (1851) and other nineteenth- and early twentieth-century orphan fiction, Pollyanna endears herself to neighbors in the community, particularly through a game she learns from her deceased father called the glad game. Players find "the glad" in every situation, and in the work of finding gladness, they come to actually feel it. The game is particularly useful for Pollyanna given Aunt Polly's punishments and the abundant chores around the house that leave Pollyanna little time to "live" (59). Pollyanna tells the housekeeper Nancy about the game: "It began in some crutches that came in a missionary barrel. . . . You see I'd wanted a doll . . . but when the barrel came the lady wrote that hadn't any dolls come in, but the little crutches had. O she sent 'em along as they might come in handy for some child sometime. And that's when we began it" (43). Sensibly, Nancy disputes Pollyanna's glee: "I can't se anthin' ter be glad about—getting a pair of crutches when you wanted a doll!" But Pollyanna explains that although she couldn't see it at first, what should make her glad is that she doesn't "NEED—'EM" (44).

The start of the game and the retelling of its first lesson foreshadow the game's ultimate challenge: Pollyanna is struck by a car and it becomes doubtful that she will ever walk again. "On the last day of October . . . the accident occurred. Pollyanna, hurrying home from school, crossed the road at an apparently safe distance in front of a swiftly approaching motor car" (232). Pollyanna is struck by the automobile and loses the use of her legs. The injury tests her sunny disposition: the accident, her inability to walk, and her radically curtailed mobility are obstacles that she finally can't find anything to be glad about. "Why, Miss Hunt, if I can't walk, how am I ever going to be glad for—ANYTHING?" (262). Against Pollyanna's growing pessimism, her extended family, friends, and neighbors join together in mutual aid. Much like Margaret's martyrdom in Spofford's "The Black Bess"—the offering of her wrists to her beloved engineer and his recovery over her bloody body—Pollyanna's injuries bring the community together; her suffering becomes an offering to heal their assorted wounds. With this achievement in community forgiveness, and, ultimately, the recovery of her legs, Pollyanna once again feels glad.

Critics have read *Pollyanna*, if they have studied it at all, in the contexts of larger leitmotifs in children's literature such as the cultural construction of childhood or the Bildungsroman.[17] I want to place *Pollyanna* in the context of crash lit and its preoccupation with the contours of vulnerability and emerging discourses on resilience. As her popularity grew and Pollyanna became an American industry—from comic book characters to international glad groups—she also became part of the American idiom; a "Pollyanna" according to the *OED* could "find cause for happiness in the most disastrous situations"; she is "a person who is unduly optimistic or achieves happiness through self-delusion" (*OED*). Porter, who recognized the disagreeable connotations that her character might inspire among critics, fiercely defended her protagonist against the charges of self-delusion: "I have been placed often in a false light. People have thought that Pollyanna chirped that she was 'glad' at everything ... I never believed that we ought to deny discomfort and pain and evil; I have merely thought that it is far better to 'greet the unknown with a cheer'" (qtd. in Harde and Kokkola 3).

Eleanor Porter's suggestion that *Pollyanna* might instruct its readers to "greet the unknown with a cheer" both acknowledges the collective vulnerability of a "risk society" and issues a corresponding charge for resilience. What Porter calls the insecurity of the "unknown," which in the *Pollyanna* novels lends itself to an obsession with accidents and disabilities, is met with acceptance rather than resistance. Indeed, the glad game and its emphasis on turning the terrible into the tolerable is intended to build resilience in its characters. Nancy reminds Pollyanna at a particularly trying moment and in an appropriately "dull voice" that "she used ter say the game was all the nice to play when—when it was hard" (251). Yet, resilience in the novel is not solely a coping strategy in the face of calamity, it is also in danger of becoming a method of social compliance. Characters who play the glad game in the novel all conveniently conform to social convention, whether through courtship, adoption, or social courtesy. What was once Pollyanna's personal well of resourcefulness after the death of her father becomes in the wider community of the novel and in American culture what Brad Evans and Julian Reid have called in a different context, "a technology of governance" (Evans and Reid 1930).

Pollyanna's ability to accommodate herself to circumstances often beyond her control—some more injurious than others—leads her to accept the "imperative *not to resist* but rather to adapt" (Evans and Reid 1634 my emphasis). Resilience in the original novel and its subsequent series operates to quell social discord and to advocate for the ready adaptation to social norms. Adaptation was particularly important in the context of automobility, in the integration of technology across landscapes, and in the facilitation of industry and the discourse of "progress," which often came at the expense of the environment and the very communities that industries claimed to serve. It is notable, for example, that in a novel that pivots on an automobile accident, particularly a collision involving a child, very little detail emerges about the impact and its aftermath beyond Pollyanna's trials of resilience. Yet, Porter wrote *Pollyanna* at the height of public outrage against automobility for accidents precisely like the one that Pollyanna suffers and their frequent and more deadly outcomes.

At the turn of the twentieth century, pedestrians, not cars, dominated the streets. Pollyanna's accident, readers are told, is a result of her miscalculation of the speed of the oncoming car as she moved to cross the road, thinking "it was a safe distance" (Porter 232). For children, streets were often community playgrounds, and pedestrians would "stride right into the street, casting little more than a glance around them," writes historian Peter D. Norton, in *Fighting Traffic: The Dawn of the Motor Age in the American City* (2006). With the release of Henry Ford's Model T in 1908, the first fast and affordable car, public thoroughfares no longer privileged pedestrians and frequently imperiled their safety. In little over ten years, from the appearance of the Model T and just as *Pollyanna* was capturing the public imagination, auto accidents climbed to two-thirds of the entire death toll in cities with populations over 25,000. The public outcry over motor vehicle accidents was well publicized. Similar to the railroads and the running accounts, by newspapers of railway slaughters nationwide, reports on automobiles decried "the homicidal orgy of the motor car." In a typical *New York Times* story, "The Nation Roused Against Motor Killings," a New York City traffic court magistrate exclaimed, "The slaughter cannot go on. The mangling and crushing cannot continue."[18]

Quite often the mangled and crushed bodies belonged to children. With the vast increase in automobile accidents, the emerging literature on public safety featured mothers grieving over their dead children. By the early 1920s, children accounted for one-third of all traffic deaths; "half of them were killed on their home blocks" (Norton 83). During New York's 1922 "safety week" event, "10,000 children marched in the streets, 1,054 of them in a separate group symbolizing the number killed in accidents the previous year" (Thompson "When Pedestrians"). At a similar safety parade in Cleveland, one float carried a woman representing the "Goddess of Safety" standing with her arms extended "over two children in an attitude of protection against the menacing figure of death" (Norton 29). When personified in newspaper cartoon editorials or in public safety campaigns, death was always a reckless driver; a child, very much in the image of Pollyanna, was most often his victim.

In order to convince the public to adapt to the new vehicles that sped across the very roadways that they once passed with little caution, automobile makers needed to persuade pedestrians that road safety was the responsibility of individuals and not machines, that bodies that collided with automobiles were themselves at fault. For automobiles to populate the American landscape required a vast conceptual transformation; carmakers saw that in addition to introducing road safety for drivers, they also needed to change the attitude and behavior of roadway pedestrians. Automobility only works because its accidents are negated; like the traffic accident in *Pollyanna*, they must be eclipsed in order for the technology to thrive (Wajcman 49). Carmakers appealed to individual autonomy over collective vulnerability, and searched for a way to cast pedestrians as self-endangering rather than as victims of indifferent machines and their drivers. This set off one of the most successful branding campaigns on behalf of the automobile: the "jaywalker." Introduced in the early 1920s by the growing automobile industry, the idea was adapted from the derisive term the "hayseed." The "jay," unaccustomed to urban city streets, would casually hop along, generally inattentive to his or her immediate surroundings, increasing the likelihood of accident and injury. Car companies used the "jaywalker" image and the self-regarding snobbery of city-dwellers against themselves; cosmopolitan urbanites were eager to distance themselves from connotations of unworldliness (Norton 77–82). Like the language of resilience and adaptation (*Pollyanna*), the jaywalker became a figure fundamental to the growth of automobility in the early twentieth century. Within a few years, "jaywalker" joined "Pollyanna" as part of the American lexicon.[19]

Crash lit helped to acculturate new vocabularies of vulnerability, risk, resilience, and adaptation in the American imagination. As Pollyanna became a beloved character to many Americans, her lessons about resilience underscored an entirely new ecosystem, one that emphasized the fantasy of self-mastery and suggested that "unforeseeable systemic disruptions are natural and survivable, if not by everyone then by some . . . some who will perhaps even thrive."[20] Even as her name came to represent a comportment toward the world that could be too sunny, her popularity in the early decades of the twentieth century conveyed the growth of a new technology of self: training, through imagination and play, to overcome the shocks and hazards of a violent new world.

I close this chapter by turning to a brief look at of one of literature's most indomitable jaywalkers, Dorinda Oakley in Ellen Glasgow's *Barren Ground* (1925). Like *Pollyanna*, the turning point of Dorinda's story comes when she is struck by a car. As the title suggests, *Barren Ground* is far less sunny than *Pollyanna*, yet it too is a glad tale, although not as Pollyanna might have taught. Like the shocking blow that awakens Louise Mallard in Chopin's "Story of an Hour," the sudden impact of crushing tires frees Dorinda Oakley from a failed relationship and the reproduction, through marriage and motherhood, of the same. The strategic use of the automobile crash allows Dorinda to imagine herself outside the dictates of social conventions like marriage and motherhood. When Ellen Glasgow published *Barren Ground* it was a departure from her earlier work such as *The Descendant* (1893) and *The Wheel of Life* (1906) that featured male protagonists and the environmental forces that sealed their successes or failures. Glasgow was thoughtful about a different fate for her modern female protagonist: "For once, in Southern fiction," she wrote, "the betrayed woman would become the victor instead of the victim. In the end, she would triumph through that deep instinct for survival, which had ceased to be a negative quality and had strengthened into a dynamic force" (qtd. in Campbell 160). Once again, the crash, the impact of body and machine, facilitates critique: Dorinda reflects on her past, rejects biological inevitability, and redefines her once static identity. Glasgow embraces the cultural contradictions central to the culture of acceleration: the mobility and freedom to escape social strictures may also incite violence and destruction.[21]

When the novel begins, Dorinda is stuck in a Virginia community that seems only to sow failure; she perceives herself "caught like a mouse in the trap of life," held hard by "circumstances as by invisible wires of steel" about which she can change "nothing" (Glasgow 56). As a young woman Dorinda embraces a conventional hope that marriage will rescue her from a bleak cultural and economic inheritance. When her fiancée Jason jilts her for a woman with "a pile of money," Dorinda, alone and pregnant, boards a train for New York City; she swaps "invisible wires of steel" for an urban metropolis (Glasgow 16). In Broomsedge, Virginia, where the novel begins, and in New York City where it leads, industry and technology appear dangerous and potentially deadly. The agrarian critique of modernity and industrialization with which the novel begins reaches its climax in the collision and traumatic injury that Dorinda suffers after a short time in New York City.

Glasgow's Dorinda Oakley is a Benjaminian subject, a country "jay" escaping to the city, whose very first steps in New York quite literally recall Benjamin's description of nineteenth-century Paris as a "series of shocks and collisions" (Luckhurst 20). Dorinda walks the city streets "exhausted" and in search of work. Overcome by "winking" lights, loud noises, and endless streams of traffic, she is far from her agrarian home (Glasgow 210). "As one among many tides of nausea subside," she steps forward into a stream of traffic and is hit by something "so swiftly that it felt as if an earthquake had flung the pavement up against the back of her head" (Glasgow 210). Dorinda is struck by an automobile. Not only has Dorinda suffered a head injury with the collision, but the impact also causes her to miscarry. The accident and her injuries put her in the hospital under the care of a celebrated surgeon, Dr. Farraday. When she awakes in her hospital bed, she is informed in oblique language of the loss of her fetus. The nurse, with little comfort, suggests to Dorinda that the accidental miscarriage is a misfortune waiting to be reread: "I thought you would take it sensibly," she says to Dorinda (Glasgow 214). The nurse implies that the chance collision actually saves Dorinda from another more dangerous condition, the unwed mother; it also saves her from a more damaging label: the ruined woman. This argument need scarcely be made. Dorinda already perceives motherhood as grotesque and a source of pain. She recalls with racist disdain, for example, the "mulatta woman" in Broomsedge with her "half breed swarm," and later she watches as Geneva, Jason's wife, loses a child, which leads to her suicide (Glasgow 63). As the (accidental) collision that causes Dorinda to miscarry puts an end to an unwanted (accidental) pregnancy and one potential source of social ruin, her head injury leaves her scarcely able to remember it: "all at once she had forgotten what she wanted to know . . . there was something I wanted to ask the doctor . . . I don't seem to be able to remember what it was" (Glasgow 214). The nurse instructs Dorinda to forget it all, and Dorinda, the dutiful patient, observes that "relief and regret faded together" (Glasgow 215). Dorinda, in fact, awakens from the accident stitched up and sore, but also like Louise Mallard, "monstrously" renewed.

Barren Ground is a naturalist novel to its core; as Donna Campbell has noted, it is "filled with epiphanies about the brutal nature of the world" (Campbell 162). Yet, the emergence of feminist subjectivity at a moment of technological and biological crises—one of the shocks that *Barren Ground* deals its readers—complicates what Donald Pizer, one of the most influential scholars on American literary naturalism, has argued are the genre's "deep roots": "the failings of the nation's industrial system" (Pizer 201). Naturalism, Pizer has argued, threatened the "established order" because writers like Stephen Crane and Theodore Dreiser, who are the subjects of subsequent chapters, "boldly and vividly depicted the inadequacies of the industrial system which was the foundation of that order" (Pizer 201). In the crash lit examined here, women writers likewise engage what Wolfgang Schivelbusch has called "industrialized consciousness"; they not only expose the risks of industry and technology, but also their works allow these potential dangers to unsettle hegemonic notions of masculine force and biological determinism. These texts articulate new avenues for understanding the self, psyche, community, and nation (Schivelbusch 159).[22]

Dorinda recovers and thrives but not through the vehicle she originally thought: marriage. With Dorinda's bodily injury, the novel abandons its attention to conjugal affection; indeed, the accident leaves her with a noted "revulsion" at the thought of physical intimacy and, for a long while, marriage (Glasgow 232). As a victim of a violent physical shock, Dorinda is permitted this idiosyncrasy, one that is substantially different from how she would be received as a fallen woman. Her vulnerabilities as an accident victim and as an unwed mother are very different. Once again, recalling cultural debates about accidents and after effects, Dr.

Farraday, the noted surgeon who finds Dorinda after the accident and saves her life, believes that her revulsion to marriage is one such aftershock, her delayed traumatic response to a violent impact. The novel connects Dr. Farraday to the medico-legal debate about such injuries; he considers Dorinda's case "unusual" and is "very much interested" in its outcomes (Glasgow 213). Of course, such accidents, as we have seen, were far less "unusual" and far more commonplace in the nineteenth century. The vehicles that provided the catalyst for mobility and freedom of movement, allowing Dorinda to escape rural Virginia for New York City, also transformed accidental injury from discrete individual events into a collective cultural experience (Welke 80). With the revolution in mobility and the increase in technological violence, physical and emotional injuries were suffered by men and women alike. As injury law emerged in response to industrialization and the growing dangers of a congested and mechanized public sphere, as we saw in the prior chapter, it also began to articulate the legal obligation that persons had to one another and to recognize that the shocks of the human sensorium impacted physical and emotional health and well-being. With women's increased mobility and, subsequently, their growing role as protagonists in accident cases, tort law began to acknowledge, however reluctantly, something different in scope from its institutionalized patriarchal conventions.[23]

Through accident and the changing face of vulnerability, liability, victimhood, and human agency, Glasgow reimagines Dorinda's place in a new technological modernity and with it a more radical expression of feminist subjectivity. Surviving her bodily injuries and limitations, Dorinda Oakley is given a fresh capacity for change. The physical wound that that leaves her "barren" inspires other forms of fulfillment: she returns to Broomsedge and restores the family farm to its "true fertility" (Campbell 162). Like Chopin, Glasgow challenges readers to reconsider what constitutes the narrative's traumatic event. The accident, the sudden impact, is not solely a literary metaphor, it is also part of an official language through which to implore what was previously invisible and seemingly impossible, the cultural recognition of women's physical and emotional integrity. While Dorinda's accident and its aftermath spark a rejection of biological determinism, they also invite readers to envision how the cultural recognition of women's wounds might, in turn, shape modern sensibilities. Dorinda steadfastly refuses to be the trodden young housewife that William Carlos Williams's poem fancies at the start of the chapter. Against the metaphor of tires crushing fallen leaves, women's critique of crash culture imagines the machinery of resistance and urges speed toward social change.

NOTES

1. Although the speaker in the poem is nameless and genderless, the narrator's position of privilege suggests his masculinity.

2. Sidonie Smith, x. Also see Smith, "The Masculine Logic of Travel," 1–15, and Stephanie C. Palmer, *Together by Accident*, 4–5. For more on women's travels see, Deborah A. Clark, *Driving Women*; Anna Despotopoulou, *Women and the Railway*; Amy G. Richter, *Home on the Rails*; Virginia Scharff, *Twenty Thousand Roads*; and Wesley, *Secret Journeys*.

3. Arthurs and Grant, "Introduction," in *Crash Cultures*, 7. The addition of "women" in the sentence is my own.

4. Nancy Bentley argues in *Frantic Panoramas* that writers like Edith Wharton and Henry James were media theorists, able to combine analytic thought with the wild sensory experiences of mass culture.

5. See Bill Brown, *The Material Unconscious: American Amusement, Stephen Crane, and the Economies of Play*: "These machines in the garden—merry-go-rounds, roller toboggans, epicycloidal wheels—marked a shift in America's symbolic relation to technology, which could now signify not just the production of more 'free time' but also the pleasures produced within that freedom," 49. For more on this idea, see also Mohun, "Introduction," in *Risk*, 5.

6. Writing about insurance, François Ewald argues that "societies come to analyze themselves and their problems in terms of the generalized technology of risk. . . . Societies envisage themselves as a vast system of insurance, and by overtly adopting insurance's forms they suppose that they are thus conforming to their own nature." Ewald, "Risk and Insurance," 210.

7. Harriet P. Spofford, *Galaxy* 5, 1868, 517–28. Future references are to this edition.

8. African American women had a very different relationship to railroad mobility. Anna Julia Cooper describes her experiences in *A Voice from the South*: "She has seen these same 'gentlemanly and efficient' railroad conductors . . . deliberately fold their arms and turn round [*sic*] when the Black Woman's turn to alight—bearing her satchel, and bearing besides another unnameable burden inside the heaving bosom and tightly compressed lips. The feeling of slighted womanhood is unlike every other emotion of the soul," 90.

9. For a discussion of male hysteria and its connections to industrial injuries, see Mark Micale's *Hysterical Men*, 49–70.

10. M. Sheffy Peters, "Danger Ahead!". *Godey's Lady's Book* 108 (1884), 470–75. All references are to this edition.

11. See John Fabian Witt, "Crippled Workingmen, Destitute Widows, and the Crisis of Free Labor," in *The Accidental Republic*, 22–42.

12. See Nell Nelson, "In an Engine Car: Nell Nelson's Midnight Ride on the Washington Express," *New York World*, Sunday January 5, 1890, 9. All future references are to this column.

13. For more on malingering and "soldier's heart," see Joanna Bourke, *Dismembering the Male*; and Jennifer Travis, *Wounded Hearts*.

14. Chopin, "The Story of an Hour," http://archive.vcu.edu/english/engweb/webtexts/hour/. All references are to this digital edition.

15. For more on middle-class mobility and accidents, see Stephanie C. Palmer, *Together by Accident*, 9–15.

16. See Paul Virilio, *The Original Accident*: "The local accident, precisely located here or there, has been replaced by the global accident," 33.

17. See Roxanne Harde and Lydia Kokkola, eds., *Eleanor H. Porter's* Pollyanna*: A Children's Classic at 100*. In their introduction, Harde and Kokkola note the paucity of scholarship on the novel. "Introduction," 3–26.

18. See Clive Thompson, "When Pedestrians Ruled the Streets," https://www.smithsonianmag.com/innovation/when-pedestrians-ruled-streets-180953396/

19. "Jaywalker," like "Pollyanna," became so well ingrained in American culture that it soon garnered a place in the dictionary: "One who crosses a street without observing the traffic regulations for pedestrians." Norton, *Fighting Traffic*, 79. In the 1922 Detroit safety week parade, the Packard Motor Car Company produced a huge tombstone float: "Erected to the Memory of Mr. J. Walker: He Stepped from the Curb Without Looking." Peter Norton, *Fighting Traffic*, 77.

20. For more on the concept of resilience, see Stephanie Foote and Stephanie LeMenager, "Editors' Column," *Resilience: A Journal of the Environmental Humanities* 1, no. 1 (January 2014), http://www.resiliencejournal.org/past-issues/issue-1-1/. Foote and LeMenager caution against the romanticization of resilience, noting that the term has been used as a paternalistic catchphrase. See also Sarah Bracke, "Bouncing Back: Vulnerability and Resistance in Times of Resilience," in *Vulnerability and Resistance*, 62; and Brad Evans and Julien Reid, *Resilient Life*.

21. "While the velocity of machines increasingly came to signify the driving force of progress and economic growth, the euphoria of constant motion also became associated with violence and destruction. These cultural contradictions remain central to the dynamics of acceleration," Wajcman, 38. For more on women and automobility, see Virgina Scharff, *Taking the Wheel: Women and the Coming of the Motor Age*.

22. Work by literary critics such as Donna Campbell and Jennifer Fleissner have argued for the recognition of more women writers of naturalism and have complicated the genre's gender politics as well as its narrative techniques and concerns. See Fleissner, *Women, Compulsion, and Modernity*, 3–30.

23. Glasgow's novel reflects the medico-legal debate in which such accidents and injuries were increasingly widespread. Collisions of the sort Dorinda suffers were among the most prominent medical and legal tort cases, adjudicated throughout law courts in the late nineteenth and turn of the twentieth century. See chapter 1 for discussion of similar legal cases.

THREE

"Hurts That Will Not Heal"

Theodore Dreiser, Masculinity, and Railroad Labor

> I never open a newspaper that does not contain some account of disasters and loss of life on the railroads. They do a retail business in human slaughter. (1844, New York diarist Philip Hone, qtd. in Rozario 62)

The young Theodore Dreiser, aspiring to a career as a reporter, studied *The Chicago Daily News* and practiced his hand at depicting newsworthy events, especially the "accidents, shootings, [and] fires" that he witnessed across the city and whose reports flooded mass circulation magazines and newspapers in the late nineteenth century (Nostwich 335). When Dreiser concluded that his ability to capture calamity was as compelling as the stories he read in print, he pursued work as a journalist. "The city editors wanted not so much bare facts, as became the rule later," Dreiser notes, "as feature stories—color . . . romance—and although I did not myself see it clearly at the time I was their man. Write?—why I could write reams on any topic, once I discovered that I could write at all" (*Newspaper Days* 77). From 1892 to 1895, Dreiser wrote over one hundred articles and columns for magazines and newspapers in Chicago, St. Louis, and New York. As a journalist, he joined a fraternity of young writers, including Stephen Crane (chapter 4), Jack London (chapter 5), Upton Sinclair, and Abraham Cahan, among others, for whom newspaper work became the foundation of later literary success. Well before the novels that would make him famous, Dreiser not only published short sketches on art, literature, and music, but also on fires, lynchings, and train wrecks, the indices of a "wound culture" that became the inspiration for his later fiction.[1]

The urban beat and its crimes and calamities provided ample material for newspapers and their journalists/novelists. Newspaper reporting helped to professionalize literary work; it was a way "to assert the manly nature of an occupation, that, some worried, had been overtaken by women in the nineteenth century," as Jean Lutes has argued ("Lynching Coverage" 457). A substantial body of scholarship has underscored the centrality of journalism to the male literary imagination in the late nineteenth and early twentieth centuries. From Christopher P. Wilson and Bill Brown to Jean Lutes and Shelley Fisher Fishkin, the crucial role that newspapers have played in American fiction is well covered. Dreiser scholars too have studied the extent to which the "themes, subjects, and style" of his fiction can be traced to his earlier journalism. Thomas P. Riggio has argued that an astonishing amount of Dreiser's "literary sensibility and ideas" grew out of his newspaper days (Nostwich xii). Given the intimate connection scholars have drawn between factual reporting and the fictional imagination in American letters, it is surprising that little attention has been paid to Dreiser's preoccupation with the subject matter that would launch and, subsequently, sustain his career: those very same accidents and injuries, fires and collisions, crimes and outrages on which he apprenticed and that fomented his career as a writer, witness, and inhabitant of loss.[2] Accidents in the nineteenth century "go a long way toward defining the newspaper's epochal success and distinctiveness as a form of communication," argues Paul Fyfe in his study of Victorian culture, *By Accident or Design* (2015) (Fyfe 28). As newspapers became fundamental in the daily lives of their readers, so too did "accidentalness" become "integrated into a sense of the metropolitan everyday" (Fyfe 28).[3] As a developing artist, Dreiser recognized that he could creatively harness the growing cultural fascination with accidents while also addressing social conflicts. The threat of violent accident was never far in Dreiser's imagination; it shaped his early career as a journalist and was the foundation of his later fiction.

The article that launched Dreiser's livelihood as a journalist was a front-page report of a train collision and explosion, "Burned to Death," on January 22, 1893, in the *St. Louis Globe Democrat*.[4] In the article, Dreiser reports with imaginative flourish on a devastating railway collision and explosion. From the anticipation of the accident, which the engineer and fireman could not stop, to the passengers who are violently thrown to the floor of the train car but recover their footing and escape, Dreiser titillates his readers with many of the suspenseful and gory details of a railway crash, as in this description of the oil tanker explosion subsequent to the crash:

> An explosion followed that shook the ground for miles about. Seething, blazing oil was showered upon the onlookers. The scene that follows beggars description. Many forms were instantly transformed to blazing, screaming, running, rolling bodies, crying loudly for mercy and aid . . . they threw their burning hands to tortured, flame-lit faces, from which all semblance to humanity had already departed. They clawed

and bit the earth, and then, with an agonizing gasp, sunk, faint and dying, into a deathly stillness. (Dreiser, *Journalism*, 40)

The article's depiction of a sea of seething, rolling bodies in the aftermath of the crash earned Dreiser a twenty-dollar bonus and five-dollar raise. Following this crash scene, Dreiser trails the wreck victims to the hospital, interviews witnesses, and solicits public commentary on what witnesses and first responders think about the responsibility and negligence of the railroad itself. "The man that had charge of the switch at that place was a fellow by the name of R. Gratten," one of the onlookers tells Dreiser. "He kept a barbershop and attended the switch at the same time. The company hired him simply because he was cheap. I know that he has gone out of the country already, and they won't find him soon. It's a shame that a railroad company should be allowed to hire men to do work in that manner, risking the lives of passengers, simply because it is cheap" (*Journalism* 44). Dreiser reported on the collision's fatalities in his follow-up article "Sixteen Dead," continuing to cover one of the most appalling and disastrous train wrecks in years. In this article, Dreiser details the "scope of the sad disaster" as hospitalized accident victims await their all but certain fate: "It isn't a question of remedy or nursing," the doctor on the scene tells Dreiser. "It is simply a question of physical strength and time, and no body, no nervous system, however strong, can stand the ceaseless irritation and stinging pain that accompanies their every move. This has been a peculiar and awful accident. . . . Such aggravated cases of physical agony I have never witnessed before and I never want to again" (*Journalism* 49).

The sensational and heartbreaking stories of disasters, the "awful accident[s]" and "physical agon[ies]," sold papers, as Dreiser and his editors well knew. Even a more staid paper like *The New York Times* featured regular columns like "The Record of Accident," which detailed the dreadful and sensational accounts of fires, railway collisions, drownings, and other injuries that led to mortal wounds.[5] In Dreiser's early years as a young journalist, he wrote bylines on sexual assault, lynching, kidnapping, fire, murder, and all manner of crash culture, with dramatic titles like: "Girl Frightfully Outraged, "Neck in a Noose," "Sufferings of a Deserted Family," Kidnapped," "Burned in Bed," "Shot by a Mad Husband," "Ten Foot Drop," "Awful Wreck!," and "Girl under the Wheels," among many others. When Dreiser left the *Globe Democrat* for the *Republic*, a paper even more invested in the exploitation of sensational stories, he continued a reporting career notable for its narration of accident, fire, arrest, neighborhood crime, and violence against women and blacks (*Journalism* 340). Amid Dreiser's growing awareness of technological and industrial, as well as racial and sexual violence, the repetitive appearance of the railroad became a form of insistent critique.

By the time Theodore Dreiser became a laborer on the very railroad that he once reported about he was himself in dire need, not only of work and money, but also of relief from what he described as a great pain that tortured most of his waking moments: his sudden inability to write. In the few short years after Dreiser moved to New York City to report for the *New York World*, he quit journalism and beat reporting to pursue long-form fiction, and he went from a prolific correspondent who could "write reams on any topic" to a neurasthenic author racked by debilitating literary silence. A short time after the publication of *Sister Carrie* (1900) Dreiser suffered from nervous anxiety, which plagued many Americans at the turn of the twentieth century.[6] *An Amateur Laborer* (1904) is Dreiser's first-person account of the loss of his status as professional writer and journalist and his search for a position as an amateur "hand," a manual laborer. For Dreiser, work on the railroad promised to be a form of recovery; he connected his need to revive his literary skill with his capacity to work his body, holding fast to the promise that the metonymic dismemberments of head and hand might literally be made whole, and what better job of bodily work than the seemingly infinite task of building the railroad in the United States? Many of those from whom he sought work believed he was not up to the charge: he wore his "cultured" status on his sleeve; moreover, few believed that a man of the mind could handle the tough labor of the road. For Dreiser, however, the work of the intellect and the work of the hand, imagination and industry, were intimately allied. If writing itself would not cure his misery, he thought that manual labor would help relieve his literary silence.

Theodore Dreiser's brief account of his "amateur labor" on the New York Central Railroad not only tells the story of a neurasthenic's personal quest for a "cure," it also underscores how the railroad helped to shape the meaning and gendering of pain and injury, safety and danger, vulnerability and resilience in the United States in the nineteenth and early twentieth centuries. Railroads were technological wonders, collapsing space and time, and they were ubiquitous sources of potential violence. The railway disaster was never far from its laborers' or its passengers' minds. Dreiser joined a fraternity of railway workers facing enormous physical risk: "At the turn of the century, one worker in fifty was killed or disabled.... By one contemporary estimate, no fewer than 42 percent of railroad workers involved in day-to-day operation ... were injured on the job each year" (Witt 2–3). The vocabulary of accident and the sheer number of railway wounded provided a potent context for Dreiser's understanding of what he would describe in *An Amateur Laborer* as his own debilitating psychological injuries, his psychic rather than physical wounds. With the railroad as his vehicle, Dreiser mapped the vulnerable masculine psyche onto the physical dangers of the industrial age.

This chapter describes how Dreiser harnessed depictions of the injured male body in industrial capitalism and the glaring tragedy of railroad wounds in order to rewrite and to reimagine the stigma of the vulnerable male psyche. It examines his painstaking account of recuperative failure in *An Amateur Laborer* and his subsequent short narratives on railroad labor, "The Mighty Burke" and "The Mighty Rourke." The railroad and its discourse of accident inspired Dreiser to add an innovative vocabulary to the culture of masculine re-embodiment; not only did men like Dreiser seek medical cures for psychological injuries associated with railway collisions, as this chapter will describe, many also turned to the vocabulary of injury to assert cultural authority and to articulate legal and cultural claims about their psychic wounds. Some rode from "camp cures" straight into court. In so doing, men embraced injury's presence—rather than desperately trying to affect its absence—embracing expressions of vulnerability as constitutive of masculinity itself.

Dreiser's self-proclaimed literary silence was mildly overstated. Beginning in October 1902, he wrote a meticulous account of his neurasthenic illness while a patient of Dr. Louis A. Duhring in Philadelphia. Within months, what started as a shorthand depiction of various physical discomforts developed into a methodically crafted lexicon of sorrow. "The beauty, the comfort, the affection of the world," Dreiser observed, "How the sign of it or its semblance pricks the soul in want" (*American Diaries* 107). Dreiser regularly grieved the "failure" of his pen, what he called the absent "recrudescence of the literary spirit," and he saw his depressive illness and his inability to produce "reams" of writing as a failure of his masculinity: "some men have so much," he mourned, "I have . . . so little" (*American Diaries* 71, 109). Throughout his early diaries, Dreiser grappled with how to narrate his struggle, wishing at once to share his story but also wondering how to best represent it: "I came out thinking how I would write all this. What a peculiar story my life would make if all were told . . . it isn't pleasant I'll admit but it can be done. How I am trying to tell you" (*Diaries* 108–12).

The beat reporter who could write reams on any subject suddenly perceived himself voiceless and incapable of telling his own story. Dreiser's brother, Paul, thought he found a cure: he sent Teddy to William Muldoon's sanatorium "Olympia" near White Plains, New York. Muldoon, a former wrestler turned motivational speaker, had a reputation as a "rebuilder of rundown bodies," and he prescribed manly physical labor as the sure remedy for what he and others diagnosed as Dreiser's effete condition (Coltrane 382). Muldoon, like the railway foreman Burke/Rourke whom I describe later in the chapter, was memorialized as a subject in Dreiser's *Twelve Men* (1919). Although Dreiser would call his portrait "Culhane, The Solid Man," Muldoon was not easily disguised; he was a well-known sportsman who commanded public attention for the "sporting sanitarium" that he called "the repair shop" (*Twelve Men* 136). Dreiser describes his first impression of Muldoon as a man who was "very virile, very intelligent, very indifferent, intolerant, and even threatening" (*Twelve Men* 138). Most of Muldoon's fellow patients, like Dreiser, were men from the "so-called learned professions or the arts": manufacturers, politicians, doctors, lawyers, actors, and merchants (*Twelve Men* 138). "Out in the world," Dreiser "sadly" muses, "they all wore the best of clothes, had their cars, servants, city and country houses perhaps, their factories, employees, institutions. Ridiculous! Pitiful! As lymphatic and flabby as oysters without their shells, myself included. It was really painful" (*Twelve Men* 142). Muldoon's method was to systematically strip his patients of the trappings of their lives outside Olympia: "However grand an osseous, leathery lawyer or judge or doctor or politician or society man may look out in the world addressing a jury or a crowd . . . glistening in his raiment," writes Dreiser, "here, whiskered, thin of legs, arms and neck, with bulging brow and stripped not only of his gown but everything else this side of his skin—well, draw your own conclusion" (*Twelve Men* 146). Dreiser and his cohort ate their "frugal meals," slept in meager "cells," and partook in various forms of rigorous physical daily activities. Muldoon celebrated physical industry as the antidote for masculine depression, a prescription similar to physician S. Weir Mitchell's, who also treated male neurasthenics with the "camp cure," a stark contrast to the infamous rest cure he most often prescribed for women.[7] Muldoon's method was to remove the "ability, agility, authority, [and] worth" that accompanied social status, brainwork, and material success, and replace it with physical prowess by any means necessary. Dreiser wonders at his methods: would "a preacher or judge, who, offended by Mr. Culhane's [Muldoon's] profanity and brutality," someday be able to convert the "gladiator" to more gentile views of society "as readily as the gladiator is able to rid him of his ailment?" (*Twelve Men* 146, 186).

Despite his scorn for Muldoon's methods, Dreiser absorbed his lessons well. Upon Dreiser's departure from the sanatorium, he continued his quest for physical revitalization with a job on the New York Central Railroad, trusting that physical work would continue to improve his health and ultimately help him to regain his ability to write. For Dreiser, however, this "work cure" proved fruitless. In *An Amateur Laborer* (1904), Dreiser's autobiography of his railroad days, he labels himself psychologically "maimed" and, literary form mirroring his fragile psyche, he leaves his memoir in fragments (*Amateur Laborer* 149). Although railroad labor proved empty in its promise of re-energizing and re-masculinizing Dreiser's ailing body and mind—after the experiment Dreiser called himself more "maimed insect" than man—the advancing railroad signaled a new vocabulary and inspiration for Dreiser, one in which the cultural vocabulary of industrial injury and its technocratic iterations supplemented the medical model of neurasthenic illness and disease. Dreiser's railroad labor was not merely debilitating, in other words; it gave him a vehicle through which to re-conceptualize and to rewrite masculine woundedness, to rethink the nature of success and failure, and to reappraise the meaning of vulnerability and resilience.

The culture of the railroad and its discourse of masculine embodiment offered Dreiser an occasion to reformulate his own illness. While he began his railroad days with the idea of reviving body and mind, spirit and pen, the railroad in *An Amateur Laborer* also became a vehicle through which he explored and described his most intimate psychological wounds. Dreiser used both the promise and the peril of the railroad: its endless labors could be invigorating but also grim and dangerous. At the start of his narrative, Dreiser identifies his neurasthenic depression with the advancing railroad. His job piling railroad tracks is the dialect through which he describes his personal suffering: he "launched upon a recreative career of labor and humm[ed]," he notes, through "the grimness of it" (*Amateur Laborer* 113). Dreiser's account turns from thoughts of recovery to scenes of self-alienation and recrimination. The "deafening and disagreeable" noises of railroad work do not crowd out his mind's clutter as he had hoped, rather he finds himself "compelled to suffer, blood-raw, the agonies of its weight" (*Amateur Laborer* 121, 122). If the railroad promised Dreiser work, food, and shelter, in *An Amateur Laborer* it also became his iron horse upon which to stride a seemingly unlocalizable hurt: "He is injured. Therefore he is not morally whole. Let him wander by himself. He does not any longer belong to the sane and healthy order of society" (*Amateur Laborer* 124). Referring to himself in the third person, Dreiser suggests that his injuries cast him beyond community; in his fragile mind, he labors alone. Dreiser seizes metaphors of the railroad's record of physical maiming and disability in order to express his psychological injury and sense of isolation. Ultimately, he casts himself as "unfit" for the railroad's multiple dangers: "I was unfitted to be a hewer of wood as I was to be the president of the railroad" (*Amateur Laborer* 160). Dreiser's memoir records the failure of recovery and confirms the irreparable: "I went over in my mind the various afflictions of recent days," Dreiser notes on the last page of *An Amateur Laborer*, "and wondered if I should ever really recover from them. . . . To be maimed as an insect. To get a hurt that would not heal. How disastrous it was in this or any other society" (*Amateur Laborer* 124). On the memoir's last page, he laments what he sees as his permanent inability to translate "what he was then feeling" into words, and he worries that he may never offer readers a glimpse into his psychological pain; the aesthetic encounter may not bring readers comfort or connection in their potential joint afflictions.

"Maimed" as he may have been by his railroad experience, Dreiser did not leave his labors with a gaping wound. He returned, revised, and re-scripted his railroad work over the next two decades in "The Mighty Burke" (1911), "The Toil of the Laborer" (1913), *The Genius* (1915), and the revised and republished "The Mighty Rourke" (1919) in *Twelve Men*. If in form and content *An Amateur Laborer* denied its author the ability to regain putative wholeness and with it his sense of his place among men, with his depictions and adaptations of railroad labor—Dreiser would come to write and rewrite his railroad experiences throughout his career—he began to embrace a different emblem of masculine status. Despite Dreiser's descriptions of his "misery" and his sense of himself as an "outcast," he returned to the iron horse and re-imagined his exile from the "sane and healthy" in his narratives "The Mighty Burke" and, later, "The Mighty Rourke."[8] Teddy, the fictionalized autobiographical narrator of "The Mighty Burke" and "Rourke," seeks out physical labor to help allay his troubled mind; yet, over the course of the narrative, the exercise of his mind more so than his body allows Teddy to become injury's accountant rather than its victim. Teddy records for the railroad company as well as the wider community the physical and psychological costs of industrial labor.

Dreiser's inventive alliance between building the railroad and rebuilding his own ability as a writer was keenly ironic; it was industrial culture, with the railroad the most visible vehicle, which was considered the impetus for so much pain and suffering according to many physicians who treated patients like Dreiser. Henry M. Lyman, responding to George Miller Beard's *American Nervousness* (1880), attributed the symptoms of nervousness that seemingly pervaded late nineteenth-century culture to industrial progress: "The Arcadian farmer," he cautioned, "who has been lulled to sleep by the hum of his wife's spinning wheel is awakened by the shriek of the locomotive" (Lyman 81–82). Far from recuperative, the shrieking of the railroad in Lyman's account is understood as unnerving, disorienting, and even dangerous. Moreover, the physical pains suffered by workmen building the railroads, the exploding injuries of an industrial economy, as Burke and Rourke memorialize, were understood not as Dreiser might have wished, as relief from the pressures of the authorial imagination, but as the cost, most often to manual laborers, of greater economic good for the nation. Progressive rhetoric was particularly fervent in the United States, where the transportation revolution was seen as a method for advancing a "new civilization from a hitherto worthless (because inaccessible) wilderness" (Marx 94).[9] Published accounts of the railroad hailed its sublime nature within America's cultural imagination, coupling endless possibility with sheer terror; it was the vehicle to assure that the United States would fulfill its promise as a nation. In the words of one *Scientific American* writer, the railroad was the "benefactor of man," and it was built to stay.[10]

For most railroad laborers, even for Dreiser who at the start of his work cure was inclined to look upon manual labor with what he called a "gentle and melancholy eye," the injuries that accompanied railroad work, the increasing number of accidents mapped upon the bodies of its builders, were meant to be suffered silently; pain often remained legally unrecognized and, hence, uncompensated (*Amateur Laborer* 121). While tort or injury law expanded in order to cope with the growing negligence claims for industrial accidents, particularly the escalating number of incidents attributed to the railroad, new legal principles often made the recognition and compensation of physical pains unavailable to the laborers most afflicted.[11] Only when the threat of physical injury became a truism for the general and predominantly middle-class traveling public was the need for relief and recompense more fully addressed, as I described in chapter 1. As men building the railroads were battered by hazardous and life-threatening work, its passengers bridled with terror as they read in the daily papers about the numerous accidents crippling the natural landscape and its inhabitants. The threat of violent accident fanned the anxiety of the railway public.

As a vehicle of industrial accident and cultural upheaval, the railroad symbolized the multiple dimensions of injury not only in the law but also in the emerging discipline of psychology. An icon of technological modernity, the railroad was linked to an emerging discourse on shock and trauma. The train accident, a newly emerging leitmotif of nineteenth-century literature, generated a range of novel and puzzling disorders. In *The Trauma Question* (2008), Roger Luckhurst locates the conceptual emergence of trauma in nineteenth-century industrialism and Victorian reactions to modern technology, particularly the accidents associated with the railroad. The magazines that published imaginative fiction on railway disasters, which I discussed in the preceding chapter, routinely published non-fiction accounts of transportation accidents and condemned the state of fright for the weary traveler, as in this 1865 *Harper's* account: "Every man or woman who steps out of a railway car unhurt does so with a feeling of sensible relief. It is a fact that more lives have been lost by accident this year than in some of the severest battles of the war."[12] This "accident cosmology," in which danger and catastrophe threatened to become the cultural norm, underscored what Mark Seltzer has dubbed in another context America's "wound culture" (Luckhurst 213–14; Seltzer *Serial Killers*). Although the railroad held out the promise of taming nature, creating new markets, and unifying an expansive landscape, it also was in danger of crushing the national psyche. John Eric Erichsen's *On Railway and Other Injuries of the Nervous System* (1867) established that the train crash could result in a series of aftershocks for its victims, injuries to the nerves that he diagnosed as "railway spine." Erichsen's account helped shift post-accident symptomology from the body to the mind as a primary pathological site. Soon neurologists and surgeons were locating a host of once invisible wounds, from "fright" and "psychic harm" to "emotional shock" and "terror," decades before Freud's and Breuer's work in *Studies on Hysteria* (Caplan 32). Erichsen's case histories included accounts of melancholia, fitful dreams, disordered memory, impotence, and a "sudden loss of business sense," among its extensive symptoms (Luckhurst 22). Moreover, prominent sufferers of "railway brain" included Charles Dickens, Sigmund Freud, and Emile Zola.[13]

By 1904, the same year that Dreiser abandoned his memoir and began writing his story "The Mighty Burke," the *Central Law Journal* published an article titled "Neurasthenia, The Result of Nervous Shock, as a Ground for Damages." This article and others like it compiled lists of the compensable conditions for railway injuries, with "sidero dromophobia," or fear of a railway journey, and "traumatic neurasthenia" (railway brain) among the most auspicious. Anticipating Freud, the article argued that "traumatic neurasthenia" might take weeks after an accident to develop. "The injury may be of nervous shock only. . . . Insomnia, brain fag, headache, mental confusion, muscular weakness, despondency and irritability develop gradually. He declares he is unable to work finally and stays in bed a good deal from pain and weariness."[14] With the railroad and modern technologies came new and controversial forms of mental sentience: "More delicate than other parts of the human organism," the mind, many argued, is susceptible to "lasting injury through external impressions without direct physical impact" ("Neurasthenia" 88).

Numerous railway accidents gave Americans their first real glimpse of a vast and delicate landscape—the psyche—that seemed as immense as the endless network of railway lines and eminently susceptible to what Freud, building upon the work of earlier railway critics, would call years later in *Moses and Monotheism* (1937), "traumatic neurosis." Wound culture responded to Freud's earliest descriptions of hysteria and trauma, descriptions that were themselves inspired by the debates over railway accidents in which passengers walked away from the scene of an accident only to be haunted in the weeks, months, and years to follow by various psychological symptoms, most invisible to the naked eye. If it should happen that a traveler escapes "unharmed" from the scene of a "shocking accident"—Freud's example, of course, is a train collision—he or she may in the next several weeks suffer a series of "grave psychical and motor symptoms," symptoms that can be ascribed "only to his shock or whatever else happened at the time of the accident" (84). Freud, himself, was one of the most famous accident victims, and his analysis of the return of repressed traumatic scene is perhaps today the most well-known theory in what was then a growing professional conundrum concerning the nature of psychic injury debated in European and American journals in the late 1860s.[15] The railroad collision, a recurring image in Freud's work, did not simply represent technological violence, as Cathy Caruth argues in her reading of Freud, it also conveyed "the impact of its very incomprehensibility" (Caruth 6). Beyond the mechanical blow and at the heart of traumatic experience, in other words, is a crisis of representation: "what returns to haunt the victim, these stories tell us, is not only the reality of the violent event but also the reality of the way that its violence has not yet been fully known" (Caruth 6). The preceding chapter on women's crash lit argued that through literature this cognitive dissonance is made manifest; women's narratives used shock, fright, and a new sensibility, collective human frailty in the face of technological change, as a crucial challenge to their protagonists' historical invisibility and other women like them.

Dreiser embraced the railroad's promise of re-masculinizing the body and repairing the mind while recognizing the railway's place as a very public symbol of grave physical and psychical harm. Along with the promise of industrial progress, the railroad was the most cogent exemplum of industry's power to inflict irreparable damage. Dreiser knew the effects of industrial accident first hand. Not only did he witness and report on these accidents for several newspapers early in his journalism career, but his father had been seriously injured in a mill fire and was left "chronically unemployed," workers' compensation still a distant dream (Loving 5).[16] In "The Toil of the Laborer," Dreiser contemplates his fate as a railroad employee and those he left behind: "not to be a tool in the hands of their indifferent masters who could not or would not interest themselves in them, was something, even though my ceasing could not relieve them of their toil" (106). Dreiser recognized that the railroad often was an "opulent despot," as he explains in his *Harper's* article "The Railroad and the People": they were "all that the dictionary of iniquity involves—dark, sinister, dishonest associations which robbed the people 'right and left,' as the old phrase put it, and gave nothing in return" (*Selected Magazine Articles* vol. 2 161). This article, which qualifies the railroad's "soulless" image by lauding its efforts at expanding markets for small businesses, also perpetuates Dreiser's earlier associations with the railroad industry as "dark," "sinister," and dangerous. These contradictory associations made their way into Dreiser's long fiction, from the menacing character Frank Cowperwood in *The Financier* (1912), who was modeled after Charles Yerkes, a mass-transit mogul, to *Sister Carrie* (1900), which famously begins with the protagonist riding a train to Chicago to embrace a new future; the thrill of the train's approach to Chicago lifts "the burden of toil" (*Sister Carrie* 10).

Dreiser's fictionalized memoir "The Mighty Burke," and its revision and expansion into "The Mighty Rourke" in *Twelve Men*, narratives on which he labored on and off for nearly two decades, offers an alternative ending to Dreiser's account of neurasthenic illness. These stories are narratives of loss, modest success, and physical and psychological vulnerability, and readers are led on a search for the meaning of injury beyond Dreiser's own lonely "wander[ings]" (*Amateur Laborer* 124). Both narratives offer rejoinders to the last line of *An Amateur Laborer* in which Dreiser wonders if he "could ever make anyone feel what [he] was then feeling" (124). For Dreiser, railroad work did not relieve his "hurts" in the way that Muldoon promised and Dreiser vainly hoped, by making a "man" out of him: curing his psychological ills through physical labor.

The railroad, in fact, only amplified the scope of his woundedness. Yet, in its very democratization of wounds and its universalization of vulnerability—its sufferers included laborers, conductors, passengers, and bystanders, many of whom suffered physical and mental pains—Dreiser also recognized that woundedness did not necessarily preclude manliness. Through his railroad experiences, remembered and rewritten on multiple occasions throughout his career, Dreiser reformulated the stakes of psychological illness. The culture of the railroad and the questions it inspired about injury, negligence, and responsibility opened a pathway for his recovery.

"The Mighty Burke," written shortly after Dreiser quit his railroading memoir, may have been intended for inclusion in *An Amateur Laborer*. Stephen C. Brennan has argued that the biographical portrait might be thought of as "the book's . . . climax" ("Myth in the Making" 77). His months working as a laborer on the New York Central Railroad "had such a powerful impact on [Dreiser] that he wrote about it in several versions, the most successful being the character sketch about . . . Burke" (Coltrane 365). Although "The Mighty Burke" met with repeated rejection by publishers, Dreiser did not abandon the piece. He resubmitted it in 1910 to *McClure's Magazine*, the same magazine that rejected it six years earlier; it was finally published in May 1911, fully seven years after the magazine had turned down the initial sketch twice. Dreiser's work with Mike Burke, a masonry foreman on the New York Central Railroad, inspired Dreiser's literary imagination. From his experience on Burke's crew in *An Amateur Laborer* (written in 1904 and published in 1983), to "The Toil of the Laborer" (written in 1904 and published in *Call Magazine* in 1913), *The Genius* (1915), and "The Irish Section Foreman Who Taught Me How to Live" (1924), Dreiser returned to Burke, Rourke, and his own railroad labors throughout his career; these experiences influenced how he thought about physical and mental work, and they shaped his craft as a writer. Dreiser's revision of "The Mighty Burke" became the first piece that he reworked toward the publication of *Twelve Men*. In this series of portraits, Dreiser was doing more than "merely updating or expanding old material"; he created a cohesive vision by employing a unifying narrative voice throughout the sketches (Coltrane 367). Joined by their embrace of the physical life and their desire to "shock men out of their mental apathy," the portraits of William Muldoon and Mike Burke (Rourke) form a pair in the collection; both men had a profound impact on Dreiser's life and work.

Writing about the railroad and industrial labor's "burden of toil" allowed Dreiser to externalize his own anxieties and sense of ontological vulnerability, to relocate self-blame, and to reformulate the meaning of manly labor. Much as Dreiser did in *An Amateur Laborer*, the narrator of "The Mighty Burke" works on the railroad for his health "at fifteen cents an hour" (41). Seeking a transfer from a foreman who is a "torture to [his] soul," he appeals to Burke, the foreman for "all that part of the railroad that lay between New York and fifty miles out, on three divisions" (41). The narrator is able to befriend Burke by "conversing upon railroad subjects," and he becomes part of Burke's "gang" (41). In Dreiser's story, railroad work is less alienating and more manly than in *An Amateur Laborer*: "If ye were to get up [my] way every day fer a year," Burke tells Teddy, "it would make a man of ye" (41). Rather than "homely" and "humbl[e]" as in Dreiser's memoir, the "little station on the Harlem" where the narrator works is "a pretty place," "a veritable haven of rest" (*Amateur Laborer* 124; "Burke" 41). Before the narrator is able to start his "manly" labor, he is called away to check some paperwork that Burke leaves unfinished. Although Burke is an "A-1 workman," he is "not skilled" in the office technicalia and accounting required of the foreman (42). To Burke the railroad signals physical fortitude, to the clerk who faults Burke's labor, "railroad work mean[s] figuring" (42).

The narrative foregrounds the distinction between the railroad's financial accounting (the work of the mind) and its physical accounts (the work of the body). Part of the foreman's job is to track materials, schedule labor, and record workplace injuries. The foreman is vested with the authority to estimate labor recovery time and to manage the general business of the road. Burke rejects such demands of accounting; his philosophy is dismissive of industry bookkeeping and as for any possible workplace injuries, Burke dismisses their importance: "ye can't always go unhurted" (48). When Teddy, the narrator, happily takes Burke's "clerical work into his own hands," Teddy becomes, in essence, injury's accountant. Unlike the railroad clerk who threatens to fire Burke for refusing the full responsibilities of a foreman, Teddy admires and, indeed, saves Burke's job.

Teddy protects Burke's "masterful" physical labor: "he would toil for hours at a stretch with his trowel and his line and his level and his plumb-bob, getting the work into shape, and you would never hear a personal complaint from him concerning the weariness of labor" (43). The narrator sees in Burke that "work was the thing, the direct accomplishment of something tangible"; this is the kind of satisfaction that Dreiser sought but did not find in his own "amateur" labors (43). Burke commands respect from his gang, and despite his belief that physical injury is inevitable in his line of work, he cares for his crew's safety and shows a keen interest in their health. Knowing that Teddy works to "gain health," Burke asks after Teddy's "feelin" and tells him that a "year or two at this work . . . would be the makin' uv ye" (46). It is only when the masons come on the job that Teddy's accounting acknowledges that work on the railroad requires more than singular displays of strength and manly comradeship.

The masons' arrival and their expectations about the workplace undermine the predominant focus on heroic physical labor and manly idealism first privileged in the story. They introduce workplace concerns: salaried hours, measures of productivity, and timely compensation. Although satirized early on, the fraternal masons introduce a different vocabulary of masculinity than Burke's into the story; it is one that includes labor rights, workplace fairness, and collective responsibility rather than merely physical dexterity and bodily strength. The narrator describes how the masons bring with them "bickerings on all conceivable subjects: the number of bricks they were to lay in an hour; the number of men they were to carry on one line, or wall, the length of time they were supposed to work, or had worked, or would work" (48). Teddy calls these labor negotiations a "comic opera" (48). Yet, within weeks of the freemasons' "comic opera," and within only a few paragraphs of their appearance in the story, Burke suffers "a most dreadful accident" that will soon take his life (48). The "boiler of the hoisting engine" explodes, and Burke and some of his men are trapped beneath the rubble of a building. While Burke desperately tries to save his men, he is fatally injured, "grim and bleeding" (48). The juxtaposition of Burke's "desperate wounds" and "dreadful pains" with the masons' labor disputes reminds readers that their demands are not so "comic" after all (48). Although Burke from his hospital bed declares, "Ye have to expect thim things. . . . Ye can't always go unhurted," the narrator no longer unquestioningly accepts that physical injuries are "the [manly] way of things" (48). While Burke lies in a hospital bed dying, Teddy ponders suffering, negligence, and responsibility, confessing that he "frequently spoke of what [he] deemed the dreadful carelessness of it all" (48).

In "The Mighty Burke" Dreiser describes physical work as manly and physical injury in heroic terms, yet he also qualifies the narrative's idealized renderings of physical prowess by introducing the railroad's labor pains and liabilities. The freemasons, like Burke, are "proud" of their work; yet, they also bring to the line their questions about labor's recompense. Unlike Burke, these men exact "rights" and demand recognition (48). Initially sketched as an individual portrait of manly strength, "The Mighty Burke" ends with the physical suffering and death of its hero, a death that the narrator ultimately finds "careless" (48). Not only Burke's wife, who is introduced at the very end of the tale, but also the narrator and the rest of the gang are described as physically and emotionally distraught and "hot with tears" (48). They are left with no recognizable redress other than the memory of Burke and what the narrator describes as the "dreadful" pain of his loss (48). Such an outcome, readers are encouraged to believe, the masons would not easily endure.

When Dreiser republishes "The Mighty Burke" as "The Mighty Rourke" in *Twelve Men*, he significantly expands the discussion of Burke's failures of accounting and develops a more detailed depiction of the freemasons. By examining multiple versions of this story and attending to the repetition of its narrative elements, its cultural significance in

Dreiser's oeuvre becomes clear. In Dreiser's extensive revisions, we can read a renewed emphasis on mental work, the character and quality of the workplace, and the emotional development of Teddy, the narrator. In telling and retelling the story of Teddy and Burke, Dreiser demonstrates his desire to interrogate masculinity, industry, and labor. If "Burke" begins to question the conventional script that physical prowess defines manhood and that physical injury is the only acceptable expression of masculine pain, Rourke corrects it further. Teddy, who joins Rourke's gang in order to purge his psychic wounds, regains his physical and emotional strength without physically laboring "every day fer a year" as Burke prescribes ("Burke" 13). Critics, however, have disagreed about the portrait of Burke/Rourke. Robert Coltrane has written that the portraits in *Twelve Men* form a meditation, we might call it a jury of sorts, on the definition of masculine success. Next to William Muldoon and Peter B. McCord, a newspaper artist and close friend of Dreiser's, Coltrane reads Michael Burke/Rourke as a failure. Far from a celebration of manly strength, Coltrane suggests that Burke's physical prowess ultimately unmans him; it cannot save him from an untimely death. In contrast, Stephen C. Brennan has argued that Rourke "assumes a tragic stature" and that the narrative, which privileges his noble suffering, ends with a sense of optimism rather than failure ("*Twelve Men*" 142).[17] Reading the narrative through the loosely fictionalized character of Teddy, I want to underscore the story's depiction of this character's crucial transformation: from laboring dilettante to indispensable auditor, from sickness to "good" health, and from insignificant "hand" to substantive voice. Through the autobiographical character of Teddy, Dreiser is able to work through the meaning of injury and responsibility and to complicate personal and cultural ideas of masculinity and vulnerability.

When Teddy introduces himself and his friendship with Rourke at the start of the revised portrait, he calls himself a "nominal laborer" (one whose salary drops by three cents an hour, from fifteen cents in "Burke" to twelve in "Rourke"): "Since I was only a nominal laborer here, not a real one—permitted to work for my health, for twelve cents an hour—we fell to conversing upon railroad matters, and in this way our period of friendship began" ("Rourke" 289). Teddy's characterizations of his own work as "nominal" underscores the importance of the task he will eventually take on as Rourke's clerk and accountant. Unlike "Burke," Teddy freely critiques the railroad in "Rourke," calling "the great railroad company for which [Rourke] toiled . . . no gentle master" (290). Rourke worked "twenty-two years, 'rain or shine'" (290), and Teddy is "forcibly" struck when he learns of Rourke's meager remuneration for his work: "perhaps, as we say in America, he had 'a right to be happy,' only I couldn't see it" (290). What Teddy quickly does see is that Rourke is considered a "failure" at work despite his "masterful" physical skill (296). Although Teddy holds fast to his idea that physical "work is the thing, not argument, or reports, or plans, but the direct accomplishment of something tangible, the thing itself," this mantra proves an empty promise (297). Rourke's physical ability is undervalued by the railroad and his accounting failures highlighted. Rourke, it seems, can't keep his "records straight" (292). He is found guilty of the "infraction of railroad rules" (292), and Teddy observes, "although [Rourke] was a better foreman than most, still, because of his lack of skill in this matter of accounting"—Teddy labels it "office technicalia"—"he was looked upon as more or less a failure" (294–95).

Teddy's assumption of accounting duties is particularly notable given the important role that railroads played in the birth of finance and the development of professional accounting in the late nineteenth and early twentieth centuries. The growth of public interest in railroad reports gave rise to a growing field of financial analysis. Thomas Woodlock's book *The Anatomy of a Railroad Report* (1895) emerged as a popular authority on railroad operations and financial accounts (Previts and Merino 80). John Moody, a pioneer financial analyst who became best known for Moody's Investors Services, also began his career in financial management with the analysis of railroad operations, including *Moody's Manual of Railroads and Corporation Securities* (1900) and *How to Analyze Railroad Reports* (1912). According to Moody, corporate secrecy and the absence of transparent financial accounting in the railroad industry endangered the public welfare as much as the neglect of safety measures like train signals and car couplers. These early financial analysts likened the railroads' corporate financial dealings to another kind of deadly crash. Railroads used private ledgers to keep accounts of sales, purchases, salaries, and capital expenses, and the policy of keeping income and expenditures private and unavailable to public scrutiny often meant that railway safety and maintenance lacked transparency: "it is one of the strong arguments in favor of uniform accounting requirements that railroads coming under the jurisdiction of the interstate commerce commission . . . are now required to charge to maintenance the items which properly belong there and can only put in improvement or betterment accounts the actual expenditures of such nature" (Previts and Merino 840). Railroads could no longer cook their books and neglect safety for the sake of profits.

Neither Dreiser's employer, the New York Central Railroad, nor any other railroad line offered an annual report to its stockholders. Moreover, when the railway industry did begin to publish annual reports, they were virtually illegible. *The Railroad Gazette* reported in 1893 that "the annual report of the railroad is often a very blind document and the average shareholder . . . generally gives up before he begins" (qtd. in Previts and Merino 81). Critics decried that the secrecy surrounding private ledgers threatened the public safety, physical and financial.[18] The profession of accounting emerged in light of the railroad industry's financial inscrutability, asserting some measure of control over a disparate and complicated financial landscape. As businesses like railroads became more widely capitalized by the public, investors demanded financial statements that periodically synthesized corporate earnings or changes in the asset position of a firm: "statement extracts of the journals and ledgers were being required in concise, uniform, and understandable form" (Previts and Merino 87). With the birth of modern public accounting came new innovations like loose-leaf and columnar books that made it possible to arrange, amend, and manage information. Moreover, regulatory agencies like the Interstate Commerce Commission (1887) were formed to combat the dangers of corporate secrecy. The system of accounting advocated by the ICC, particularly "The Classification of Operating Expenses" (1894), was hailed by many in the financial industry as the birth of "the fourth branch of modern federal government" (85). In "Rourke," Dreiser imagines the charge to render the railroads financially legible and, therefore, less dangerous. Teddy spends his days in a little woodshed by the tracks "keeping the mass of orders and reports in shape" ("Rourke" 294).

It is important to note that in Dreiser's narrative Teddy excels at "office technicalia" where Rourke disappoints. Teddy quickly abandons his position as "nominal laborer" and railroad hand to handle the reports that "cover every possible detail of [Rourke's] work" (294). Teddy manages the railroad reports with precision and descriptive integrity. Whereas Burke tells Teddy that physical work would make a man of him, in "Rourke" it is not Teddy's body but his brain that defines his manhood. Rourke assures Teddy that he is "the right man in the right place now" (310). "As time proved, this [Teddy's help with the accounting] was [his] sole reason for being there" (293). In fact, it is no longer physical labor but mental work that promises to repair Teddy's health. Rourke, inquiring after Teddy's "feelings," tells him, "Ye'll have plenty to do there to relave yer mind" (310). "The Mighty Burke" glorifies physical prowess—Burke ensures Teddy that "if ye were to get up [my] way every day fer a year it would make a man of ye" (41)—"Rourke," however, valorizes and cultivates Teddy's mental labor, his keeping of railroad accounts.

As "The Mighty Rourke" recognizes the value of mental labor, it also draws a more detailed portrait of freemasonry, which, like Teddy, offered itself as a mediator between capital and labor. "Rourke" pictures the freemasons as "discontented labor," and the story dwells in detail on their depiction as potential antagonists; for example, a drunk "ex-workman" and "non-union mason" accosts Rourke on a Sunday for pay that the mason believes he is due (306). While Rourke explains that this "stranger" left "without finishin' [his] work, an [will] get no more time" (305), this incident, which involves a scuffle and eventually the police (although Rourke refuses to press charges, saying, "what can you do with a loafer like that? He has no money, an' lockin' him up won't help his wife an' children any"), represents an extreme response of a disgruntled laborer (309). The "stranger" who is drunk and bellicose seems to prove

Rourke and Teddy's disparaging initial depictions of the masons well founded. Yet, this vignette also provides a stark contrast to a later discussion in which readers learn that although Burke/Rourke often maligns the masons, the foreman was once among their numbers. Regardless of the loafing "drunk" who tears Rourke's Sunday coat, the foreman is really "enthralled" about the "coming of the masons" (311). Freemasonry underscored the equality of "moral" men, writes Lynn Dumenil: "Masonry reassured men that despite the inequalities and immorality of the profane world, moral behavior was still the best ideal, and masonry honored them for it" (96).

Although Rourke's encounter with the drunk mason contrasts with this ideal, masonry offered prestige and status to those men whose economic standing brought them little recognition from the outside world (Dumenil 110). "We are in troublous times," writes a mason in one of its magazines, *Dispatch* (1886): "The sky of the commercial world is dark. Clouds have arisen. The breeze of discontented labor has grown to a fearful magnitude." Recognizing that the "working man has much to complain of," the author asks, "what then, can Masonry do now?" (Dumenil 94). Voluntary associations like the freemasons provided men with greater measures of political and economic power in "troublous times" by establishing new patterns of social organization. Rourke quickly corrects Teddy when Teddy tries to diminish the masons' demands: "There's no sinse in allowin' another man to waalk on ye whin ye can get another job" (314). The rights talk that was quickly dismissed in "Burke" crucially consumes Teddy's and Rourke's conversations in the later version of the narrative. Rourke is "never weary of talking of [masons]," and he defends their interests when he declares his shared sensibility: "I have my rights. . . . What kind av man is it that'll let himself be waalked on? . . . . It's nacht natural" (314). Rourke does manage to "pick a quarrel" with a "lusty mason" every now and then, but Teddy recounts that the roadwork as well as paperwork just hum along.[19]

Just as Teddy is "about to announce [his] departure," with his "health good" and his "purse" "lean," "a most dreadful accident occur[s]" (316). The boiler of a hoisting engine explodes, burying Jimmie, Matt, and Rourke, along with several others, under thousands of bricks. Most of the men, save Jimmie, are seriously injured or killed. Rourke, who Teddy describes as a "fabled giant," "half-god, half-man, composed in part of flesh, in part of brick and stone," makes it to the hospital, where he lingers for a week in "very serious condition" (319). Teddy tells us that he "frequently spoke of what [he] deemed the dreadful uncertainty of life and the seeming carelessness of the engineer in charge of the hoisting engine. [Rourke], however, had no complaint to make" (319). Teddy, in the later narrative, adds more detail to his general lament about the "dreadful carelessness of it all"; his comments intensify from an abstract observation about negligence to the direct assignment of responsibility in the figure of "the engineer in charge of the hoisting engine" (319). In this detail, and in the introduction of the language of negligence and responsibility, Dreiser draws upon a very real transformation in the development of industries like insurance and law, both expanding to cope with the growing number of industrial accidents like the one that kills Rourke and wounds many of his co-workers.

Similar to the masons who are "obstreperously conscious of their own rights," Teddy's entreaty against "carelessness" is precisely what was coming to drive U.S. culture and its industries. The insurance industry, for example, took the logic of industrial risk and subjected every contingency to mathematical probability tables and actuarial statistics. The Travelers Insurance Company of Hartford, Connecticut, which began in the 1860s to insure travelers against accidents, particularly those associated with railroad travel, soon offered "personal insurance" to white male workers (black men were often deemed uninsurable, as I will discuss in the following chapter). In Dreiser's telling and retelling of the story of Mike Burke, the freemasons' appearance introduces the discourse of workplace rights and accountability; yet even fraternal societies like the freemasons that sought to protect its members were soon surpassed by an actuarial worldview that would consolidate risk and compensate individual policy holders based on lost time (or in some cases lost body parts) due to accident and injury.[20]

Teddy, whose own "hurts" are scarcely visible and nearly mended, becomes the voice and accountant that keeps the larger consequences of psychological injury and Rourke's physical and fatal wounds alive. In his job as injury's accountant, Teddy not only reports to the railroad about the gang's injuries and Rourke's death, he also finds himself "frequently" speaking of "dreadful carelessness"; in both portraits, Teddy "speaks" toward the care of wounds and the vulnerability of labor in a society from which Dreiser deemed himself, on the very basis of his own "pains," an "outcast" (*Amateur Laborer* 124). Both narratives end, not as Dreiser's memoir does, by turning attention inward, by conveying a sense of hopeless personal "hurts" ("could I ever make anyone feel what I was then feeling?"), but by casting pain beyond the scope of the personal by assigning wider cultural responsibility. Increasingly, this petition played itself out in courts of law, where railroad laborers, employees, passengers, and bystanders narrated their own stories of physical as well as psychological harm. Like Dreiser's description of disastrous "maiming" in *An Amateur Laborer*, legal narratives asked courts to recognize the damage done not only to the bodies of its many plaintiffs, but also to acknowledge what Dreiser dramatically described on the last pages of his railroad memoir as "hurts that would not heal" (*Amateur Laborer* 124). Unlike Burke who died acquiescing to the "way of things," the cultural demands for the recognition of injury brought its sufferers out in increasing numbers, from sick beds, private homes, and places of work, into courts of law.

Teddy's accounting and Dreiser's storytelling introduced new avenues for understanding suffering and its modes of potential redress.[21] Rourke, Teddy's model of the manliest of men, suffers dreadful injuries and, shortly thereafter, senselessly, if valiantly, dies. The collective sadness and despair at the death of Burke (Rourke) at the end of the narrative brings the whole town out in mourning. Mourning his own sense of loss, "The Mighty Burke" and "Rourke" may have provided some closure for Dreiser's internalized sense of fragmentation by dramatizing and imploring a cultural accounting for what Teddy labels the "carelessness" of a society marked by its wounds ("Burke" 48). It is precisely this cultural accounting and the narrative's ability to recast injury from a mark of personal failure to an impetus for collective responsibility that provides Teddy and, in turn, Dreiser, with the promise of healing his psyche and restoring his manhood. Yet, public accounting, actuarial methods, and the rise of accidents and their legal redress do not tell the whole story.

The railroad in Dreiser's literary imagination helped to demonstrate that pain was not solely an individual cry of bodily harm. It was a problem of cultural compensation and evidentiary representation; its incitements as well as its consequences—what Dreiser in *An Amateur Laborer* might have described as a "call to harms"—demanded attention. Unlike James Fenimore Cooper, who imagined "regeneration through violence," Dreiser demonstrates that the pains pervading turn-of-the-century culture required treatment, especially as they were suffered by everyone from society's most valued writers to the nation's most invisible workers.[22] Dreiser's railroad narratives, rewritten and reworked over numerous years, encapsulates the transition from the sentiment held by Burke early on, "you can't always go unhurt," to Safety First, the new slogan and corporate campaign for workplace safety. Inspired by workmen's compensation laws and the insurance industry, "employers of labor and their insurers worked together in the National Safety Council to prevent industrial accidents," writes Peter Norton (Norton 31). Safety first spread beyond the railroad and factory walls to become an "admonition not only to industrial workers but also to motorists, streetcar patrons, and pedestrians," as I described in the previous chapter (Norton 32). By 1907, the American Museum of Natural History in New York City opened the first public exhibit on safety innovations in the United States, which in 1911 became the American Safety Museum.[23] Dreiser's preoccupation with the railroad and his obsessive revision and retelling of the story of the foreman Mike Burke speaks to a changing cultural mood, one that led to an increase in insurance claims, legal cases, and the industrial safety movement's growing stake in accident prevention. It also introduced a discourse on risk, responsibility, and compensation that remains with us to this day.

For Dreiser and many others equally compelled and repulsed by the iron horse, the railroad embodied all that was new and exciting about modern culture, while it also symbolized the universal fragility of body and mind. Dreiser's lament in *An Amateur Laborer* that "others" would "never feel" what he was "feeling" is proven a false fear, however, as men increasingly subjected their experiences of vulnerability to public scrutiny, not only by publishing personal accounts of "hurts that [would] not heal" but also by voicing such narratives in courts of law and through insurance claims (*Amateur Laborer* 124). In light of men like Dreiser, laboring with the isolation and shame of their psychological pain and searching for sense against the "carelessness" of industrial culture's damaging wounds, the dominant language of the law cast psychic injury with greater legitimacy; it completed, by measuring and awarding compensation, a narrative of pain that might otherwise be left in fragments. Although Dreiser's memoir, *An Amateur Laborer*, was left in such a state, that is, unfinished, and he never took his own story of injury and the railroad into a court of law, he labored for years on publications associated with this industry, writing articles and fictionalized accounts of railroad laborers, imagining that through their stories he might complete and compensate his own. Like Southworth's serializations, published for decades corresponding to the expansion of injury claims, Dreiser returned again and again to the railroad as a vehicle through which to explore and to understand his own pain, and, in turn, to recognize masculine vulnerability in a growing technological culture. While many of his narratives met with resistance from publishers, especially Dreiser's narratives that looked upon railroad laborers (rather than the business of the railroad) with a "gentle and melancholy eye," Dreiser persisted (*Amateur Laborer* xxix-xxxii). The wounded yet still manly men of Dreiser's narratives confirm that Dreiser was not a social "outcast" and that his injuries did not denote failure; rather, we might think of Dreiser as a vital interlocutor, who, like his narrator Teddy in "The Mighty Burke" and "The Mighty Rourke," "frequently spoke" toward the recognition and reevaluation masculine wounds, physical and psychic.

NOTES

1. See Mark Seltzer, *Serial Killers: Life and Death in America's Wound Culture*.
2. Dreiser's writing about lynching has interested scholars. See Jean Lutes, "Lynching Coverage and the American Reporter-Novelist"; and Debbie Lelekis, *American Literature, Lynching, and the Spectator in the Crowd: Spectacular Violence*. See also Lutes, *Front Page Girls*, for a discussion of gender and reporting styles, "Introduction," 1–11.
3. See Paul Fyfe, "Accidents in the News," 31–61.
4. When he worked for the *St. Louis Globe Democrat*, Dreiser was given "a police precinct for a regular beat" as was "customary for a new man on a big-city paper," Nostwich, 337.

5. See Paulette D. Kilmer, "*The New York Times* Accident Stories: Sensational Coverage Warns of Consequences," in *Sensationalism: Murder, Mayhem, Mudslinging, Scandals, and Disasters in 19th-Century Reporting*, 253–64.

6. See Tom Lutz's classic, *American Nervousness: 1903*; and, more recently, Justine Murison, "Cui bono? Spiritualism and Empiricism from the Civil War to American Nervousness," in *The Politics of Anxiety in Nineteenth Century American Literature*, 136–70.

7. See Hildegard Hoeller's "Herland and Hisland: Illness and 'Health' in the Writings of Charlotte Perkins Gilman and Theodore Dreiser" for a discussion of the similarities between Charlotte Perkins Gilman's and Theodore Dreiser's experiences of neurasthenia, 24–43. For Dreiser's experience in Muldoon's "sporting sanitarium," see Kathy Frederickson, 'Working Out to Work Through': Dreiser in Muldoon's Body Shop of Shame," 128. See also John Pettegrew, "Rugged Individualism," in *Brutes in Suits: Male Sensibility in America, 1890–1920* for discussion of male neurasthenia and the "regenerative powers of the wilderness," 45–76.

8. Theodore Dreiser, "The Mighty Burke," *Electronic Text Center, University of Virginia Library*, 41–48. http://wyllie.lib.virginia.edu:8086/perl/toccer-new?id=DreMigh.sgm&images=images/mod. All future references are to this edition.

9. Wolfgang Schivelbusch in his study of railroad culture, *The Railway Journey* (1977), argues that in the United States the railroad, at least in its infancy, infrequently registered as a symbol of harm. For the railroad's legal and economic impact, see Morton Horwitz, *The Transformation of American Law, 1780–1860*, 201–10. See also Leo Marx, "The Machine," in *The Machine in the Garden* for more on this progressive rhetoric.

10. Quoted in Marx, *The Machine in the Garden*, 205. See also *The Railway Age Gazette's* publication, *Sayings and Writings about the Railway—By Those Who Have Managed Them and Those Who Have Studied Their Problems*. "It is not an exaggeration to say that in the past history of this country, the railway, next after the Christian religion and the public school, has been the largest single contributing factor to the welfare and happiness of the people." Quoted in Lynn Kirby, *Parallel Tracks*, 32.

11. Horwitz, Friedman, and others writing about injury, accidents, and the law describe how new legal doctrines regarding negligence often made compensation of bodily injury claims far more difficult for men like Rourke and his gang. See Morton Horwitz, *The Transformation of American Law, 1780–1860*, 201–10; Lawrence M. Friedman, *A History of American Law*, 409–27; see also G. Edward White, *Tort Law in American History* for a history of what he describes as "the changing ethos of injury in America," xx.

12. See "The Horrors of Travel," *Harper's Weekly*, 594. James O. Fagan, author of *Confessions of a Railroad Signalman* (1909), implored: "The people are now beginning to comprehend that the unexplained death-toll and suffering peculiar to American railroads is a situation in which the self-respect of the nation is intimately concerned," 135. An 1867 study in *The Lancet* estimated that in that year alone 5,600 persons were killed on U.S. railroads, a number that jumped dramatically by 1898 when 47,729 persons were killed or injured. These statistics are quoted in Denuta Mendelson, *Interfaces of Medicine and Law*, 36.

13. Charles Dickens writes in *Dombey and Son* (1848): "Though characterised as an 'earthquake,' th[e] devastation and ruination of 1840s Camden Town has little to do with nature. The catastrophe is the result of the monstrous, mechanical shadow being cast over Europe: the Railway." Dickens, *Dombey and Son*, 120–21.

14. See "Neurasthenia, The Result of Nervous Shock, as a Ground for Damages," 86. See also Herbert Oppenheim's *Textbook of Nervous Diseases* for cases of men who worked on the railway and were involved in collisions that resulted in severe neuroses. Herbert Page's *Injuries of the Spine and Spinal Cord and Nervous Shock* also lists hundreds of nervous shock cases.

15. The fear of physical injury and bodily violation displaces what Freud argues is the foundational fear: castration. See Freud, *Moses and Monotheism*, 84. Mark Seltzer in

Bodies and Machines accords the railroad privileged status in what he calls the "erotics of uncertain agency": the anxieties that accompany machine culture that manifest themselves on the body, particularly, Seltzer argues, in problems of production and reproduction, 18.

16. For a discussion of the development of workplace safety regulations and compensation, see R. Rudy Higgens-Evenson, "From Industrial Police to Workmen's Compensation: Public Policy and Industrial Accidents in New York, 1880–1910," 365.

17. For more on Dreiser's depiction of success and failure in his biographical portraits, see Thomas P. Riggio, "Dreiser and the Uses of Biography," 34.

18. Accounting was a symbol of big business and in its mission to develop the railroad's financial accountability it was crucial to the progressive movement. See Previts and Merino, *A History of Accounting in America*, 128.

19. For more on voluntary fraternities and the freemasons, see Lynn Dumenil, *Freemasonry and American Culture, 1880–1930*.

20. The growing culture of bureaucratized responsibility gave Dreiser a vocabulary for restoring his manhood, but it also inaugurated a new form of fungibility, particularly of persons and body parts. Dreiser speaks progressively in his desire to associate manliness with psychological wounds, but the growth of legal claims also indicates a new cultural ethos, one that sought to monetize all aspects of the human condition.

21. For analysis of sentimentality in the age of managerial capitalism, see Aaron Ritzenberg, *The Sentimental Touch*.

22. George F. Drinka in *The Birth of Neurosis* argues that "the progressive symbols of society, such as the railways, seemed to be responsible for the breakdown of the human nervous system . . . in which the human psyche collided with the changing nineteenth-century environment and gave birth to an epidemic-like neurotic illness whose form and severity are rooted in the Victorian era," 122. See also Tom Lutz's *American Nervousness: 1903*, which provides an extensive collection of neurasthenia sufferers.

23. The museum focused on the conservation of human life and featured safety equipment and methods of accident prevention that would become a big business in the twentieth century. The exhibitions not only educated workers but also served as advertisements for safety equipment.

FOUR
Burning Down the House
Comets, Hurricanes, and the Fire to Come

Stephen Crane, like Theodore Dreiser, began his writing career as a journalist, reporting on scenes of catastrophe and turmoil on the urban landscape. On November 25, 1894, Crane published an article in the *New York Press* titled "When Every One is Panic Stricken/A Realistic Pen Picture of a Fire/In a Tenement." Submitted for publication as a factual report on a Greenwich Village fire, Crane's journalistic fiction—an editor later complained that there was "no fire at all, no baby, no hysterical mother"—drew upon the iconography of conflagrations reported in the daily papers.[1] Often spectacular, urban fires were all too common events in the nineteenth-century city. In fact, the very first illustrations printed on the front pages of the New York dailies were images of fires and their ruins by illustrators like Corwin Knapp Linson, who was a friend of Crane's and shared a studio with him during part of the time Crane wrote for the *New York Press*.[2] Metropolitan growth, and with it the factories, warehouses, and tenements, meant that the threat of fire was demonstrable, and few dangers ignited the public imagination quite like it. Tourists and city dwellers alike would plan their evenings around fires much as they would a theatrical event: "It was like deciding to go to the theater to see a play that has been announced and that could be counted on with certainty to come off," wrote one New York City tourist (qtd. in Rozario 111). As fires and other calamities became lead features in the daily papers, it kindled the public's fascination with urban disasters.

The narrator of Crane's "realistic pen picture" is deep in "some grim midnight reflections upon existence" as he walks with a "stranger" down the "shadowy" streets of New York City ("Panic" 97). Spotting a crowd "excitedly" running toward an "old four story structure," the narrator

Figure 4.1. Art and Picture Collection, The New York Public Library. "Saving lives at a tenement-house fire [(a)n actual scene]." *New York Public Library Digital Collections.* Accessed October 24, 2017.

notices "a deep and terrible hue of red, the color of satanic wrath, the color of murder" seeping from the basement window of a nearby building ("Panic" 98). Like the image of flames that Crane returns to when he writes another story with fire as its catalyst, "The Monster," the neighbors are "awakened" and rush from their houses to "lookut'er burn" ("Panic" 98). From the crowd of spectators on the street a woman emerges, her "features lined in anguish," calling out "My baby! My baby!" A nearby policeman hears the woman's cry and "plunge[s]" into the building. Crane describes the onlookers as "full of distress and pity" for the fire victims and "cynical scorn for their impotency" ("Panic" 99). All the crowd can do is watch as the "demons of the flame" engulf the structure ("Panic" 98). "They felt the human helplessness that comes when nature breaks forth in a passion, overturning the obstacles, emerging at a leap from the position of a slaver to that of a master, a giant" ("Panic" 99). Emphasizing human vulnerability, inconsequence, and bondage to the "pitiless" fire, Crane ends his fictionalized account with a description of the valor of heroic fire fighters against the "fury" and dominion of nature. Leaving the reader uncertain as to the fate of the baby or the policeman, Crane's final pages are not a resolution to the calamity, but rather a paean to the fire company whose "magnificent" engine was led by "three white horses" dashing down the street and whose "graceful" hook and ladder truck made it "obvious that these men who drove were . . . charioteers incarnate" ("Panic" 102). Crane ends his pen picture with a "battle" raging between the fire and its "veterans," while the "new nerves" of the "populace" reeled from the "thrill and dash of these attacks" ("Panic" 102). The sketch, despite its fiction, intensified some of the most salient features of newspaper reports on urban conflagrations. In it we see the spectator's sublime horror and fascination with fire, the extraordinary heroism of those dedicated to extinguishing it, and the community's vulnerability in the face of a "common enemy, the loosened flame" ("Panic" 102).

In 1894, the year that Crane published his newspaper sketch of a tenement fire, the National Board of Fire Underwriters reported that the number of fires in New York City reached 3,984, with damage estimates of over four million dollars (there are no available estimates of the loss of life) (*Proceedings* 143). In cities and towns from Poughkeepsie to Utica, the number of fires and their financial cost were likewise staggering. As Crane well knew, the ubiquity of conflagrations was the mainstay of urban experience. In 1894, the year he published "Everyone Is Panic Stricken," several blazes made national news: the Roxbury fire destroyed Boston's baseball stadium and close to two hundred nearby buildings; farther west, in Hinkley, Minnesota, a fire killed hundreds and razed 350,000 acres, a tragedy recounted in newspapers across the country. In January 1894, fire even destroyed the Columbia exhibit at the Chicago World's Fair, the very event intended to celebrate Chicago's triumphant return after the catastrophic 1871 fire destroyed the city. The threat of fire and its calamitous costs pervaded the cultural imagination well into the twentieth century as "thousands of onlookers gathered to watch the action at fire scenes; stories of blazes filled newspapers, provided the subject of theatrical performances, and appeared in the early films of Thomas Edison" (Tebeau 4). The problem was particularly acute in cities, which saw themselves united by the fear of fire: when Chicago burns, wrote one *Harper's* editor, "New York trembles" (qtd. in Puskar 17).

Numerous publications emphasized new and glorious futures for cities like Chicago that were razed by fire; indeed, builders and businessmen descended on these urban ruins aiming to make them anew. Transforming "apocalypse into profit," Chicago, for example, subordinated the suffering caused by the fire—the injuries, deaths, displacements, homelessness, lost fortunes, and physical ruins—in favor of the "myth of an ever resurgent city" (Miller 195, 37). Post-fire narratives of triumph and stories of rebirth and reconstruction grew increasingly commonplace in the wake of urban conflagrations. Joseph Schumpeter, the Austrian American economist, labeled this dynamic "creative destruction." According to Schumpeter in *Capitalism, Socialism, and Democracy* (1942), modern capitalism thrived on replacing the old with the new, and the calamities and disasters that befell urban centers and precipitated reconstruction were quite often good for business.[3] Feeding the public fascination with these urban conflagrations, Crane's sketch, like many similar accounts in the daily newspapers, helped to establish some of the conventions of creative destruction, particularly, as in Crane's example, the triumph of common humanity through heroic deeds. In this storyline, fire and other natural disasters are indiscriminate phenomena; they impact the rich and the poor, black and white, immigrant and natural born citizen alike. Just as heroic firemen carry men, women, and children to safety, narratives of creative destruction glorify the businessmen, builders, and insurance executives who, ashes still smoldering, restore the integrity of property, making the world whole again. The first volunteer and municipal fire companies and, later, the insurance industry were themselves built on nascent narratives of creative destruction.

By representing themselves as "bastions of virile male virtue, whose members voluntarily performed an obligation of citizenship," firemen preserved the social order at a time when uncontrolled fires threatened to destroy the economic, political, and moral order of the nation, argues historian Marc Tebeau in *Eating Smoke* (2006, 17). The daily newspapers and magazines that reported on these conflagrations heightened these representations; Theodore Dreiser's New York City sketch "The Fire" is another example:

> Groups of hook-and-ladder handlers are unhooking and making ready to invade the precincts of danger at once. The art of balancing on one foot while tugging at great coils of hose that are being uncoiled from speeding vehicles is being deftly illustrated. These men like this sort of thing. It is something to do. They are trained men, ready to fight the fire demon at a moment's notice, and they are going about their work with the ease and grace of those who feel the show as well as the importance of that which they do. Once more, after days of humdrum, they are the center of a tragedy, the cynosure of many eyes. It is exhilarating thus to be gazed at, as any one [sic] can see. They swing down from their machines in front of this holocaust with the nonchalance of men going to dinner. (Dreiser, "The Fire," 61)

Both Dreiser's and Crane's accounts of fire in New York City emphasize the firefighters' speed, ease, and superior performance at "the center of a tragedy." They are "trained and ready to fight," and the object of an admiring "gaze." Like Crane and Dreiser, Jacob A. Riis, the well-known muckraker and documentary photographer, honed his craft writing about sensational fires. His short magazine article "Heroes Who Fight Fire" (1898) is an even more comprehensive hagiography of the firefighter than Dreiser's "Fire" or Crane's "Panic." Celebrated in the magazine's byline as "the author of *How the Other Half Lives*" (1890), Riis's report describes numerous conflagrations in New York City and the valiant efforts of its firefighters to extinguish blazes and save lives. It recounts the dash and daring of New York City firefighters and sets the tone for heroic firefighting narratives that have continued in the decades after September 11, 2001.

In one of the stories Riis recounts, drawing heavily on the language of social amity in the face of catastrophe, a firefighter saves a young boy from a fire in a building's upper floor. Once safety is assured:

> Such a shout went up! Men fell on each other's necks, and cried and laughed at once. Strangers slapped one another on the back, with glistening faces, shook hands, and behaved generally like men gone suddenly mad. Women wept in the street. The driver of a car stalled in the crowd, who had stood through it all speechless, clutching the reins, whipped his horses into a gallop, and drove away yelling like a Comanche, to relieve his feelings. The boy and his rescuer were carried across the street without anyone knowing how. Policemen forgot their dignity and shouted with the rest. Fire, peril, terror and loss were alike forgotten in one touch of nature that makes the whole world kin. (Riis 483)

Riis's rhetoric is suffused with the idea that social kinship is stirred by calamity, noble collectivity is evident in the crowd, and, summoning Shakespeare, Riis argues that the scene exhibits a "touch of nature that makes the whole world kin."[4] Like Crane's "When Everyone Is Panic Stricken," Riis's report is representative of a genre of newspaper account that establishes the iconography of fire and the hagiography of the fireman: at the spark of danger to life and property the fireman rushes in to stamp out the fire, coming to the rescue of women and children. It is also representative of what Ross Miller, describing the literary boom after the 1871 Great Chicago fire, has called "boosterature": literature intended to inspire post-fire reconstruction of a new and glorious city (Miller 49). The extraordinary efforts of the New York City Fire Brigade bring "The Other Half" to safety. In Riis's account, fire draws strangers together and intensifies their shared humanity; importantly, the collective vulnerability of the crowd and the unselfish heroism of the firefighter is presented as an antidote to the social inequality evident in the hordes of onlookers. "Fire, peril, terror and loss were alike forgotten in the one touch of nature that makes the whole world kin" (Riis 483). Riis's narrative echoes the final line of Crane's fire sketch: on the urban landscape, monstrous flames make "a common enemy."

Both Crane and Riis cultivate the iconography and rhetoric of fire and both sketch remarkably similar portraits of their heroes. Riis's fire Captain Thomas J. Ahearn responds to the pained cry of a parent, which quickly draws him into a burning building. Arriving at the fire, Ahearn is confronted by a desperate man shrieking "My child! My child!" (Riis

486). Like Crane's earlier *New York Press* portrait and his later description in "The Monster" of Mrs. Trescott "waving her arms" to "Save Jimmie," the cry of a parent for a child ignites Henry Johnson's leap into a burning house enveloped by smoke. Both Riis's Captain Ahearn and Crane's fictional Henry Johnson are heroic figures irreparably disfigured by their daring. Ahearn and Johnson "all but [lose their lives] in a gallant attempt to save the life of a child" (Riis 486). Rescued by a second wave of firefighters, both are alive but badly burned. Ahearn's coat is "burned off his back" and "of his hat only the wire rim remained" (486). Riis tells his readers that Ahearn "lay ten months in the hospital, and came out deaf and wrecked physically" (Riis 486). Unlike Henry Johnson in Crane's story, a black man who becomes the monster of Whilomville after his near fatal injuries, the white firefighter Ahearn maintains his heroic stature and, despite his disfigurement, is "retired" to the "quiet of the country district" at the age of forty-five. In Riis's portrait of firefighting heroism, Ahearn is successfully protected from becoming a public spectacle and suffering the horrified stares of his fellows. However, Henry Johnson's heroism is immediately overshadowed by his double disfigurement as a black man without a face. The fate that awaits Johnson is far from retirement in the country. Whereas Riis informs his readers that Ahearn is awarded the first formal resolution of heroism issued by the New York City Fire Department to acknowledge his sacrifice, Johnson, in Crane's story, is dehumanized as a "monster" and expelled from Whilomville society (Riis 486).

Crane publishes "The Monster" in *Harper's Magazine* in 1898, well aware of how conflagrations and firefighters have been represented in the press and by his fellow writers. It too is a story with a fire and the disfigurement of its protagonist at its center. Crane's fiction, however, unsettles the customary representations of fire, firefighting, and the discourse of danger so prevalent in the daily press. His story invites readers to unfold a less tidy narrative, one that burns of social prejudice and racial violence. Against the paradoxical promise that disasters and destruction may generate social harmony and economic progress, and against the widespread narrative of creative destruction that sees only the flame the "common enemy," Crane returns to the spectacle of fire in his literary fiction, illustrating how catastrophe threatens to reinforce social inequities rather than to extinguish them.

This chapter examines how the threat of fire, the discourse of danger, and the state of ecological risk imagined in Crane's fiction, in the work of W. E. B. Du Bois, and, more recently, in Ta-Nehisi Coates's writings reflect deep trepidations about social injustice and cultural methods of recompense. Like Dreiser, Crane schooled himself in daily press depictions of urban despair, social violence, and environmental calamity. His account of accident and ecological emergency animates his newspaper work as well as his literary imagination. Paul Sorrentino's biography of

Crane, with its subtitle "A Life of Fire" (2014), offers a fitting description—Crane's own—of his sensibilities. Critics like Michael Robertson, Bill Brown, and Shelly Fisher Fishkin have skillfully shown how Crane's newspaper sketches of New York City life became the inspiration for longer fictions like "Maggie" (1893) and "The Open Boat" (1897). This chapter argues that the spectacle of fire that Crane deftly describes in his "realistic pen picture" and again in "The Monster" is a mechanism for exposing the spectacle of racism in turn-of-the-twentieth-century America. For Crane, systemic disruptions brought on by unforeseeable events like a building fire bring stories of precariousness into sharper focus. Using the cultural fascination with "demons of the flame," Crane likens it to another cultural obsession at the turn of the twentieth century, the perception of dangerous otherness that draws attention away from potential real threats, whether environmental, social, or political. Although recent criticism on Crane's "The Monster" has been led by efforts to connect Henry Johnson to historical figures like Robert Lewis (lynched in Port Jervis) or Levi Hume (his face ravaged by cancer), reading Crane's fiction through the iconography of fire and the cultural ideology of creative destruction illuminates how catastrophe often reinforced rather than remedied the social prejudices that plagued the fictional town of Whilomville and, by extension, the nation.[5] The volatile climate imagined in Crane's story forecasts later prophesies of racism and ruin by writers like W. E. B. Du Bois and Ta-Nehisi Coates.

CREATIVE DESTRUCTION: FICTIONAL FIRES TO HURRICANE KATRINA

Crane's fictional fire in the *New York Press* glorified the "thrill" and "horror" of a tenement fire as spectators watched it burn. From the industriousness of the police and firemen to the piety of the crowd, the rhetoric of disaster in the newspaper sketch recalls a long genealogy, harking back to American jeremiads, in which orators invoked the threat of calamity in order to incite discipline and productivity, as Sacvan Bercovitch famously described.[6] From colonial to modern America, the discourse of disaster and catastrophe often served ideological functions, promoting what literary critic Philip Fisher, echoing Joseph Schumpeter, has described as a "society of permanent newness" (Fisher 18). Fisher argues that American culture is marked by its repeated desire to watch the old world burn, from Emerson's rejection of the "sepulchers of the past" in the nineteenth century, to Schumpeter's celebration of the entrepreneur in the twentieth. American cultural history embraces a "destructive restlessness" that serves "technological capitalism" well (qtd. in Fisher 18, 3). In Schumpeter's economic theory of creative destruction, destruction is the agent of invention and calamities are opportunities, "nothing less than instruments of progress" (Rozario 85). Unlike Marxist theorists who see capitalism propelled by class struggle, Schumpeter's vision of capitalism is animated by the "restless, innovative, and heroic entrepreneur who create[s] new products, open[s] new markets, promote[s] new industries, and destroy[s] old ones in the process'" (Lipartito 151). Schumpeter's theory has fascinated literary critics, economists, anthropologists, and historians, many who have turned to him to explain and analyze urban development, the boom and bust cycles of American capitalism, and its entrepreneurial spirit. Much like Mark Woolston in James Fenimore Cooper's *The Crater*, with which this book began, Schumpeter's heroic entrepreneur opens new markets, settles new colonies, and remakes disaster into a development opportunity. Notably, Woolston's colonialist epistemology, described in the introduction, privileged development over sustainability and war over peace with notably deleterious effects.

In *The Shock Doctrine: The Rise of Disaster Capitalism* (2008), Naomi Klein demonstrates the relentless reach of the dynamic of creative destruction, reading contemporary catastrophes like Hurricane Katrina (2005) through the discourse of "disaster capitalism."[7] Disaster capitalism is the rapid-fire political and corporate re-engineering of societies still reeling from wars, terrorism, market meltdowns, and environmental disasters. Klein argues that U.S. free market policies thrive through the manipulation of disaster-shocked peoples and countries.[8] In the contemporary scenarios Klein describes, disaster's most vulnerable subjects remain tragically at risk. The "creative" work by government, industry, and institutions to respond to destruction—whether fiscal, ecological, or institutional—often leads to policy designs and state-mandated systems that render people more vulnerable and, often, increasingly unsafe. When governments and industry commodify catastrophe, Klein argues, human rights often are sacrificed in the name of safety and security.

Disaster theorists urge a different kind of response to catastrophe; rather than reading ecological dangers as so-called "natural" phenomena demanding "technocratic solutions," solutions that often increase risks to vulnerable populations, they argue for responses that attend to and examine the social processes that "generate unequal exposure to risk by making some people more prone to disaster than others" (Bankhoff 3). Policy makers, in other words, must look more closely at human and social actions and at the structural inequalities and power relations that "place people at risk in relation to each other and their environment" (Bankhoff 3). The damage wrought by a fire, hurricane, or, as we shall see in the next chapter, an earthquake always depends on intricate interactions between environmental factors and the social, political, and economic determinants of vulnerability. Disaster studies treats as axiomatic that "natural" catastrophes are fictions; so-called "natural disasters" always reveal pre-existing weaknesses.

One of the nation's more recent and egregious illustrations of what it means to be disaster prone, Hurricane Katrina and its devastating impact on New Orleans and its residents, exposed the "deeply structured inequalities (in housing, in environmental exposures, in access to health care and transportation, and in media coverage)" (Wailoo 1). The hurricane and its aftermath amplified a vast web not only of environmental dangers but also of racial inequalities and injustices that recalled the nation's reprehensible past, the literal destruction of homes and lives symbolic of the sustained racism embedded in local communities as well as in federal systems of governance (Wailoo 2). As the hurricane heightened a dangerous landscape made all the more vulnerable by humans, it also revealed a wider cultural refusal to see the most vulnerable among us, and this dynamic escalated the catastrophe.[9] News accounts of the hurricane and its aftermath—like the stories of fires filling the daily papers in cities across America at the turn of the twentieth century— reported the tragedy and also cultivated the spectacle. Katrina survivors were imperiled both by environmental danger and public display. In the Superdome in New Orleans, where resources like food and water were scarce, survivors were supposed to be sheltered from the storm; yet, their plight made spectacle also revealed their perpetual exclusion from the sanctuary of citizenship. The disaster exposed a vast web of vulnerabilities for the nation's poor and the deep inequalities in access to resources that recall a deeply racist American past.

Written over one hundred years before Hurricane Katrina, Crane's fictional story of conflagration and the exclusion of its protagonist from the "shelter of citizenship" is a small instance of counter-narrative; it is an imaginary adaptation of a growing and pervasive cultural logic, one that Katrina, and more recently Hurricane Maria (2017), demonstrates is still in evidence today. Crane's story calls into question the growing ideology of civic renewal in the wake of catastrophe, and it depicts how the terrifying experience of disaster may disclose social divisions and cataclysmic violence. By the late nineteenth and early twentieth centuries, fires and other ecological dangers were mechanisms for a nation, at once socially volatile and increasingly vulnerable to widespread hazards given rapid urban growth, to embrace capitalism's promise of a more glorious future and to narrate social cohesion and national security in the face of universal vulnerability and social divisiveness. Historian Kevin Rozario has called this the "catastrophic logic of modernity"; drawing on the dynamics of creative destruction, he argues that this logic valorizes the endless cycles of ruin and renewal, and bust and boom, regardless of the potential collateral damage and destroyed lives (Rozario 10). Journalists and writers like Crane, Dreiser, and Riis played important roles in disseminating nascent narratives of creative destruction, particularly given the fires and other catastrophes they covered for various magazines and presses. It is striking, therefore, that Crane's repetition of the spectacle of fire in his story "The Monster" writes against the mounting cultural discourse that represents disaster/accident as a secular path to prosperity and cultural cohesion, an event that makes "the whole world kin." Environmental destruction and racial tyranny are twin scourges within the fictional community of Whilomville, and Crane uses the ecology of fire and the discourse of danger as a means to link environmental vulnerability with the social politics of race. In exposing the discourse of racial and ecological hegemony, Crane joins and also anticipates the blistering critiques of American racism by Du Bois in the twentieth century and Coates in the twenty-first; moreover, Crane forecasts the critiques that would emerge in disaster studies and ecocriticism: namely, the dream of mastery over nature or, indeed, over other human beings, leads to unpredictable and uncontrollable irruptions.

WHITE FIRES BURNING

Crane's use of fire and fire fighting in "The Monster" counters several of the dominant tropes of the culture of catastrophe: fire as a source of urban/rural renewal, disasters as common enemies that ignite community cohesion and progress, and the image of unassailable, heroic, white

Figure 4.2. The Miriam and Ira D. Wallach Division of Art, Prints and Photographs: Print Collection, The New York Public Library. "The life of a fireman: The Metropolitan System." Currier & Ives, Lithographer. Date Issued: 1866. *New York Public Library Digital Collections.* Accessed October 24, 2017.

masculinity. In contrast, his early newspaper report of fire, "Panic," much like Riis's "Heroes," establishes the rhetoric and discursive power of valiant, white manhood in chronicles of calamity. The victims in these pieces may be poor tenement dwellers of various ethnic and racial descents; yet, the noble men fighting the fires are almost exclusively white. Heroism in these accounts is reserved for the white firefighter, and his valorization follows a long history. When Ben Franklin started the first fire company, the Union Fire Company, in 1736, he "rhapsodized about those who exerted themselves at fires: 'here are brave Men, Men of Spirit and Humanity, good Citizens, or Neighbors, capable and worthy of civil Society, and the Enjoyment of a happy Government'" (Carp 785). Colonial fire companies were considered model communities, encouraging principles of voluntarism, mutual endeavor, public safety, active self-government, civic obligation, manliness, courage, and duty, indeed, all that was laudable and virtuous in one's fellow man. Fire companies assumed a great share of the responsibility for the "safety, welfare, and prosperity of all" (Carp 785).

From their earliest days, membership in a fire company came with a mark of distinction and established the firefighter as a dutiful citizen. John Hancock was a fire ward, and numerous firemen would be signatories of the Declaration of Independence, including Samuel Adams, Benjamin Franklin, Benjamin Rush, James Wilson, Robert Morris, and Francis Hopkinson.[10] Fire safety, moreover, was fundamental to the language of liberty and to the image of the nation from its earliest days. Thomas Jefferson used the idea of an unstoppable conflagration to describe the urgency of the American Revolution: "The flames kindled on the 4th of July 1776 have spread over too much of the globe to be extinguished by the feeble engines of despotism. On the contrary, they will consume those engines, and all who work them" (qtd. in Carp 815). As the fires of freedom raged, it was the civic duty of the fireman/founding father to know when and how to bring the flames under control. Firefighters were hailed as national heroes willing to sacrifice their lives for the preservation of good and innocence, usually in the figure of a woman or child. This hagiography continues. Recent examples include the images of firefighters at "ground zero" taken by photographers like Joel Meyerowitz and Thomas E. Franklin, the latter's *Newsweek* cover image of three firefighters raising an American flag amid the ruins of the World Trade Center has become iconic.[11]

From Benjamin Franklin's *Philadelphia Gazette* through the early twentieth century, books, pamphlets, songs, broadsides, certificates, policies, prints, and even the earliest films celebrated the bravery of the fireman: rushing to a fire, directing his hose against the flames, preserving property, and saving the lives of women and children (Cooper "The Fireman" 139). The fireman was a cult hero and a model of civic virtue, especially as fire threatened to destroy the property on which a new national faith was built: security, prosperity, and progress (Cooper "The Fireman" 143). Written to commemorate New York's "bravest," books like *Reminiscences of the Old New York Fire Laddies* (1885) responded to the public's fascination with fires, firefighting equipment, techniques, and, of course, the fireman himself. On stages across the country beginning in the 1840s, Mose the fireman recued damsels in distress, while on film, Edwin S. Porter's *Life of an American Fireman* (1903) brought audiences in close proximity to danger. Currier & Ives's popular series of twenty-five hand-colored lithographs of firemen and scenes of conflagrations featured dramatic rescues and the latest firefighting technologies. American Insurance of Newark, New Jersey, used *The Life of a Fireman* (1854) as part of its early advertising campaign.[12] By the 1870s, firemen "graced the cover of *Harper's Weekly* and appeared in other national magazines in poses that replicated firemen's understanding of their manhood" (Tebeau 224). *The American Fireman: Prompt to the Rescue* (1868),[13] for example, depicts the daring rescue of a woman overcome by smoke. Reporting on virtually every fire, newspapers featured the "heroic feats of firemen on their front pages" (Tebeau 224).

The images of firefighters in theater, painting, journalism, literature, and film represented their brotherhood and bravery; yet, these ideals were perceived threatened once black firefighters sought to enter the ranks and to establish their own companies in the mid-nineteenth century. "Volunteer firefighters uniformly agreed that firefighting was the purview of white men, and their beliefs about race explicitly structured how they provided service. With few exceptions, firefighters denied African Americans the opportunity to join fire companies or to establish their own companies" (Tebeau 37). Currier & Ives, the firm that had produced the popular print series *The Life of a Fireman*, followed their iconic portraits of heroic white firefighters with the "comic" and deeply racist *The Darktown Fire Brigade* (1884).[14] These prints ridiculed the idea that African Americans could perform as successful firefighters.[15] In a print titled *The Rescue* (1884), the black brigade is clueless about firefighting techniques and incompetent at their task. The firemen struggle to get the fire truck up the road as a building in the distance burns, forcing the victim to jump from a window. The truck called "Niagara" gushes water, and the scene implies that before these hapless "firefighters" reach the site only ashes will remain. The series of images in Currier & Ives's *Darktown Fire Brigade* portray black firefighters as unskilled, ineffectual, and powerless to extinguish fires. These firefighters are *Taking a Rest* (1894) and smoking pipes around the fire truck as flames envelop a house behind them, or in *Hook and Ladder Gymnastics* (1887) the company is barely able to control and raise a ladder meant for rescue.

These scenes are far different from Riis's description and the accompanying sketches of the first use of scaling ladders to rescue a young boy from a burning building. In Currier & Ives's rendition, black firemen hold out a tablecloth and catch a cast iron skillet rather than a woman or child, a stark contrast to virtually every depiction of the white firefighter. "The heroic, chivalrous image of firefighters presented by journalists and artists for a national audience enhanced the stature of white fire-fighters in their transition from a volunteer service to a professional department; conversely, disparaging, racist representation reinforced the negative perception of their black counterparts" (McWilliams 111). From exaggerated features and bodily distortions to clattering equipment, the imagery is recognizably racist: the black firefighter is portrayed as timorous, bungling, and useless.

Stephen Crane's pen picture of the unlikely hero Henry Johnson, a black man in lavender trousers running to rescue a young white boy from a house fire in "The Monster," employs images similar to those of Currier & Ives's *Darktown Fire Brigade*. Throughout the pre-fire narrative, Johnson is described in a comic and occasionally scornful manner: he is likened to a child; he is depicted as an occasional drunk, a bully, a dandy, a narcissist, and an inadvertent clown. Johnson and the young Jimmie Trescott are "pals"; not only do they share a deference and subordination to Dr. Trescott, but "in regard to almost everything in life they seemed to have minds precisely alike" (344). This derision evaporates the moment that Henry Johnson leaps into the Trescott's burning house, a straw fedora crushed in his hands.

From the story's opening accident in which Jimmie damages a flower, to the narrative interlude on fire companies, "The Monsters'" attention to a discourse of calamity and destruction functions not to mask class or racial hierarchies or to sell social cohesion for the sake of industrial/capitalist growth. Rather, Crane reimagines the contours of the accident, the vocabulary of vulnerability and risk, and the aftermath of the fire in order to encourage readers to raise fundamental questions about the nature of community, interdependence, and social value in America. Who and what is worth saving? Who or what should be repaired? The narrative quickly recognizes that there is a compensatory mechanism in place to restore the property of the white and privileged; the Trescott house is swiftly rebuilt: "The black mass in the middle of the Trescott's property was hardly allowed to cool before the builders were at work on another house. It had sprung upward at a fabulous rate. It was like a magical composition born of the ashes," while simultaneously, human life marked by race or disability is devalued, deemed monstrous, and destroyed (366). Indeed, just as the Trescott's house is magically reconstructed, Henry Johnson, the "monster" of the story's title and the other "black mass" who is "born of [the fire's] ashes," is rendered homeless. What Eric Wertheimer calls "the fantasy of insurance underwriting"—that no loss goes uncompensated—is demonstrable for the Trescotts; their property is "swiftly rebuilt," while Johnson's humanity just as quickly chars. Trescott cannot compensate his employees and neighbors amply enough to shelter a "monster," and after the fire Johnson is glimpsed outdoors in the cold, sitting far out of sight on a "box behind the stable," or peeked at with terror through closed windows. The narrative follows Johnson as he haunts the town; he is always outside and beyond the structures of home. Reading the "long history of black's physical and cultural displacement," particularly in the context of post-Katrina dislocations, Evie Shockley calls this experience "gothic homelessness." The historic denial of access to and participation in domestic ideologies, particularly the idea that home is a "safe haven from the dangers, diseases, and degradation of the street" — a denial amplified in the aftermath of catastrophes like Katrina — produced a "specter of terror" in black communities (Shockley 98). In Crane's text, Henry Johnson is a forebear of this persistent trope: he is cast out of Whilomville society, rendered precarious, and is treated as a specter of terror in a town unwilling to recognize his humanity.

Not only does Crane's fire link environmental danger and destruction with racial vulnerability, but also Crane's invented conflagration, by implicating concepts of safety and danger, property and compensation, risk and loss, is a small piece of a much larger narrative about how individuals as well as industries come to assess and impose ideas about the human and the non-human, and about value and worthlessness in the decades following the Civil War.[16] Insurance companies like those that "swiftly rebuilt" the Trescott house preyed on cultural anxieties about the destruction of property by fire, injury and disability through occupational hazards, and, of course, premature mortality. "The vast impersonal forces of the universe . . . crush many," wrote Rufus M. Potts, an early twentieth-century insurance executive, "while those not thus destroyed are disabled or become diseased so that their bodies are filled with pain and misery and their souls with despair. The ways in which humanity is injured or destroyed are innumerable" (qtd. in Puskar 231). What Potts and other insurance men described as the near certainty of disease, destruction, and despair over the passage of a human lifetime helped to drive the public toward new and emerging kinds of insurance — fire, accident, and life — in which the vast tide of human vulnerability might be soothed by the compensatory mechanisms of insurance policies.[17]

In the wake of conflagrations like the one that destroyed the Trescott's home and endangered their son, insurance companies erected a global industry that sold the public policies promising protection against inevitable loss and calamity. The efforts to contain the great problem of fire in America conjoined the labor of both firefighters and underwriters: the heroic and the banal, people and property, labor and business (Tebeau 3). In fact, advancements in fighting the scourge of fire across the nation moved in tandem with developments in fire insurance in the nineteenth and early twentieth centuries. As information technologies like actuarial tables made methods for evaluating and categorizing danger more reliable, the insurance industry's application of statistical reasoning and predictive mechanisms eclipsed the depiction of the heroic physical labor of the firefighter. The insurance industry rather than the valiant fireman came to dominate the discourse on fire safety and prevention (Tebeau 90).

The insurance industry was at the center of defining new forms of risk and marketing these to the public. By the end of the nineteenth century, writes philosopher and historian François Ewald, insurance signified "at once an ensemble of institutions and the diagram with which industrial societies conceive their principle of organization, functioning and regulation."[18] Ewald's observations about the vast reach of the insurance industry in modern industrial and post-industrial societies is indicative of a paradigmatic shift far too extensive to recount here. For the purposes of this chapter, I want to draw attention to the significant role that insurance companies played in the discourse about human *value* at the turn of the twentieth century and the ways in which writers like Stephen Crane and W. E. B. Du Bois engaged and critiqued its logic. In Crane's "The Monster," for example, the promise that fire-damaged property would be repaired at a "fabulous rate" appealed to a public fearful of uncontainable conflagrations; yet, insurance company policies also seemed to support the assessment—reached by Crane's fictional "jury" of twelve men on behalf of the town of Whilomville—that a black man who bravely risks his life in order to rescue a child should nonetheless be classified as a monster not worth saving.

How a man's value was assessed for insurance purposes became a particularly pressing question at the turn of the twentieth century, particularly as insurance companies practiced the relative evaluation of white and black lives. Louis I. Dublin, statistician, scholar, and vice president of the Metropolitan Life Insurance Company, argued for what he called the "social value" of man, observing in *The Money Value of Man* (1930) that an individual's worth to his dependents, family, and community is more nuanced than an actuarial account of his future labor can provide. While life insurance sold itself as the guarantee of the lost value of the insured's future industry, for example, Dublin questioned the notion, developed by fellow analysts at the turn of the twentieth century, that a singular monetary figure "should form the basis of an estimate of a man's social value" (Dublin 19). Dublin described his unqualified optimism that "the modern economic structure" of life insurance will, in due time, recognize man's full social importance (Dublin 4). Despite Dublin's optimism in the insurance industry's expanding vocabulary, when it came to discriminations about human value according to race, "life insurers designated 'white' to be the default standard category encompassing the vast majority of Americans, while 'black' or 'colored' became, by a cruel data logic, substandard," as Dan Bouk describes in *How Our Days Became Numbered: Risk and the Rise of the Statistical Individual* (2015, 185). Insurance companies were built on a long history of racist practices, including the commodification of slaves. Literary critics like Ian Baucom and Tim Armstrong as well as historians such as Jonathan Levy, Sharon Murphy, and Dan Bouk have examined the connections between the slave economy and the rise of insurance in the eighteenth and nineteenth centuries.[19] By the early twentieth century, scientific racism became a tool of the trade.[20] American actuaries teamed with doctors and statisticians to institutionalize discriminatory practices against blacks, and they used "white data politics" to court white working-class men while refusing to recognize and insure their black counterparts (Bouk 185). Fire, accident, or life, few insurance companies solicited black risk. In a cruel irony of the insurance industry, in less than fifty years African Americans went from the class of human beings most insurable—as human chattel—to least insurable as free men.[21]

To the town elders in Whilomville, Henry Johnson's life has no value. He is a monster, a faceless black man in burned lavender trousers who becomes a specter of terror haunting the town. Dr. Trescott is accused of birthing a monstrosity: "He will be your creation, you understand. . . . You are making him, and he will be a monster" (346). While Johnson haunts the narrative as a specter of gothic homelessness, the eugenics discourse adapted by the insurance industry agitates the men's exchange. The medicalization of racial difference preyed upon fears of the abnormal, the defective, and the inferior, declaring the monstrous birth of the "Other" a danger to the nation. Yet, insurance assessments also were mutable depending on the stories actuaries told about the value or risk of certain human "characteristics." Political scientist Brian Glenn has called this "the myth of the actuary," and he describes how insurance adjusters used subjective evaluations of social norms and conditions, undermining the purported objectivity of risk assessment. These practices formed the systemic bias against blacks in the insurance industry and, in turn, the racist narrative of human social value that the industry perpetuated.

In the late nineteenth century, insurance companies were particularly concerned about how to assign value to black and white lives, and they were furious about a wave of new anti-discrimination laws that were growing in popularity in states like Massachusetts, New York, and New Jersey, laws that required life insurance companies to offer insurance policies to blacks and whites at the same rates.[22] Enraged by what they perceived as the incommensurability of valuing black lives on par with white, insurance companies sought to ground their discriminatory practices in statistical research. Prudential Life Insurance Company hired a young statistician and social Darwinist named Frederick L. Hoffman to prove the insurance industry's contention that black lives equaled bad risk. Hoffman's study of black risk communities, "The Vital Statistics of the Negro" (1892), published in Boston's *The Arena* magazine, seemed to prove the insurance industry's case by statistically confirming blacks as an exceedingly high-risk group.²³ Citing congenital deficiencies, sexual debauchery, and susceptibility to disease, Hoffman's article concluded that blacks were not on a path to equality after the Civil War, rather they were on a sure "path to extinction" (Bouk 49). Prudential Insurance hired Hoffman to expand his work in "Vital Statistics" into a book-length study. Published by the American Economic Association, *Race Traits and Tendencies in the American Negro* (1896) became an immediate cultural sensation (Bouk 50). In its wake, life insurers abruptly stopped insuring blacks throughout the North. One of the few exceptions was Metropolitan, which continued to "actively sell policies to blacks at standard rates, but only for those applicants who passed the most strenuous medical scrutiny" (Bouk 51).²⁴ Hoffman applied statistical methods to make wide-ranging claims about the health, welfare, and social productivity of black communities; *Race Traits* became an influential example of the insurance industry's assessment methods, methods based on social narratives that embraced racial prejudices and masqueraded them as universal truths.²⁵

The most vocal and formidable critic of Hoffman's work and the treatment of blacks by the insurance industry was W. E. B. Du Bois. Drawing attention to Hoffman's misuse of data, his methodological inconsistencies, and the study's inherent racism, Du Bois exposed its specious logic, including the ways that the report was used for political and cultural discrimination. In "How to Figure the Extinction of a Race" (1897), Du Bois decries Hoffman's use of social Darwinism and his hyperbolic predictions of black extinction. "With great-patience, energy, and zeal," Du Bois writes, Hoffman has prepared an "elaborate brief in support of the proposition that the American negro, like the New Zealand Maori, is doomed to extinction" (Du Bois 246). Du Bois counters Hoffman's argument with his own well-researched statistics that show black population growth, and he chides Hoffman for excluding "forgotten articles which, a few years ago, demonstrated to the satisfaction of their authors that the negroes were increasing so rapidly that their ultimate and speedy preponderance in every Southern State was a melancholy certainty" (Du Bois 246). Although high mortality rates did affect black communities in the late nineteenth century, Du Bois demonstrated that Hoffman's study willfully ignored the economic conditions of his subjects: "If the population were divided as to social and economic condition the matter of race would be almost entirely eliminated."²⁶ The life expectancy and health outcomes of blacks were quite similar to immigrant groups with comparable economic resources. For example, Du Bois presented actuarial data from an early twentieth-century Atlanta University study that examined thirty-four leading life insurers and demonstrated that blacks and working-class immigrants had analogous health outcomes. Why did insurers single out blacks for rejection while accepting and even soliciting other groups with similar mortality statistics at ordinary industrial rates?

In magazine articles and reviews, Du Bois steadily debunked Hoffman's celebrated statistical analysis and the ideas circulated by insurance companies and their actuaries about the extinction of the black race; indeed, Hoffman's spurious claim that blacks were doomed to disappearance became fruitful ground for Du Bois's incisive critique of American racism and his turn to speculative fiction. Du Bois ends his book *Darkwater* (1920) with "The Comet," a short story in which New York City and its inhabitants are destroyed by the combustible deadly gas of a comet's tail. Narrating environmental disaster and a post-apocalyptic landscape was another strategy by which Du Bois blasted the discriminatory practices of institutional racism and interrogated the uncertain future that such racial oppression and exploitation portends. Du Bois's "The Comet" challenges the science of racial traits and the idea of extinction so prominent in Hoffman's insurance work. Amid the ruins of New York City, Du Bois demonstrates the duplicity rather than the scientific certainty of racial difference; against the certitude of black extinction, he imagines a black man as the sole survivor of a dramatic mass annihilation event.

When "The Comet" begins, we see Jim, a messenger for a Wall Street Bank, suffering the injustices of institutionalized racism. Because he is black, he is treated as a "nobody" and sent to do the company's most dangerous work: "Of course, they wanted *him* to go down to the lower vaults. It was too dangerous for more valuable men" (253). The irony in the story is that in this instance the least "valuable" man compelled to do the most dangerous work is spared from environmental catastrophe and instant death. When the gas from a fiery comet engulfs the city, Jim is deep inside the "dangerous" dungeon vaults, saving him from the comet's mortal gases. He emerges, for all intents and purposes, the last man on earth. Wandering up Fifth Avenue, past "crowds and groups" of dead bodies, he encounters the only other survivor among the throngs of the deceased: Julia, the privileged white daughter of a Metropolitan Life Insurance executive (258). Given Du Bois's critique of the insurance industry and its duplicitous practices, the story revels in the irony that no matter of statistical reasoning can predict this sudden human wasteland, and, crucially, the survival, rather than the extinction of one of its most scorned members. Believing themselves the last of the human race, they begin to imagine rebuilding the world, Jim the "All-Father of the race to be," and Julia "mother of all men," standing atop the Metropolitan Life Insurance building, one of the many institutions that perpetuated racial hierarchies (269). Before they can consummate their union, however, Julia's father and her fiancé return from outside the city having survived the gas, as does Jim's wife, and with her, their dead son. With these "rescuers" the old world returns, and so too all its racism, divisions, and injustices, starkly symbolized by the dead body of a young black boy and any hope for a different future. *Darkwater* begins with Du Bois's vision of a united world, "I believe in God, who made of one blood all nations that on earth do dwell. I believe that all men, black and brown and white, are brothers, varying through time and opportunity, in form and gift and feature, but differing in no essential particular, and alike in soul and the possibility of infinite development" (3). It ends, however, with Julia's fiancé whisking her away from Jim, but not before threatening to lynch him for insubordination. What Du Bois shows his readers is that the promise of social justice, or an American landscape free of racism, is another kind of apocalyptic fantasy.

The comet that strikes New York, "indiscriminately exterminating black and white, blue- and white-collar, male and female alike," reveals the artificiality of racial difference rather than the inherent racial traits of its two surviving heroes, which the scientific racism of the insurance industry purports to demonstrate (Yablon, 275). Through "The Comet," Du Bois again critiques the discriminatory science perpetuated by an industry that sought to adjust for and administer to human precarity, conceptually unsettling how humans and their possessions were defined and valued.[27] Du Bois challenged a legacy of racist representation that excluded black men from normative categories of manhood and bureaucratic assessments of human value.[28] Using race and environmental ecologies as intertwined themes, both Crane and Du Bois predict a future for black Americans that is always in danger, undervalued, and at risk of death and disfigurement, corporeal and social. The universal vulnerability of humans in the environment—whether by risk of a house fire or a fiery comet—was the ecological thought through which to represent and challenge the social and political precariousness of people of color in America.[29]

The toxic climate of racism persists. In the mid-twentieth century, James Baldwin continued to describe an American landscape that had been defined and, indeed, scorched by slavery and racism. In *The Fire Next Time* (1963) Baldwin's forecast of a "cosmic vengeance" is echoed in Ta-Nehisi Coates's book-length essay *Between the World and Me* (2015), which again turns to the idea of the "natural disaster" to articulate the continuing plague of structural racism in twenty-first-century America (Baldwin 105). Americans, Coates argues, naturalize racism the way we most often naturalize disasters: as the handiwork of God rather than the machinations of human beings. "Racism is rendered as the innocent daughter of Mother Nature, and one is left to deplore the Middle Passage or the Trail of Tears the way one deplores an earthquake, a tornado, or any other phenomenon that can be cast beyond the handiwork of men" (Coates 7). Describing himself, like Du Bois's Jim, a "survivor of some great natural disaster," Coates contemplates the terror, insecurity, and vulnerability of living in a black body in America and describes the attendant feelings of perpetual danger (129). Like the "menaces of nature," the "fire, the comet, the storm," America can, "with no justification—shatter my body" (87). Only when the privileged and powerful realize that they too are "not inviolable," when a hurricane destroys a city or a fire scorches the earth, does the "vulnerability [of all people] become real" (107). "Vengeance," Coates argues, echoing Baldwin, will not be "the fire in the cities but the fire in the sky" (150).[30] In Coates's narrative, mutual vulnerability in the face of environmental catastrophe, "cosmic vengeance," may be the only model by which Americans learn and respect reciprocal interdependence. Coates's text is a lamentation: such recognition will surely come too late.

Like James Baldwin's *The Fire Next Time*, Stephen Crane's "The Monster" and Du Bois's "Comet" are crucial preambles to Coates's recent requiem on race. Crane's novella starts with a small accident that foreshadows the compound catastrophes with which "The Monster" concludes. Little Jimmie "playing train" runs over a peony in his father's garden. Recalling the railroad accidents and injuries that pervaded the American landscape, the broken flower forecasts Henry Johnson's fate: Johnson, "floral" in his "lavender slacks," soon will be broken (351). The opening of the narrative anticipates the deadly conflagration to come. Engine number 36, Jimmie's imagined train, foreshadows the fire companies featured later in the story. Moreover, Jimmie's accident and his subsequent "effacement" prefigure Johnson's sacrifice and "effacement," the literal loss of his face, as he saves Jimmie from the fire. "It was apparent from Jimmie's manner that he felt some kind of desire to efface himself" after he tramples the flower (344). Johnson is Jimmie's solace, and he and Jimmie are described as friends, for which Johnson derives "great joy from the child's admiration." Jimmie's admiration turns to abhorrence after the fire; Jimmie joins the community in mocking Henry as a monster (345). The start of the story establishes the significance of accident and injury in the narrative; for Jimmie, "the importance of the whole thing [the accident] had taken away the boy's vocabulary" (344). Jimmie at the start of the story and Johnson at the end are relegated to silence.

The narrative presents readers with vignettes of the community prior to the conflagration, suggesting that the townspeople gave "no particular social aspect to th[eir] gathering[s]," be they in the barbershop, the park, or at a band performance (347). It describes how the people of Whilomville "gathered at the corners, in distinctive groups, which expressed various shades and lines of chumship, and had little to do with any social gradations" (345). Their "public dependence upon one another" was their "inheritance." (347). The story does not bear out this glib camaraderie, however; it routinely reminds readers of the distinctions, the "shades and lines" between people: Giscom is the white businessman, Reifsnyder the Dutch immigrant, Bella the "saffron" love interest. The image of Johnson in the community prior to the fire is riddled with comic disdain: "It was not a matter altogether of the lavender trousers, nor yet the straw hat with its bright silk band," but rather the overall spectacle of a man who seems not to know his proper place (11). As much as Johnson is admired by "Watermelon Alley" women like Bella Farragut, who calls him "divine," he is mocked by the men at the barbershop as he saunters past.

The fire in the story at first becomes an opportunity to show community "chumship." From the ringing of the fire bell to the gathering of the fire laddies, Whilomville becomes a model of community interdependence. By the "twist of the wrist," the Trescott's neighbor sounds the alert at the corner fire-box. Scarcely moments later, a factory whistle produces a "hoarse roar" that the narrative likens to the band that plays in the park: it "raised and swelled to a sinister note, and then it sang on the night wind one long call that held the crowd in the park immovable, speechless" (348). The crowd recognizes the sound of the fire alarm and waits to hear where the fire is located. They shout out "One" and then the "sound swelled," "Two." "Second district! In a flash the company of indolent and cynical young men had vanished like a snowball disrupted by dynamite" (349). Recalling the crowd that gathers outside the Greenwich Village tenement in Crane's earlier newspaper report, men who are "cynical" with "scorn for their impotency," the "indolent" and "cynical" young men in the Whilomville park disperse toward the scene of the fire. The narrative turns its attention to the volunteer fire companies, which are described in swift bursts: Tuscarora Hose Company Number Six "swept a perilous wheel into Niagara Avenue, and as the men, attached to the cart by the rope which had been laid out from the wind glass under the tongue, pulled madly in their fervor and abandon, the gong under the axle clanged incitingly" (349). Chippeway Hose Company Number One, the "hook-and-ladder experts from across the creek," also begin their journey to the second district. Never Die Hose Company Number Three too: "it was fine to see the gathering of the companies, and amid a great noise to watch their heroes perform all manner of prodigies" (355). The fire displaces all other community gatherings and lures everyone to its spectacle. As the church bells ring the alarm, young boys and their mothers bound out of houses; they join the "dark wave" and the "black crowd" (349). Amid disaster the community frantically coalesces; the narrative even pauses to feature a young boy, Willie, who, desperate to watch the events unfold, runs to the street corner with the rest of the crowd, despite his mother's admonition that it is past his bedtime.

These short vignettes are summarily pieced together, anticipating the editing style of Edwin Porter's film, *Life of an American Fireman* (1903). Writers like Crane, Dreiser, Du Bois, and others at the turn of the twentieth century were aware of how literary texts competed with emerging mass-media forms; this is reflected in the style, syntax, and grammar of their work, as Katherine Biers describes in *Virtual Modernism: Writing and Technology in the Progressive Era* (2013). Readers follow the excitement of the crowd and the preparations of the firefighters, although the cult figure of the firefighter proves largely ineffectual in Crane's story. Indeed, it is not the fire companies competing to reach the scene, or the fire captains contending for their jobs, who arrive at the fire first. Henry Johnson alone enters the burning house. Only "one man . . . ran with fabulous speed." He wore "lavender trousers" (351). The chosen "heroes who perform all manner of prodigies" do not make it to the conflagration as quickly as Johnson, and in Crane's narrative the tone of comedic scorn shifts from Johnson and the derisive laughter in the barbershop about a black man not knowing his proper place, to the fire companies, with risible names and "heavy apparatus" that almost cause one company to "stall" on Bridge Street's hill, much to the scorn of the crowd. John Shipley, the chief of the department, was known to move "leisurely around a burning structure surveying it, puffing meanwhile at a cigar" (355). Apart from these crowds, Henry Johnson dashes past a "screaming" Mrs. Trescott and into the house, where a print of the Declaration of Independence immediately falls from the wall and bursts with a "sound of a bomb" (351). Johnson's actions, like the smoldering fire, explodes what Bill Brown has called the allusion to America's originary moment of racism, the Declaration of Independence, which imprinted inequality into the founding of the nation. Henry Johnson in this narrative moment is the heroic firefighter poised to dampen the engines of racial despotism. Johnson, recalling Crane's earlier pen picture, "emerged at a leap from the position of a slaver to that of a master, a giant" ("Panic" 99).

From the destruction of the Declaration of Independence to the "red snake" (first described by Crane in "Panic") that flows "directly down into Johnson's upturned face," the imagery of the fire scene has garnered considerable critical attention. Gregory Laski has argued that Crane's description of Johnson "submitting" to the smoke, "bending his mind in a most perfect slavery to the conflagration," is meant to invoke the "unexplored path" between Johnson's injury in the fire and "the fundamental injury of slavery" (Laski 40). "The Monster," writes Laski, is an extended rumination on reparations and the historical debt incurred in a slave economy, a debt, physical and psychic, that can never be adequately remunerated.[31] It is important to note that the narrative's preoccupation with fire purposefully draws readers' attention to evolving concepts of risk, loss, and compensation. Indeed, the metaphors of slavery that Crane employs in "The Monster" echo his earlier fire report, "Panic." In both pieces by Crane, the volatility of the fire and the constant danger of it obtaining dominion constitutes a threat to humanity's power over nature. Man and woman, black and white, become "slaver" to the "master," fire. Crane emphasizes human inconsequence and human vulnerability in the face of environmental danger, and he questions the cultivation of hegemony: human over nature and white over black. Although Johnson is initially described in "The Monster" as being in "perfect slavery to this conflagration," this is but a "momentary apathy" (Crane 352). Once Johnson spots Jimmie, he is "no longer creature to the flames," and he is "without fear" (Crane 352). Crane redeploys and reassigns the common tropes of heroism that he and fellow journalists developed when they covered fires and other disasters for local newspapers. The unstable and fragile environments imagined in Crane's "The Monster" and Du Bois's "The Comet" advance critiques of social inequality and racial injustice, showing them to be morally and ecologically unsustainable.

The fire acts as an alternate register through which black masculinity is re-inscribed; at first, it imbues Henry Johnson with a fleeting authority he otherwise does not have in the community. Although Johnson is fearless as he leaps into a burning house and momentarily heroic in the community's eyes for saving Jimmie Trescott's life, his disfigurement by chemicals in Trescott's laboratory swiftly turns him into a monster. Johnson is viewed as dangerous and deranged, and, consequently, he is denied the status of hero or victim; he is rendered a specter, a ghost, a monster. Dr. Trescott, moreover, is accused of a Frankensteinian feat in nursing Johnson back to life: "He will be your creation, you understand," Trescott is warned. "He is purely your creation. Nature has very evidently given him up. He is dead. You are restoring him to life. You are making him, and he will be a monster, and with no mind" (353). Trescott is accused of birthing a monster and warned that he saves Johnson's life at his own risk. Elizabeth Young's *Black Frankenstein* (2008) brilliantly demonstrates how Mary Shelley's 1818 novel and its eponymous character became a powerful political metaphor for racial anxiety in America, in which numerous cultural scripts, including Crane's novella, "linked monsters to black men" (82). This chapter also has been arguing that "The Monster" critiques the racial imaginary at the turn of the twentieth century, particularly a culture that deadens blackness into monstrosity, devalues black lives, and cultivates racial fear. In "The Monster," Henry Johnson bravely risks his life; in saving Johnson, Dr. Trescott risks his reputation and livelihood. What makes the conflagration a powerful focal point in Crane's story is the way it encourages readers to contest emerging cultural values, from what risk and vulnerability mean to the way a common house fire binds these men's fates. For Crane, Du Bois, and Coates, anxiety about environmental catastrophe and universal vulnerability help to illuminate social fissures. The fire in Crane's novella and the comet in Du Bois's story reveal the community's failings; the literary imaginary is a warning and a premonition of the fires yet to come.

NOTES

1. "The facts are: there was no fire at all, no baby, no hysterical mother, no brave policeman, no nothing," John S. Mayfield, qtd. in Stallman and Hagemann, *The New York City Sketches*, 97.

2. Crane's "realistic pen portrait" also anticipates the work of his *New York Press* colleague Everett Shinn, who painted later scenes like "Fire on Twenty Fourth Street" (1907) and "Night Life—Accident" (1908), and who was part of a group of ashcan alley

artists so named because of their depiction of New York City street scenes. See Mecklenburg, Snyder, and Zurier, *Metropolitan Lives*.

3. "The opening up of new markets, foreign or domestic, and the organizational development from the craft shop to such concerns as U.S. Steel illustrate the same process of industrial mutation—if I may use that biological term—that incessantly revolutionizes the economic structure from within, incessantly destroying the old one, incessantly creating a new one. This process of Creative Destruction is the essential fact about capitalism." Joseph Schumpeter, *Capitalism, Socialism, and Democracy*, 83. For discussion of this phenomenon in the context of American culture, see Kevin Rozario, *The Culture of Calamity*.

4. In Shakespeare's "Troilus and Cressida," Ulysses says to Achilles, "One Touch of Nature Makes the Whole World Kin" (Act III, Scene iii). O'Henry also wrote a short story, "Makes the Whole World Kin," published in *The World*, September 1904.

5. Robert Lewis was murdered in Port Jervis on June 2, 1892. For a discussion of "The Monster" and Levi Hume, see Susan Schweik's, "Disability Politics and American Literary History: Some Suggestions," 217–37.

6. See Bercovitch, *The American Jeremiad*.

7. "The original disaster—the coup, the terrorist attack, the market meltdown, the war, the tsunami, the hurricane—puts the entire population into a state of collective shock . . . shocked societies often give up the things they would otherwise fiercely protect." Naomi Klein, *The Shock Doctrine: The Rise of Disaster Capitalism*, 20.

8. Klein writes that in less than two years, while most of the city's poor residents were still unable to return to New Orleans, its public school system was almost completely replaced by a charter school system that produced an "educational land grab." Klein, *The Shock Doctrine*, 6. Anthony Lowenstein also analyzes how corporations and governments profit from disasters; the subtitle of his book *Disaster Capitalism* (2015) is *Making a Killing Out of Catastrophe*.

9. As I am completing this manuscript, Puerto Rico is facing a similar fate from Hurricane Maria (2017).

10. "Franklin, Adams, and many of their brother firemen applied these principles of equality, voluntarism, mutual endeavor, public safety, and active self-government to their understanding of the American Revolution and consequently paved the way for a republican political system independent from Great Britain." See Benjamin Carp, "Fire of Liberty," 814.

11. Franklin's *Newsweek* cover appeared on September 24, 2001. See Thomas E. Franklin *(The Record), Firefighters Raise the American Flag at Ground Zero, 2001. Thomas E. Franklin Portfolio:* http://www.thomasefranklin.com/#a=0&at=0&mi=2&pt=1&pi=10000&s=0&p=3. Joel Meyerowitz was the sole photographer to have continued access to the 9/11 site. His photographic collection, *Aftermath* (2006), is a memorial to those who lost their lives and a celebration of the thousands of firefighters, police, construction workers, and volunteers in the days and months after the attack.

12. The print is in the collections of the Springfield Museums, Springfield, MA: https://springfieldmuseums.org/collections/item/the-life-of-a-fireman-the-fire-now-then-with-a-will-shake-her-up-boys-nathaniel-currier/.

13. In the collections of the Springfield Museums, Springfield, MA: https://springfieldmuseums.org/?s=american+fireman+prompt+to+the+rescue.

14. In the collections of the Springfield Museums, Springfield MA: https://springfieldmuseums.org/?s=darktown+fire+brigade. See also: "The darktown fire brigade-taking a rest: Foreman-right you is parson dis terbakker beats de deck": https://www.loc.gov/item/91724465/ and "The darktown fire brigade-hook and ladder gymnastics: Brace her up dar! and cotch her on de fly!": http://www.loc.gov/pictures/item/91724452/.

15. Marc Tebeau, *Eating Smoke*, 229. For more on black firefighters and the campaigns against them see Tebeau, *Eating Smoke*, 224–40.

16. "In America, the poetics of underwriting fostered an understanding of creative originality and authority that had property ownership as its primary ground, and the loss of property as a constant source of anxiety," Eric Wertheimer, *Underwriting*, xiv.

17. See Ian Baucom, *Specters of the Atlantic*; and Tim Armstrong, *The Logic of Slavery*.

18. François Ewald, "Insurance now really signifies not so much a particular, distinctive type of institution as a form, an organizing schema of management and rationality capable of being realized in any and every kind of provident institution," "Insurance and Risk," 209.

19. See, for example, work by Tim Armstrong, Ian Baucom, and Dan Bouk. See also Sharon Ann Murphy, *Investing in Life*, 184–206, and "Securing Human Property," 615–52.

20. See Bouk, "The Science of Difference: Designing Tools for Discrimination in the American Life Insurance Industry, 1830–1930," 717–31.

21. Jonathan Levy makes this observation in his dissertation "The Ways of Providence," 311. See also his published book on this material, *Freaks of Fortune*. Like fire insurance, life insurance companies derived their success from harnessing the vulnerability and fear of the public.

22. In 1884 Massachusetts successfully passed a law requiring insurance companies to offer the same rates to blacks and whites. Similar laws were being passed around the nation. See Hoffman, *History of the Prudential*, 139; Levy, *Freaks of Fortune*, 310.

23. For more on Hoffman and *Race Trait and Tendencies of the American Negro* see Megan J. Wolff, "The Myth of the Actuary: Life Insurance and Frederick L. Hoffman's *Race Traits and Tendencies of the American Negro*," *Public Health Reports*, 84–91. "*Race Traits* immediately became a key text in one of the central social preoccupations of the turn of the century: the supposed Negro Problem. Numerous turn-of-the-century tracts (including Hoffman's) stipulated that minority racial groups were not only biologically inferior but also barriers to progress." Wolff, 84. See also Wolff, "The Money Value of Risk," chapter 1.

24. "John Hancock had stopped soliciting blacks in 1884 now Prudential and most of the industry followed. . . . At the same time, new black-run fraternal societies and insurers expanded to pick up some of the slack and in the process became key aggregators of capital in African American communities," Bouk, *How Our Days Became Numbered*, 51. See also Ibram X. Kendi's article, "A History of Race and Racism in America, in 24 Chapters," *The New York Times*, February 22, 2017: https://www.nytimes.com/2017/02/22/books/review/a-history-of-race-and-racism-in-america-in-24-chapters.html?_r=0. Kendi names Hoffman's *Race Traits* one of the most influential books on race in the 1890s, noting that Hoffman "blazed the trail of racist ideas in American criminology when he concluded that higher black arrest rates indicated blacks committed more crimes." See also Kendi's *Stamped from the Beginning: The Definitive History of Racist Ideas in America*.

25. See Brian J. Glenn, "Postmodernism: The Basis of Insurance," 131–43; and "The Shifting Rhetoric of Insurance Denial," 779–808.

26. W. E. B. Du Bois, "The Health and Physique of the Negro American," 272. See also W. E. B. Du Bois's reviews of Hoffman: "*Race Traits and the Tendencies of the American Negro* by Frederick L. Hoffman," 127–33; and, "How to Figure the Extinction of a Race," 246–48.

27. See Eric Wertheimer, *Underwriting*, 31. See also Nick Yablon's *Untimely Ruins* for a reading of "The Comet," 275–79.

28. As Americans continue to struggle to understand and combat the incessant police violence and mass incarceration that destroys black lives, we need the activism of movements like Black Lives Matter.

29. Here I echo Timothy Morton's book title, *The Ecological Thought*, which "imagines interconnectedness," 15.

30. See Ta-Nehisi Coates's, *Between the World and Me*. Coates's work recalls James Baldwin's *The Fire Next Time* (1963). Baldwin's book includes two essays about American racism, one in the form of a letter to his nephew. For discussion of black

writers, ecocriticism, and the ways that "slavery and racism have shaped the American landscape," see Smith, *African American Environmental Thought*. See also Jeffrey Myers, *Converging Stories*.

31. For more on the idea of debt and slavery see Tim Armstrong, *The Logic of Slavery*, chapter 2.

FIVE

The Tremblor

Disaster and Vulnerability, San Francisco, 1906

> Not to quarrel with the intelligence that reads God behind seismic disturbance, one must still note that the actual damage done by God to the city was small beside the possibilities for damage that reside in man-contrivances; for most man-made things do inherently carry the elements of their own destruction. (Mary H. Austin, "The Tremblor: A Personal Narration," 358)

Edward S. Holden's 1894 *Century Magazine* article "Earthquakes and How to Measure Them" introduced seismology, the burgeoning science of earthquakes, to the general public. The article described several new instruments for measuring earthquake energy and surveyed the damage done by recent quakes in places like Krakatoa (1883) and Charleston, South Carolina (1886). But for the limitations of space, Holden "regrets," he would have included a selection of eyewitness accounts of these "great earthquakes," which, he notes, have far "more than scientific interest," even in light of the new technologies his article promotes (759). Although they are often "simple narratives," Holden claims that they provide crucial insights about the earthquake experience. Earthquake observers capture the visceral sensations of the seismic event and are powerful eyewitnesses to the devastation. Looking "awful Death face to face," Holden writes, the earthquake observer knows in an instant "all the lingering horrors of the inferno . . . the hells of sound, of light, of darkness, of cold terror" (759). Holden's article, intended to introduce the American reader to an "entirely new department of physical or mechanical science," concludes that the Geographical Survey should emphatically embrace its "occasional observers, whose records may be of the greatest value" (759).[1] Central to the chronicle of the incipient technology to measure seismic activity is the importance Holden attaches to personal narratives in the birth of earthquake science. In the account of a new scientific discipline, the technologies for mechanical measurement and the human capacity for storytelling go hand in hand.

Long before the 1906 San Francisco earthquake, which scientists have long recognized as the dawn of the science of seismology, lay observers, of the kind to which Holden refers, meticulously recorded their earthquake impressions, experiences, and reflections. In *The Earthquake Observers* (2013) Deborah R. Coen broadly examines the growth and cultivation of the "citizen observer" of earthquakes and the development of the "felt report," from Immanuel Kant in the eighteenth century, who writes some of the first works of modern seismology, to the standardized felt reports issued by the U.S. Geological Society in the twentieth and twenty-first centuries. The challenge facing scientists in the age before the seismograph, as Edward Holden well knew, was how to transform moments of uncertainty and horror around seismic events into an arena for the cultivation of scientific knowledge (Coen 3). Written felt reports by citizen observers and the growing network of responses to seismic phenomena systematized by organizations like the U.S. Geological Society set the foundation for the development of earthquake science. Scientists enlisted ordinary people to record their feelings and sensations, registering "barely perceptible tremors to catastrophic shocks" (Coen 2). From their stories, these lay observers, "in as many places, in as many different situations as possible" helped to establish the science of seismology (Coen 2). Similar to the Lisbon quake of 1755, which elicited reactions around the world from Enlightenment philosophers in Europe to theologians in the colonies of North America, the San Francisco quake occasioned a veritable storm of first-hand impressions from citizen observers, professional authors, journalists, scientists, photographers, and insurance adjusters alike. The U.S. Geological Survey hailed April 18, 1906, the birth of a "scientific revolution" (Coen 215).

In the movement from subjective accounts to objective instruments, from amateur to professional science, and from sublime sensations to predictive mechanisms, the San Francisco earthquake not only shaped the science of seismology, ushering in a scientific revolution, it also inaugurated a vocabulary about disaster and ecological vulnerability that continues to our present moment. In the ensuing contest over the disaster's meanings, the conventional narrative that emerged in the commercial press and among public officials made sense of catastrophe according to dominant conceptions of capital. Joseph Schumpeter's celebration of creative destruction, discussed in the preceding chapter, would prevail. The San Francisco earthquake and fire is another early example of what Naomi Klein has called "disaster capitalism": the elevation of economic renewal often at the expense of vulnerable populations. The response to the San Francisco earthquake has been critiqued in these terms, inspiring numerous scholarly and popular accounts about virtually every aspect of the event and its aftermath: examination of the relief and recovery efforts; the business of rebuilding the city; the consumption of disaster as spectacle; and the birth of a new genre of cinematography, the photography of ruins.[2] This chapter builds on these foundations, reading the felt report as a powerful mechanism for helping to unsettle dominant narratives of disaster. The 1906 earthquake exemplified a rare occasion in which predictive thinking had not prevailed and first-person accounts were not dismissed as naïve; this would alter dramatically as industries dedicated to statistical management, like insurance, gained prominence and authority in the post-earthquake years and disciplinary and intellectual distinctions—humanities/science, nature/culture, and human/non-human—rather than intersections predominated. Various forms of felt reports, from fiction writers, journalists, psychologists, insurance adjusters, and environmental writers, bore witness to the inextricability of the earth and human embodiment; they also moved beyond disciplinary predispositions, as scientists reached out to storytellers, insurance adjusters employed narrative strategies familiar to literature, and citizen scientists became curators of disaster.

Earthquakes, much like the fires, comets, and hurricanes of the preceding chapter, are measures of a wider climate: social, political, and cultural. Throughout *Danger and Vulnerability*, I have examined how ideas about vulnerability and inviolability have impacted gender, race, and anti-oppressive politics. The preceding chapter argued that writers like Stephen Crane, W. E. B. Du Bois, and Ta-Nehisi Coates employed widespread anxieties about environmental danger to illuminate forms of discrimination that were rendered invisible and faceless. *Danger and Vulnerability* begins and ends with an earthquake, imaginary and real, asking how cataclysms are metaphors for and measures of power, vulnerability, and social change. We might recall that when James Fenimore Cooper imagined his dual earthquakes, one that spawned life and another that took it away, he employed environmental danger as a rationale for state-sponsored acts of racial violence. Cooper's hero and his close associates became consumed with fears of otherness and disillusioned with the community they helped to build. The colonists of the Crater took up arms against their neighbors as a way to deny the fragility of their society, which was built on an inhospitable landmass in the middle of the Pacific Ocean. Fifty years later, the official narratives that emerged in the aftermath of the San Francisco disaster continued to find ways to perpetuate illusions of mastery over the environment as well as disregard for structural inequalities, cultural differences, and those most vulnerable. Against the fantasy, evident in Cooper's work, that disasters can be contained and nature mastered, this chapter describes how literature, insurance reports, and even scientific documents recognized unique forms of human vulnerability, forms that the official narrative and its artifacts often sought to damper. This concluding chapter on the San Francisco earthquake examines how felt reports and testimony about earthquakes troubled prevailing paradigms of disaster discourse and activated cross-disciplinary alliances.

The San Francisco earthquake was the first time a so-called "natural" disaster was so meticulously recorded and collected: insurance disputes led to an abundance of photographs, magazines and penny papers collected first-person accounts, scientists solicited felt reports, spectacle books of ruins became sought after souvenirs, all inspiring early efforts to collect evidence of the destruction, which industries like insurance did for professional purposes and individuals also did *en masse*.[3] Americans far and wide not only consumed the disaster spectacle, they also accumulated its artifacts. In fact, the quake inaugurated what is arguably the nation's first disaster archive: people rushed to publish felt reports and eyewitness accounts, to produce and purchase souvenir books about the earthquake, to circulate photographs like the comparative before and after scenes of destruction, to record tales of heroism, and to deliver orations about recovery. The San Francisco earthquake quickly revealed how catastrophes are shaped by the politics of inclusion and exclusion. What stories did the official archive of the event dismiss or ignore? What stories could not be told or feelings said? Reading felt reports in their expression of ecological agency makes visible the assumptions and the vulnerabilities of institutional and disciplinary knowledge. The citizen observer, whose felt responses to earthquakes helped to launch a new field of scientific inquiry, also became the citizen collector, whose compulsion to witness the spectacle was a model for the nation's first disaster archive, a "morbid archive" of destruction that would anticipate later archives like those shaped around Hurricane Katrina and September 11, 2001.[4]

By 1906 San Francisco was notorious for its earthquakes. Edward Holden's "Earthquakes and How to Measure Them" cites 417 earthquake shocks in San Francisco from 1808–88 alone (759). Mark Twain famously recorded his experience of the 1865 earthquake, musing that "it was going to be the greatest earthquake of the century," and he hypothesized that "the city was going to be destroyed entirely" (qtd. in Carter 1000). "Looking out for the best interests of history," Twain took out his "watch and timed the event" (qtd. in Carter 1000). Rather than hunt "for something to climb," as Twain surmises most people would do in the face of such danger, he boasts of his own "coolness and presence of mind" (qtd. in Carter 1000). He would be the ultimate earthquake observer/citizen scientist. It is no wonder that when William James set off for a visiting faculty position at Stanford in 1906, his "old Californian friend B" wished him a "touch of earthquake"; it was the true California experience (James 1215). When James was awakened on the morning of April 18, he knew that B's wish was upon him. First elated, "by Jove" this is a "jolly good" quake, James's initial "glee" and "delight" give way to more "fortitude of temper," as the sixty-four-year old is thrown down on his face, the room shaking "as a terrier shakes a rat" (James 1215). Like Twain, James's famous account, "On Some Mental Effects of the Earthquake," records his quick first impressions during the event and its aftermath, including the "roaring noise" and the crack of plaster as he ducks for safety (James 1215).

Similar to other "felt reports" of earthquakes used by scientists to record their strength and duration as the field of seismology developed in the early twentieth century, James's account relied on physical sensations, first-person observations, and personal feelings. "Sensation and emotion were so strong," he writes, that "no reflection or volition was possible in the short time consumed by the phenomenon" (James 1215). In an effort to observe the human mind and body in the midst of disaster, James catalogued his perceptions, noting that the quake's duration—forty-eight seconds according to the Stanford Observatory—felt far shorter according to his own senses (James 1215). James mixes his excitement at the experience of the event with precise impressions of its character, strength, and magnitude (James 1215). To scientists, writes James, the "earthquake is simply the collective *name* of all the cracks and shakings and disturbances that happen. They *are* the earthquake" (James 1216). For James, the earthquake was not an objective set of fault lines but rather a "living agent," a dramatic force, and an aid to unique perception (James 1217). James's account emphasized what he saw as the difference between human observation and scientific explanation. Although the empiricism of nascent earthquake science and James's catalogue of sensations were more mutually constitutive than he may have represented, James was skeptical of the relationship between the scientific, technocratic, and empirical imagination. Venturing into the city a few days after the initial tremors for several hours of "observation," he decides to report on "subjective phenomena exclusively"; the description of "material ruin," he notes, he will leave to the daily papers and the insurance adjusters (James 1218). His efforts to acknowledge and record human sensation and to understand the earthquake by grasping the most intimate ways it impacts the human body, mind, and emotions stresses the immediacy of individual response—the direct feeling of the earth's ruptures in the body—against what he reasons will be the desensitization of the disaster in journals, papers, and business reports. Personal, observational, and subjective, James puts the chaos of the catastrophe in its most sensate human terms, literally rendering sense out of events that were seemingly beyond human control.

James's earthquake record, perhaps the most celebrated of the impromptu felt reports to emerge in the aftermath of the quake, is representative of a shift, made in little over a century from Lisbon to San Francisco, in the desire to understand natural disasters as intimately human rather than cosmic or supernatural. Since the Lisbon earthquake in the eighteenth century, the belief that disasters were warnings of an angry god were replaced by a rising generation of secular thinkers, many of whom would adopt a scientific vocabulary and the rhetoric of risk to analyze disasters. "Anxieties about the relationship between humanity and God," writes historian Joanna Bourke in *Fear: A Cultural History* (2005), were supplanted by "trepidation about the place of humanity in this world" (Bourke 56). If disasters were no longer manifestations of supernatural wrath, they became cultural predicaments that raised questions about how human societies create, recognize, and relate to their own vulnerability. So-called "natural" disasters were, more pointedly, social and political. As Marie-Helene Huet writes in *The Culture of Disaster* (2012), "if volcanoes erupted and the earth shook without divine intent, humans made the damages greater and more grievous to bear" (Huet 2). In an effort to make sense and meaning of the damage wrought by the San Francisco earthquake, numerous volumes of material were published in the months after the earthquake and fire, nearly a hundred popular books in 1906 alone (Steinberg 103). Many, like Charles Morris's *The San Francisco Calamity by Earthquake and Fire: A Complete and Accurate Account of the Fearful Disaster which Visited the Great City and the Pacific Coast, The Reign of Panic and Lawlessness, the Plight of 300,000 Homeless People and the World-Wide Rush to the Rescue as Told by Eye Witnesses, including Graphic and Reliable Accounts of all Great Earthquakes and Volcanic Eruptions in the World's History, and Scientific Explanations of Their Causes* (1906), were comparative collections of world disasters, with San Francisco as its epicenter.[5] Lamenting human frailty in the face of overwhelming catastrophe, the publisher's preface muses at what "weak" and "almost helpless" creatures humans are: "We millions of men stand upon the deck of a great ship, which goes rolling through space that is itself incomprehensible, and usually we are so busy with our paltry ambitions, our transgressions, our righteous labors, our prides and hopes and entanglements that we forget where we are and what is our destiny" (Morris xii).[6] Recalling Mark Woolston's more sinister forecast in James Fenimore Cooper's *The Crater* with which this book began—that humans are just "mites amid millions of other mites," our "temporary possessions" aboard a "globe that floats . . . in space" waiting at any moment to be "suddenly struck out of its orbit"—numerous publications after the San Francisco quake treated the disaster as an occasion for philosophical and apocalyptic pronouncements (Cooper 461). Moderating between invocations of helplessness and control, vastness and smallness, uncertainty and inevitability, some viewed the world as godlike and, others, godless. Certainly, the "destiny" of San Francisco was hardly forgotten; the "battle over the meaning of the San Francisco disaster began even before the smoke had cleared," as powerful economic forces mobilized to minimize the scope of the earthquake in the public imagination (Steinberg 104).

Influenced by financiers with stakes in urban development, state and local officials as well as reporters on the scene recast the event as an out-of-control fire in an effort to describe the disaster in terms more familiar and welcome to commercial investment, insurance compensation, and population growth. Historians and critics often tell the story of the rebuilding of San Francisco in this particular light. The scientific community watched aghast as commercial interests' "deliberate suppression of news about earthquakes" transformed a geological disaster into an urban catastrophe similar to the conflagration that destroyed Chicago more than three decades earlier (Steinberg 110). Earthquakes were not good for business, but, as the Chicago fire proved, widespread razing of the urban landscape could be an invitation to economic and commercial renewal. "Among the people with losses to adjust the fact that there was an earthquake has been forgotten. In fact, it is now tacitly understood that there never was any earthquake and the whole trouble was the fire" (Steinberg 111). With the quake, "calamity and capitalism" were intimately intertwined; the "belief in the blessings of disaster came to frame and energize (ambivalent) modern commitments to constant economic expansion and unending economic renewal" (Rozario 24, 65). The spectacle of destruction and the thrill of danger went hand in hand with the rhetoric of recovery and the business of rebuilding the city. "Disasters were not just moments of chaos to be overcome," Kevin Rozario writes, they were events that "liberated and channeled the chaotic passions that propelled the civilizing process" (Rozario 120).

Efforts to normalize the earthquake, to demonstrate cheery optimism in the face of destruction, and to frame the earthquake and its aftermath in terms of San Francisco's pioneer spirit were particularly powerful. The earthquake brought unbridled excitement (Twain, James), elicited playful, if nervous, laughter (Atherton, Austin), and was domesticated by select scientists eager to see the earthquake as a potentially beneficent force. Thomas Rowlandson, a fellow of the Geological Society of London, published his study *Treatise on Earthquake Dangers, Causes and Palliatives* (1869) shortly after the 1868 San Francisco earthquake, and, as Coen describes, it was one of the "few sources to shed light on the seismological thought in California at the time" (Coen 192). Living north of the Pajaro River in California, Rowlandson includes his "felt report" of the earthquake of 1868. Where one might expect to find catastrophic destruction, Rowlandson offers only an "image of lazy domesticity," describing how he and his wife were drinking tea and reclining in the comfort of their home when the earthquake shook (Coen 193). Instead of denying that California was seismically active, which scientists felt compelled to do by 1906, he sought to prove the "beneficence of earthquakes," linking them to the prosperity of gold (Rowlandson 58). Rowlandson's domestication of the earthquake threat offered a model for future development: businessmen and government officials followed his model, recasting the 1906 quake as a commercial opportunity.

Some writers and journalists like Jack London helped to animate the narrative of creative destruction and the "good disaster," while others, like Mary Hunter Austin, seized the quake as an opportunity for reflection on human vulnerability and environmental fragility. Jack London's report in *Collier* (May 5, 1906), published shortly after the quake, is representative of how disaster tropes—including an emphasis on heroism, the democratization of disaster, and the sublime nature of ruins—provided a mythology upon which to scaffold the discourse of recovery. When the muckraking magazine telegraphed London and asked him to write an eyewitness description, London's report joined numerous first-person narratives published in newspapers and magazines in the days, weeks, and months following the quake. London describes the post-apocalyptic quake scene in terms that immediately appeal to the public's appetite for calamity; it was a "meeting of the handful of survivors after the day of the end of the world."[7] London begins "Story of an Eyewitness" with the memorialization of a once "imperial" city in ruins. "Not in history has a modern imperial city been so completely destroyed. San Francisco is gone. Nothing remains of it but memories." San Francisco has become "like the crater of a volcano, around which are camped tens of thousands of refugees." The streets of the city were "piled with the debris of fallen walls," water mains burst, and communications systems were disrupted. "Within an hour after the earthquake shock the smoke of San Francisco's burning was a lurid tower visible a hundred miles away. And for three days and nights this lurid tower swayed in the sky, reddening the sun, darkening the day, and filling the land with smoke." London's article cultivates the aesthetics of destruction and a vernacular iconography of ruin, what Miles Orvell has called the "destructive sublime," and Kevin Rozario has described as Americans' "consumer relationship with chaos" (Orvell 647; Rozario, 136). San Francisco's "proudest structures," writes London, were "crumbled" by man himself in an effort to halt the fire, but there was no withstanding the "rush of the flames." London at once domesticates the disaster and presents it as spectacle, giving his reader the thrill of proximity without the real threat of danger, much as souvenir books sought to do. Titles like *Souvenir of the Destruction of San Francisco by Earthquake and Fire as seen through the Camera* (1906) were published quickly after the earthquake and sold across the country, catering to the public's desire for a good disaster. London's account, like Dreiser's report of the train wreck that began chapter 2, is what Paul Virilio has called "the catastrophic accident turned into a scoop" (Virilio 26).

In London's description, the earthquake and subsequent fire are democratizing forces. As people try to flee the flames, to salvage what they can, wealth is irrelevant and social distinctions are leveled. London witnesses a man offering a thousand dollars for a team of horses to haul trunks filled with material possessions to safety. From the richest to the poorest, residents of the city escape only with what can be carried. One man London meets on the street tells him: "Today is my birthday. Last night I was worth thirty thousand dollars. I bought five bottles of wine, some delicate fish and other things for my birthday dinner. I have had no dinner, and all I own are these crutches." The most affluent residents of the city describe themselves reduced to nothing in little more than an instant. A man guarding his doorstep tells London: "Yesterday morning . . . I was worth six hundred thousand dollars. This morning this house is all I have left. It will go in fifteen minutes. . . . There are no horses. The flames will be here in fifteen minutes." London describes how the city's wealthiest citizens are as vulnerable to the earthquake's aftermath as the city's poorest.

Destruction, as London tells it, has a democratic disregard for class distinctions. Just a day after the earthquake and in the midst of all the smoke and flames, London recounts himself sitting on the steps of a "small residence on Nob Hill." With him sat "Japanese, Italians, Chinese, and Negroes—a bit of the cosmopolitan flotsam of the wreck of the city." Surrounding this scene of "cosmopolitan flotsam" were the palaces of the "pioneers of Forty-nine," which London describes as just as vulnerable to fire as the city's tenements. "To the east and south at right angles, were advancing two mighty walls of flame." Regardless of ethnicity, race, or class, in London's report, all are victims and refugees of the disaster. "There was no opposing the flames. . . . All the cunning adjustments of a twentieth century city had been smashed. . . . All the shrewd contrivances and safeguards of man had been thrown out of gear by thirty seconds' twitching of the earth-crust." In London's recognition of universal vulnerability to the earthquake and fire, all are "cosmopolitan flotsam" in the wrecked city; there is no accounting for how some may be more vulnerable than others, or how the most vulnerable populations are more likely to become discarded wreckage in a city already bent on expedient rebirth. London's use of the term "flotsam" is particularly significant because it links the San Francisco quake to a long history of disasters, particularly shipwreck and marine accidents from which the term derives; it also confers value, or lack thereof: flotsam is worthless and disposable (Huet 16). In his desire to democratize the disaster and cast everyone in the city as "cosmopolitan flotsam," London ignores the unique vulnerabilities that attend cultural differences, whether of race, ethnicity, or class, differences to which London himself draws readers' attention. Indeed, London abandons an opportunity to question the city's policies and its systems for ordering social lives, to complicate the language of vulnerability that he cultivates, in order to promote a narrative of urban and economic renewal. His description of the city's flotsam does little to recognize those who are most at risk, and his hyperbolic rhetoric about the democratization of suffering fails to identify the concrete inequalities and injustices magnified by the earthquake, a failure not only of imagination but one that helped to perpetuate miscarriages of social and political policy. These failures continue to repeat themselves over one hundred years later in twenty-first-century catastrophes like Hurricanes Katrina (2005), Sandy (2012), and, more recently, Maria (2017).[8]

The disaster, as Jack London promotes it in his report, is a welcome trial of the city's character, "An enumeration of the deeds of heroism would stock a library and bankrupt the Carnegie medal fund," he writes. London emphasizes bravery, selflessness, and the triumph of the human spirit, and he describes how the intensity and danger of the quake incites an overabundance of heroic deeds. "Never in all San Francisco's history, were her people so kind and courteous as on this night of terror." Unlike London's immediate account in the days following the quake, Gertrude Atherton would make the quake and its disruption of social hierarchies the topic of her later California novel *The Sisters-in Law* (1921). Atherton re-imagines the earthquake as an opportunity to form new social alliances, the disaster as an occasion to rebuild social relations. From the safety across the bay, Atherton's protagonist, Alexina, relays her own felt report: "the crashing of steeples, the dome of the City Hall, of brick buildings too hastily erected, of ten thousand falling chimneys; of creaking and grinding timbers, and of the eucalyptus trees behind her, whose leaves rustled with a shrill rising whisper that seemed addressed to heaven; the neighing and pawing of horses in the stables, the sharp terrified yelps of dogs; and through all a long despairing wail" (Atherton 8). The "falling," "creaking," and "despairing wail" that opens the novel is the cataclysm that wakes Alexina to stifling social conventions and the artificialities of society, stirring her passions and leading to a romantic entanglement that brings her in contact with social reformers. The novel establishes social reformers as the new heroes, as the few who recognize the "cosmopolitan flotsam" and their economic vulnerability in a world of disaster capitalism.

London's account of post-quake heroism does not recognize the social reformers that Atherton describes but rather "the bankers and business men [who] have already set about making preparations to rebuild San Francisco." Many businessmen and insurance leaders were eager to accept the charge. Samuel Weed, an insurance executive, declared that businessmen would "relax no effort to make [the] city safe," and he assured audiences eager for accounts about how the city would fare after the quake that although the people of San Francisco were "dazed" by the catastrophe, they were "not cast down." Addressing an annual meeting of the San Francisco Underwriter's Association, Weed, recalling Rowlandson, boasts to his audience of the "magnificent resources" of Northern California: the "fertile valleys, the inexhaustible treasures of the mountains and the river beds and an indomitable energy in the city that no earthquake or fire could extinguish" (Weed 11). Given the "prosperity" of the city's location, there is "no such word as fail" (Weed 11–12). San Francisco, he writes, had been "the world's wonder. . . . There is no similar instance perhaps in the history of civilized society where so much had been accomplished in so short a space of time. . . . I repel the suggestion," he concludes, that "San Francisco will not be rebuilt" (Weed 25–26).

The outpouring of first-person accounts of the quake by insurance men form an important, although less examined, archive of the disaster.[9] Despite the boosterism that many business and insurance leaders like Weed voiced in the aftermath of the catastrophe, insurance adjusters also recognized extreme challenges to their ability to minister to professional demands. "No one without seeing could have believed," writes G. H. Marks in his *Reminiscence and Lessons of the San Francisco Conflagration, 18–21 April 1906* (1909), which is subtitled: "the story of the San Francisco fire from an insurance adjuster's point of view."[10] "I HAVE entered somewhat into the incidents of the three days of earthquake and fire in order, if possible, to enable you to realize the circumstances through which they had passed and the situation when we, who represented the fire insurance companies, came upon the scene." Marks describes the overwhelming difficulty in evaluating and recording the loss: "How were we to check the claims? All usual means were absent. Under ordinary circumstances we have some data to go upon—the ruins contain many evidences, but here the ruin was so complete, and everything that was consumable had so entirely vanished, that little or nothing could be learnt by a visit to the scene of the fire." Lacking evidence and a coherent statistical approach that characterized other insurance events, Marks describes a variety of methods of insurance adjustment, including thick description, close observation, and habits of composition most associated with narrative arts. For the fire adjuster "in ordinary circumstances," analysis of loss might include narrative accounts of "next door neighbours and friends" who might "confirm the Assured's statements," but in the case of the San Francisco disaster, neighbors were soon gone, some hundreds, if not thousands, of miles away, others "scattered through many a refugee camp, and almost as difficult to find as the proverbial needle in a hay-stack." All methods for detailing material loss were compromised: even the "retail or wholesale firm from whom the articles were purchased," Marks laments, "had been burnt out too."

For insurance adjusters, the inability to find substantive records led to the utilization of narrative strategies more frequently aligned with journalists, novelists, and other short- and long-form writers. Agents, Marks announces, must learn to observe closely, to record personal histories, and to describe with accuracy and vigor. The practices were improvisational and varied, and, as Marks reveals, the core occupation of insurance adjusters after the quake was not only about the appraisal of physical property but also about writing, recording impressions, and storytelling. Professional practices included short descriptive anecdotes in the absence of statistical methods. Much like the scientists who were dependent upon citizen observers for their felt reports, inviting the input of those who registered and recorded the deep convulsions of the earth in and on the human body, insurance agents and executives relied on narrative and descriptive impressions to capture the chaos and loss of disaster. Some insurance adjusters published accounts of their work in local papers, others spoke to business organizations, and still others used them to develop insurance reports. Even as professionals would be pushed to greater specialization in their fields in the aftermath of the earthquake, whether seismology or insurance, the quake also became an occasion to speak across specialized vocabularies and to include stories, autobiographical accounts, and creative adaptations in the face of the massive loss suffered by so many.

Side Lights, an insurance Bildungsroman by H. T. Lamey, published in June 1906 scarcely two months after the earthquake, emphasizes the importance of the "felt report" of the insurance adjuster against the push for statistical management: "After all, we must reckon with the equation of human judgement," writes Lamey. "In forming his conclusion each weighs the factors upon his own scales" (35). Lamey's *Side Lights* includes a "felt report" of the San Francisco earthquake in the context of his education as an insurance adjuster and agent. Likening himself to Swift, he jokes, "My mile teeth were coaxed out by an old volume of Bennett's Instructions to Aetna Agents, an excellent lance for reluctant eye teeth to this day" (6). Lamey credits his account of the earthquake and fire to the means of training, temperament, and methods of an insurance agent. "Whereas many drift into the insurance business through stress of weather . . . only a few are born to our atmosphere of risks, or if you prefer, to our risky atmosphere" (5). Lamey stresses the importance of negotiation and personal persuasion in the process of adjusting: "Adjusting is the one branch of our business where special training is a requisite to success . . . few can determine the sum accurately and fewer have the knack of convincing the claimant and securing his assent to the estimate" (89). Despite confidence in his training and skill, nothing, he notes, prepared him for the "mess set before the adjusters" in the aftermath of the San Francisco earthquake (83).

Like William James and many others who would write felt reports about the quake, Lamey was shaken out of bed at 5:17 a.m. on April 18. He "lived in the house, so lightly and cheaply built that [he] still wonder[s] how it withstood the shock . . . bricks rested a moment with me on the floor and then leisurely sought the basement. It was some comfort to know that the law of gravitation was intact; other natural and artificial laws appeared to be either suspended or abrogated entirely" (73). He confesses to feeling "scared" and describes how he fled the "quivering shack as soon as I could, and so did a few hundred thousand others" (73). Lamey describes "a panic of excitement" among the crowds, the children "sobbing," and the strong feeling that was "uppermost in all minds": the need to "get away" (73). Along with thousands of others, however, Lamey remained in the city. Like many of his neighbors, he "gravitated toward places where business was daily transacted" only to find the streets "littered with brick and debris," roofs collapsed, "cornices covered the walks, glass . . . shattered, and not infrequently entire buildings . . . collapsed into a heap of twisted timber and iron" (74). Witnessing the destruction first hand, Lamey and some of his fellow insurance men saw a pressing need; they "got together, hired a hall, [and] organized an Adjustment Bureau" (81). "You can't keep an insurance man down," he muses. At first Lamey is appointed a flue inspector; however, soon he is re-assigned by "the committee on quake evidence" to the corps of "official Kodakers" whose job it was to photograph the destruction (81). Lamey's *Side Lights* surveys, records, and narrates the quake damage; the felt report he embeds in his insurance Bildungsroman tries to approximate the photograph in its precision and detail. "This was the mess set before the adjusters," he amazes, "with blocks blown away by dynamite for desert" (83). His final assignment attending to the quake and fire damage is as assistant chief of the clipping and personal evidence bureau. "My investigations covered all phases," thus he worries that the "damage was more serious than the natives would admit" (82). Lamey observes that although "talk is [the] chief subsistence" of the insurance adjuster, there was a "universal effort" to minimize quake talk along with "quake loss" (82). Lamey's detailed felt report, along with his story of the insurance adjuster's self-making, offers too much earthquake "talk" and discussion of loss; he recognizes that his felt report provides evidence for the wrong insurance conclusions. Lamey closes his narrative by predicting that the insurance industry will fall in the public's estimation: "When the two hundred million have been apportioned and the stress and excitement and tension are but memories; when the magnitude of the payments dawn upon the people; when the new city should have arisen in all its beauty and glory," Lamey cautions, "the citizens will rise as one man and call us—scoundrels" (84).

Despite Lamey's insistence on the indefatigableness of talk about the destruction, "you can't keep an insurance man down," much of the post-quake narrative was characterized by silence, particularly silence about the earthquake itself (77). Competing claims about the catastrophe, as Lamey acknowledges, allowed for emphasis on fire evidence while other testimony regarding earthquake damage and risk were suppressed. While earthquake insurance did not exist in 1906, and the insurance industry had incentive to see the disaster as an act of god (a category of event not covered by insurance), many city residents held fire insurance policies and made claims for damages that resulted from the conflagration following the quake. Insurance companies were overwhelmed by the enormity of the loss and the resulting claims, as William Bronson notes:

"only six companies made adjustments quickly and then paid off in full without delay and without asking cash discounts" (Bronson 111–14). What Ted Steinberg calls "seismic denial" helped to facilitate insurance compensation and development, and so the story of the earthquake soon was obscured by the conflagration that followed it. On the twentieth anniversary of the earthquake and fire, the Fireman's Fund Record called April 18, 1906, "the most romantic as well as the most remarkable achievement in the history of [fire] insurance."[11]

Seismologists and geologists were dumfounded. As John Branner, a scientist at Stanford, lamented, "When efforts were made by a few geologists to interest people and enterprises in the collection of information regarding [the earthquake], we were advised and even urged over and over again *to gather no such information, and above all not to publish it*" (qtd. in Steinberg 110, my emphasis). By trying to constrain the institutional archive on and about the quake, government officials and business executives thought they could control the political narrative and, in turn, curb the growing body of information about the earthquake that suggested the folly of reconstruction and the fragility of the environment on which businesses and residents continued to build. The 1907 collection that Branner, with Stanford University president David Starr Jordan and eminent geologist Grove Karl Gilbert, published, against cautions urging otherwise, is a collection of largely academic essays that examines the quake from a variety of scientific and engineering fields. "The earthquake of 1906 is receiving the most thorough study possible, and in such a way as to give promise of important practical results. The state of California has formed an Earthquake Commission consisting of geological experts . . . the details of the earthquake rift and the effects of the shocks on buildings have been carefully recorded and photographed" (Jordan 51). With such essays as "Geology and the Earthquake," "Preliminary Note on the Cause of the California Earthquake of 1906," and "The Destructive Extent of the California Earthquake of 1906" by well-known academics, structural engineers, and geologists associated with the U.S. Geological Survey, it is striking that the collection concludes with an essay by Mary Hunter Austin, a nature writer who set her fiction in the deserts of Southern California and was best known as the author of *The Land of Little Rain* (1903). Against the widening separation of science and culture, and against the growing inclination to distinguish scientific fact from the literary imagination, these scientists repelled the official order of silence in favor of narrative. *The California Earthquake of 1906* (1907) concludes with Mary Austin's essay "The Tremblor: A Personal Narration." That Austin's account, first published in 1906 in *Out West* magazine, is included in a largely scientific collection is again a testament to the importance of first-hand narrative, in this case, the literary "felt report." Austin's account is included because of her reputation as an environmental writer; however, she too was a recognized citizen scientist, and her felt report written after the 1872 California earthquake is noted elsewhere in David Starr Jordan's collection for its precision about the size of the earth's fractures: the "fissure at Big Pine [is] 50 to 200 feet wide, 20 feet deep, extending 50 miles or more." Austin notes that she felt "numerous shocks" that she would describe as "very violent," and these violent ruptures were "preceded by weaker shocks for a year or more" (Jordan 53).

Austin's felt report of the 1906 San Francisco quake begins, like William James's, with the suggestion that the tremblor that she and others felt on the morning of April 18 was "*only* an earthquake" (my emphasis 342). Austin notes that she could hear "twists of laughter between tremblings" even though the quake was really quite "credible" (342). The efforts to normalize and downplay the quake made its first rumblings comic. Like Gertrude Atherton's character, Alexina, who "remembered that it was a rigid convention among real Californians to treat an earthquake as a joke" and began to laugh, Austin tries but fails to chuckle (Atherton 8). "Naïve delight" aside, Austin brings a human and tragic dimension to a largely scientific anthology; she contextualizes the technological renderings of her colleagues and places the reality of the earthquake experience in sharp relief (Atherton 9). "The largeness of the event had the effect of reducing private sorrow to a mere pin prick and point of time" (Austin 346). Austin is self-reflective about the writing of her impressions and the literary conventions she employs. "Everybody tells you tales like this with more or less detail" (Austin 346). Acutely aware of the abundance of first-person accounts and felt reports, she dismisses the distinction between invention and truth: "It is perfectly safe to believe anything any one tells you of personal adventure; the inventive faculty does not exist which could outdo the actuality" (343). Literary invention and "actuality" in the face of disaster are mutually constitutive; the imagination cannot "outdo" the experience of the event. Austin's account, like many others, is filled with thick description and vivid imagery: "Before the red night paled into the murky dawn thousands of people were vomited out of the angry throat of the street far down toward Market. Even the smallest child carried something, or pushed it before him on a rocking chair, or dragged it behind him in a trunk, and the thing he carried was the index of the refugee's strongest bent" (Austin 343). The city's survivors carry not only what belongings they can salvage but also the shock, pain, and trauma of loss.[12] "It was all like this, broken bits of human tragedy, curiously unrelated, inconsequential, disrupted by the tremblor" (Austin 346).

Austin's account brings to a scientific collection meant to redress seismic denial both the human dimensions of the disaster and its politicization. She notes that "the disorder of the social world threw all men back severely upon its primal institutions" as they sought out security, and she worries that "everywhere the will of the people was toward authority (Austin 357). Austin witnesses how insecurity drives policy and fear nourishes authoritarian thinking. While her account and those of her co-contributors are dedicated to changing the discourse around the San Francisco catastrophe, they also recognize that disasters result in fierce competition over which interpretations sway the collective imagination and the political establishment. "For the greater part of this disaster—the irreclaimable loss of goods and houses, the violent deaths—was due chiefly to man-contrivances, to the sinking of made ground, to huddled buildings cheapened by greed, to insensate clinging to the outer shells of life" (Austin 356). Disaster flourishes, Austin rebukes, because of human efforts to shape the environment in our image: "the actual damage done by God to the city was small beside the possibilities for damage that reside in man-contrivances; for most man-made things do inherently carry the elements of their own destruction" (Austin 358). Like James, Twain, and even the insurance adjuster H. T. Lamey, Austin emphasizes the human dimension of the quake and the role humans play in turning natural events into "natural" disasters; indeed, Austin articulates a critical point: there are no natural disasters outside of human constructs. "There have been some unconsidered references of the earthquake disaster to the judgment of God; happily not much of it" (Austin 358). Whereas London's account emphasizes rescue, relief, and recovery, Austin emphasizes ecological awareness and the intersection of natural hazards and human populations: "How much of all that happened of distress and inestimable loss could have been averted if men would live . . . with wide, clean breathing spaces and room for green growing things to push up between?" (359).

Austin writes against the fantasy of disaster containment and the mastery over nature espoused by politicians and technocrats, and she asks her readers to recognize the human precariousness and vulnerability that the official narrative and its artifacts sought to constrain. She urges precaution about the resumption of human activity and awareness of discourses of progress. In a "half burned building where activity had begun again" Austin notes a placard: "Don't Talk Earthquake Talk Business" (359). Against this invocation, Austin invites readers to look at the cracks that the San Francisco earthquake made, quite literally, visible. While the official reaction enabled an enormous concentration of government and corporate power that eroded the accountability of the state and industry to the "flotsam," and which was facilitated by cultural representations like London's, Austin invites us to see a world that is as fragile as "green growing things" amid fallen planks and re-buildable, but not in the way big business thinks. The earthquake exemplified a porous moment that quickly closed as cultural framing turned it into a symbolic event that bound an imagined community to economic triumph, professionalization, and disciplinary authority (Rozario 180). Yet, even as professionals were pushed to greater specialization, the felt report became an invitation to animate descriptive language and embodied response for the sake of ecology. The felt reports after the 1906 earthquake embraced a kind of symbiosis—science sustained by human sensations, industry actualized by the things they carry and the stories they tell—and they recognized embodiment, sensation, and forms of physical and environmental vulnerability. The interdependence of the stories told by novelists, scientists, insurance adjusters, and reporters alike suggests a subtle shift in consciousness about what kinds of stories are important; their focus on embodied sensations as a fundamental register of historical and ecological experience presents a challenge to managerial culture and to narratives of disaster capitalism.

When James Fenimore Cooper imagines his final earthquake in *The Crater*, it signals the end times; for San Francisco, the quake was reimagined as a new beginning: a glorious city would be built up from its cracked foundations. If there is a lesson to be learned from Cooper's novel (as he urges) or from the aftermath of the San Francisco quake, which continues to inspire voluminous scholarship and critique, it is that we cannot afford to maintain a collusion of silence or perpetuate the illusion of mastery over nature or each other. In our present moment, we continue to face monumental challenges, from climate change and resource depletion, to socioeconomic inequality, and the persecution of marginalized persons and groups. We live in dangerous times. What makes humans remarkable is our capacity for empathy and our ability to respond in "large numbers in times of need, stress, and emergency," even for strangers, as the artist John Sims notes as he contemplates the recent storms to hit Florida and the Caribbean. Yet, what makes humans so "self-destructive," Sims continues, is our "insatiable lust for opportunity at the expense of other folks' vulnerability."[13] As the writers and artists on these many pages illustrate, how we respond to danger and how we recognize our shared and particular vulnerabilities will be the final measure of our collective futures.

NOTES

1. "I regret that lack of space does not allow me to transcribe here some of the accounts of eyewitness of the great earthquakes. These stories have more than scientific interest. They are the direct and simple narratives of persons who have passed through the most awful of human experiences. To them the world, the solid globe, the mother of us all, can never again be the same. They have looked on awful Death face-to-face, and in an instant have known all the lingering horrors of the Inferno—its hells of sound, of light, of darkness, of cold terror. There is a peculiar quality in such accounts, which is singularly striking and pathetic." Edward S. Holden, "Earthquakes and How to Measure Them," 759.

2. The earthquake continues to attract the attention of writers and scholars. See Simon Winchester's popularization of the quake in *A Crack in the Edge of the World: America and the Great California Earthquake of 1906*; Andrea Rees Davies, *Saving San Francisco: Relief and Recovery after the 1906 Disaster*; Rebecca Solnit, *A Paradise Built in Hell: The Extraordinary Communities that Arise in Disaster*; Kevin Rozario, *The Culture of*

Calamity; and Nick Yablon, *Untimely Ruins: An Archeology of American Urban Modernity, 1818–1918*, among many other titles.

3. These observations are based on my work with spectacle books and insurance pamphlets found in the Churchill Collection at the Kathryn and Shelby Cullom Davis Library, St. John's University, New York. The Churchill Collection is a comparative archive of disaster, with emphasis on earthquakes. Acquired by the library in 1951 as a donation of its creator Heber B. Churchill, an executive at the Great American Insurance Company of New York, the archive provides detailed accounts of major natural disasters, particularly the San Francisco earthquake and fire of 1906. Churchill collected and indexed a wide array of original materials and many are not recorded or available through WorldCat. I have been working with art historian Susan Rosenberg on these materials. I also am grateful for the assistance with this collection of archivist Alyse Hennig and Davis Director Ismael Rivera-Sierra.

4. I borrow the term "morbid archive" from Jeremy Braddock, *Collecting as Modernist Practice*, 22. These artifacts did not originally constitute a conventional and/or institutional archive; they were not pristine objects curated by professionals and housed in an institutional setting. Most often they were ruins or representations of ruins marketed for profit. Yet, it is instructive to think about how recent critiques of "the archive" might inform scholars' understanding of the early impulse to collect artifacts of disaster and stories of vulnerability. Ann Laura Stoler's work on archives, for example, demonstrates the intimate relationship between archival practices of collecting and their influence on politics. Stoler calls the archive "a force field that animates political energies and expertise, that pulls on some 'social facts' and converts them into qualified knowledge, that attends to some ways of knowing while repelling and refusing others," *Along the Archival Grain*, 90. Although archives often are seen as neutral repositories of materials, a place where scholars can investigate items in order to develop objective accounts of the past, scholars acknowledge that there is distinct power involved in collecting, appraising, cataloguing, organizing, and interpreting archives. Archives are not only sites of knowledge retrieval but also sites of knowledge production.

5. Charles Morris is also author of *The Volcano's Deadly Work* and *Decisive Events in The Story of the Great Republic*.

6. For more on the etymology of disaster and the term "peril," which has complex associations with the dangers of the sea, see Marie-Hélèn Huet, *The Culture of Disaster*, 3–4.

7. Jack London, "Story of an Eyewitness." https://www.parks.ca.gov/?page_id =24206. All references are from this digital reproduction of the report, which includes photographs taken by London and his wife Charmian.

8. For more analysis of Hurricane Katrina, see Wailoo, O'Neill, Dowd, and Anglin, *Katrina's Imprint*; and Eyerman, *Is This America?*

9. See note 3 on archival collections in the Kathryn and Shelby Cullom Davis Library.

10. This was a paper read before members of the Birmingham Insurance Institute on February 26, 1909. G. H. Marks, *Reminiscences and Lessons of the San Francisco Conflagration*, in the Churchill Collection, Davis Library, St. John's University. The pamphlet, cited here, was published in New York.

11. "Fireman's Fund Record, April 1926," in the Churchill Collection, Davis Library, St. John's University.

12. A similar image would be central to Tim O'Brien's stories about Vietnam, *The Things They Carried*.

13. See John Sims, "Waiting for Hurricane Irma," in the *Los Angeles Review of Books*, https://www.guernicamag.com/waiting-hurricane-irma/.

Bibliography

Abate, Michelle Ann. "Launching a Gender B(l)acklash: E. D. E. N. Southworth's *The Hidden Hand* and the Emergence of Racialized White Tomboyism." *Children's Literature Association Quarterly* 31, no. 1 (Spring 2006) : 40–64.
Abraham, Kenneth S. *The Liability Century: Insurance and Tort Law from the Progressive Era To 9/11.* Cambridge, MA: Harvard University Press, 2009.
Adams, Henry C. "The Slaughter of Railway Employees." *Forum* 8 (1892): 500.
Agamben, Giorgio. *Homo Sacer: Sovereign Power and Bare Life.* Palo Alto, CA: Stanford University Press, 1998.
Alcott, Louisa May. "Honor's Fortune." In *Jo March's Attic: Stories of Intrigue and Suspense.* Edited by Madeleine B. Stern and Daniel Shealy. Boston, MA: Northeastern University Press, 1993.
———. *A Long Fatal Love Chase.* New York: Random House, 1995.
Aldrich, Mark. *Death Rode the Rails: American Railroad Accidents and Safety, 1828–1965.* Baltimore, MD: Johns Hopkins University Press, 2006.
Alexander Hanlon v. Philadelphia and West Chester Turnpike Road Company. 182 Pa. 115. 37 A. 943 1897 Pa. LEXIS 778.
"American Genius and Enterprise." *Scientific American* 2 (September 1847): 397.
Amper, Susan. "Male Fears and Fantasies in Harriet Prescott Spofford's 'The Black Bess.'" *West Virginia University Philological Papers* 47 (September 2001): 29–36.
Anderson, Benedict. *Imagined Communities: Reflections on the Origins and Spread of Nationalism* (Reprint 1983). New York: Verso, 2006.
Armstrong, Tim. *The Logic of Slavery: Debt, Technology, and Pain in American Literature.* Cambridge, UK: Cambridge University Press, 2012.
Arthurs, Jane, and Iain Grant, Editors. *Crash Cultures: Modernity, Mediation and the Material.* Bristol, UK: Intellect Ltd., 2000.
Atherton, Gertrude. *The Sisters-in-Law: A Novel of Our Time.* New York: Frederick A. Stokes Company, 1921.
Austin, Mary Hunter. "The Tremblor: A Personal Narration." In *The California Earthquake of 1906.* Edited by David Starr Jordan. San Francisco, CA: A.M. Robertson, 1907.
Baker, Meredith Henne. *The Richmond Theater Fire: Early America's First Great Disaster.* Baton Rouge, LA: Louisiana State University Press, 2012.
Baldwin, James. *The Fire Next Time.* New York: Vintage International, 1963.
Bandes, Susan A., Editor. *The Passions of Law.* New York: New York University Press, 2000.
Bankoff, Greg, George Frerks, and Dorothea Hilhorst, Editors. *Mapping Vulnerability: Disasters, Development and People.* London, UK: Routledge, 2004.
Baranoff, Dalit. "Shaped by Risk: The American Fire Insurance Industry, 1790–1920." *Enterprise & Society* 6, no. 4 (2005): 561–70.
Batlan, Felice. "Review Essay: Engendering Legal History." *Law and Social Inquiry* 30 (2005): 823–49.
Baucom, Ian. *Specters of the Atlantic: Finance Capital, Slavery, and the Philosophy of History.* Durham, NC: Duke University Press Books, 2005.
Bauman, Zygmunt. In *Liquid Times: Living in an Age of Uncertainty.* Cambridge, UK: Polity, 2006.
Baym, Nina. "Introduction." In *The Hidden Hand.* New York: Oxford University Press, 1997.

Beard, George M. *American Nervousness; Its Causes and Consequences, a Supplement to Nervous Exhaustion (Neurasthenia)*. (Reprint, 1881). New York: Arno Press, 1972.
Beck, John, and Paul Crosthwaite. "Velocities of Power: An Introduction." *Cultural Politics* 3, no. 1 (March 2007): 23–34.
Beck, Ulrich. *Risk Society: Towards a New Modernity*. London, UK: Sage Publications Ltd., 1992.
———. *World at Risk*. Cambridge, UK: Polity, 2008.
Beito, David T. *From Mutual Aid to the Welfare State: Fraternal Societies and Social Services, 1890–1967*. Chapel Hill, NC: University of North Carolina Press, 2000.
Benjamin, Walter. *Illuminations*. New York: Shocken Books, 1939.
Benjamin v. Holyoke Street Railway Company (1893), 160 Mass. 2; 35 N.E. 95; 1893 Mass. LEXIS 2.
Bentley, Nancy. *Frantic Panoramas: American Literature and Mass Culture 1870–1920*. Philadelphia, PA: University of Pennsylvania Press, 2009.
Bercovitch, Sacvan. *The American Jeremiad*. Madison, WI: University of Wisconsin Press, 2012.
Bergstrom, Randolph Emil. *Courting Danger: Injury and Law in New York City, 1870–1910*. Ithaca, NY: Cornell University Press, 1992.
Berk, Gerald. *Alternative Tracks: The Constitution of American Industrial Order, 1865–1917*. Baltimore, MD: Johns Hopkins University Press, 1994.
Biel, Steven, Editor. *American Disasters*. New York: New York University Press, 2001.
Biers, Katherine. *Virtual Modernism: Writing and Technology in the Progressive Era*. Minneapolis, MN: University of Minnesota Press, 2013.
Blaikie, Piers, Terry Cannon, Ian Davis, and Ben Wisner. *At Risk: Natural Hazards, People's Vulnerability and Disasters* (Second Edition). London, UK: Routledge, 2003.
Blanchot, Maurice. *The Writing of the Disaster*. Translated by Ann Smock. Lincoln, NE: University of Nebraska Press, 1995.
Bouk, Dan. *How Our Days Became Numbered: Risk and the Rise of the Statistical Individual*. Chicago, IL: University of Chicago Press, 2015.
———. "The Science of Difference: Developing Tools for Discrimination in the American Life Insurance Industry, 1830–1930." *Enterprise & Society* 12, no. 4 (2011): 717–31.
Bourke, Joanna. *Dismembering the Male: Men's Bodies, Britain, and the Great War*. Chicago, IL: University of Chicago Press, 1996.
———. *Fear: A Cultural History*. Emeryville, CA: Counterpoint, 2007.
Bracke, Sarah. "Bouncing Back: Vulnerability and Resistance in Times of Resilience." In *Vulnerability and Resistance*. Edited by Judith Butler, Zeynep Gambetti, and Leticia Sabsay, 52–75. Durham, NC: Duke University Press, 2016.
Braddock, Jeremy. *Collecting as Modernist Practice*. Baltimore, MD: Johns Hopkins University Press, 2011.
Brennan, Stephen C. "Theodore Dreiser's *An Amateur Laborer*: A Myth in the Making." *American Literary Realism* 19, no. 2 (Winter 1987): 66–83.
———. Review of *Twelve Men*, by Theodore Dreiser. Edited by Robert Coltrane. Textual Editors, James L. W. West III and Lee Ann Draud; General Editor, Thomas P. Riggio. *Resources for American Literary Study* 27, no. 1 (2001): 139–42.
Bromley, Dorothy Dunbar. "The Railroads and the 14th Amendment." *Nation* 172, no. 19 (May 12, 1951): 441–43.
Bronson, William. *The Earth Shook, The Sky Burned—A Moving Record of America's Great Earthquake and Fire—San Francisco, April 18, 1906*. New York: Doubleday and Company, 1959.
Bronstein, Jamie L. *Caught in the Machinery: Workplace Accidents and Injured Workers in Nineteenth-Century Britain*. Stanford, CA: Stanford University Press, 2007.
Brown, Bill. *The Material Unconscious: American Amusement, Stephen Crane & the Economies of Play*. Cambridge, MA: Harvard University Press, 1996.

Bulla, David W., and David B. Sachsman, Editors. *Sensationalism: Murder, Mayhem, Mudslinging, Scandals, and Disasters in Nineteenth-Century Reporting.* New Brunswick, NJ: Transaction Publishers, 2013.

Bullard, Robert D. *Race, Place, and Environmental Justice after Hurricane Katrina: Struggles to Reclaim, Rebuild, and Revitalize New Orleans and the Gulf Coast.* Boulder, CO: Westview Press, 2009.

Burnham, John C. *Accident Prone: A History of Technology, Psychology, and Misfits of the Machine Age.* Chicago, IL: University of Chicago Press, 2009.

Burns, Grant. *The Railroad in American Fiction: An Annotated Bibliography.* Jefferson, NC: McFarland & Company, 2005.

Burton, Antoinette, Editor. *Archive Stories: Facts, Fictions, and the Writing of History.* Durham, NC: Duke University Press, 2006.

Butler, Judith. *Frames of War: When Is Life Grievable?* New York: Verso, 2010.

———. *Precarious Life: The Powers of Mourning and Violence.* New York: Verso, 2006.

Butler, Judith, Zeynep Gambetti, and Leticia Sabsay, Editors. *Vulnerability in Resistance.* Durham, NC: Duke University Press, 2016.

Campbell, Donna. "'Where are the ladies?' Wharton, Glasgow, and American Women Naturalists." *Studies in American Naturalism* 1 (2006): 152–69.

Caplan, Eric. "Trains and Trauma in the American Gilded Age." In *Traumatic Pasts: History, Psychiatry, and Trauma in the Modern Age, 1870–1930.* Edited by Mark S. Micale and Paul Lerner. London: Cambridge University Press, 2001.

Carp, Benjamin L. "Fire of Liberty: Firefighters, Urban Voluntary Culture, and the Revolutionary Movement." *The William and Mary Quarterly* 58, no. 4 (October 2001): 781–818.

Carrington, André M. *Speculative Blackness: The Future of Race in Science Fiction.* Minneapolis, MN: University of Minnesota Press, 2016.

Carter, Paul J. "Mark Twain Describes a San Francisco Earthquake." *PMLA* 72, no. 5 (December 1957): 997–1004.

Caruth, Cathy. *Unclaimed Experience: Trauma, Narrative, and History.* Baltimore, MD: Johns Hopkins University Press, 1996.

Cassedy, Steven. *Connected: How Trains, Genes, Pineapples, Piano Keys, and a Few Disasters Transformed Americans at the Dawn of the Twentieth Century.* Stanford, CA: Stanford University Press, 2014.

Castronovo, Russ. "James Fenimore Cooper and the NSA: Security, Property, Liberalism," *American Literary History* 28, no. 4, 1 December 2016, Pages 677–701. https://doi.org/10.1093/alh/ajw044

Cather, Willa. "Paul." *McClure's Magazine* 25 (May 1905): 74–83.

Chamallas, Martha, and Linda K. Kerber. "Women, Mothers, and the Law of Fright: A History." 88 *Michigan Law Review* 814 (1990): 814–64.

Chapman, Bruce. "Allocating the Risk of Subjectivity: Intention, Consent, and Insurance." *University of Toronto Law Journal* 57, no. 2 (2007): 315–30.

Chopin, Kate. "The Story of an Hour." In *Literature: Reading, Reacting, Writing.* Edited by Laurie G. Kirszner and Stephen R. Mandell. Boston, MA: Thomson Wadsworth, 2007.

Clarke, Deborah. *Driving Women: Fiction and Automobile Culture in Twentieth-Century America.* Baltimore, MD: Johns Hopkins University Press, 2007.

Coates, Ta-Nehisi. *Between the World and Me.* New York: Spiegel & Grau, 2015.

Cobb, Bruce. "The Nation Roused Against Motor Killings." *The New York Times*, November 23, 1924.

Coen, Deborah R. *The Earthquake Observers: Disaster Science from Lisbon to Richter.* Chicago, IL: University of Chicago Press, 2012.

Cohen, Patricia Cline. "Women at Large: Travel in Antebellum America." *History Today* 44, no. 12 (1994): 1–12.

Cole, Alyson M. "All of Us Are Vulnerable, But Some Are More Vulnerable than Others." *Critical Horizons* 17, no. 2 (May 2016): 260–77.

———. *The Cult of True Victimhood: From the War on Welfare to the War on Terror.* Stanford, CA: Stanford University Press, 2007.
———. "Victims No More (?)." *Feminist Review*, no. 64 (2000): 135–38.
Cole, Alyson M., and Kyoo Lee, Editors. *Safe:* Volume 39, Nos. 1&2 Spring/Summer 2011. New York: The Feminist Press, CUNY, 2011.
Coltrane, Robert. "Historical Commentary: The Creation of *Twelve Men*." 361–75. In Theodore Dreiser's *Twelve Men.* Edited by Robert Coltrane. Textual Editors, James L.W. West III and Lee Ann Draud; General Editor, Thomas P. Riggio. Philadelphia: University of Pennsylvania Press, 1998.
Cooper, Anna Julia. *A Voice from the South.* Xenia, OH: The Aldine Printing House, 1892.
Cooper, James Fenimore. *The Crater; or Vulcan's Peak. A Tale of the Pacific (In Two Volumes).* New York: Burgess, Stringer & Co., 1847.
Cooper, Robyn. "The Fireman: Immaculate Manhood." *The Journal of Popular Culture* 28, no. 4 (1995): 139–70.
Crane, Stephen. "The Monster." *Harper's New Monthly Magazine* (August 1898). Electronic Text Center, University of Virginia Library. http://etext.lib.virginia.edu/etc-bin/toccer-new2?id=CraMons.sgm&images=images/modeng&data=/texts/english/modeng/parsed&tag=public&part=1&division=div1
———. "When Everyone Is Panic Stricken/A Realistic Pen Picture of a Fire/In a Tenement./The Philosophy of Women/Fright and Flight—The Missing Baby/—A Commonplace Hero." In *The New York City Sketches of Stephen Crane and Related Pieces.* R. W. Stallman and E. R. Hagermann, Editors. New York: New York University Press, 1966.
Crosthwaite, Paul, Editor. *Criticism, Crisis, and Contemporary Narrative: Textual Horizons in an Age of Global Risk.* New York: Routledge, 2014.
Daly, Nicholas. *Literature, Technology, and Modernity, 1860–2000.* Cambridge: Cambridge University Press, 2004.
Daston, Lorraine. "Life, Chance & Life Chances." *Daedalus* 137, no. 1 (Winter 2008): 5–14.
Dauber, Michele Landis. *The Sympathetic State: Disaster Relief and the Origins of the American Welfare State.* Chicago: University of Chicago Press, 2012.
Davies, Andrea Rees. *Saving San Francisco: Relief and Recovery After the 1906 Disaster.* Philadelphia, PA: Temple University Press, 2011.
Davis, Mike. *Ecology of Fear: Los Angeles and the Imagination of Disaster.* New York: Metropolitan Books, 2014.
Davis, Rebecca Harding. "Anne." *Harper's New Monthly Magazine* 78 (April 1889): 744–50. https://www.unz.org/Pub/Harpers-1889apr-00744
Despotopoulou, Anna. *Women and the Railway, 1850–1915.* Edinburgh, UK: Edinburgh University Press, 2015.
Dickens, Charles. *Dombey and Son.* Oxford, UK: Oxford University Press, 1982.
Dilworth, Leah, Editor. *Acts of Possession: Collecting in America.* New Brunswick, NJ: Rutgers University Press, 2003.
Dobson, Joanne. "*The Hidden Hand*: Subversion of Cultural Ideology in Three Mid-Nineteenth Century American Women's Novels." *American Quarterly* 38, no. 2 (1986): 223–42.
Donegan, Kathleen. *Seasons of Misery: Catastrophe and Colonial Settlement in Early America.* Philadelphia, PA: University of Pennsylvania Press, 2016.
Donovan, Frank P. Jr. *The Railroad in Literature: A Brief Survey of Railroad Fiction, Poetry, Songs, Biography, Essays, Travel and Drama in the English Language, Particularly Emphasizing Its Place in American Literature.* Boston: The Railway and Locomotive Historical Society, Inc., 1940.
Douglas, Mary, and Aaron Wildavsky. *Risk and Culture: An Essay on the Selection of Technological and Environmental Dangers.* Berkeley, CA: University of California Press, 1983.

Dreiser, Theodore. *An Amateur Laborer*. Edited by Richard W. Dowell, James L. W. West, and Neda M. Westlake. Philadelphia: University of Pennsylvania Press, 1983.
———. *American Diaries, 1902–1926*. Edited by Thomas P. Riggio, James L. W. West, and Neda M. Westlake. Philadelphia, PA: University of Pennsylvania Press, 1982.
———. "Burned to Death." *St. Louis Globe-Democrat*, January 22, 1893. *Theodore Dreiser's Journalism. Volume One. Newspaper Writings, 1892–1895*. Edited by T. D. Nostwich; Thomas P. Riggio, General Editor; James L. W. West, Textual Editor. Philadelphia, PA: University of Pennsylvania Press, 1988.
———. "The Mighty Burke." Electronic Text Center, University of Virginia Library, 41–48. http://wyllie.lib.virginia.edu:8086/perl/toccer-new?id=DreMigh.sgm&images=images/mod
———. "The Mighty Rourke." In *Twelve Men*. University of Pennsylvania Dreiser Edition. Edited by Robert Coltrane, James L. W. West, Lee Ann Draud. General Editor, Thomas P. Riggio. Philadelphia, PA: University of Pennsylvania Press, 1998.
———. "Railroad and the People." *Harper's Monthly* 100 (February 1900): 479–84.
———. *Selected Magazine Articles of Theodore Dreiser: Life and Art in the American 1890s*. Volume 1. Edited by Yoshinobu Hakutani. Rutherford, NJ: Fairleigh Dickinson University Press, 1985.
———. *Selected Magazine Articles of Theodore Dreiser. Life and Art in the American 1890s*. Volume 2. Edited by Yoshinobu Hakutani. Cranbury, NJ: Associated University Presses, 1987.
———. *Sister Carrie*. The Pennsylvania Edition. Edited by James L. West III. Thomas P. Riggio. Philadelphia, PA, 1998.
———. *The Color of a Great City*. Syracuse, NY: Syracuse University Press, 1996.
———. "The Toil of the Laborer: A Trilogy." *New York Call*, July 15, 1913. Reprinted in *Hey Rub-a-Dub-Dub: A Book of The Mystery and Wonder and Terror of Life*, 92–106. New York: Boni and Liveright, 1920.
———. *Theodore Dreiser's Uncollected Magazine Articles, 1897–1902*. Edited by Yoshinobu Hakutani. Newark, DE: University of Delaware Press, 2003.
———. *Twelve Men*. New York: Boni and Liveright, 1919.
Drinka, George F. *The Birth of Neurosis: Myth, Malady, and the Victorians*. New York: Simon & Schuster, 1984.
Dublin, Louis I. *The Money Value of a Man*. New York: The Ronald Press Company, 1930.
Du Bois, W. E. B. *Darkwater: Voices from within the Veil*. New York: Harcourt, Brace, and Company, 1920. http://www.gutenberg.org/files/15210/15210-h/15210-h.htm
———. "*Race Traits and the Tendencies of the American Negro* by Frederick L. Hoffman." *Annals of the American Academy of Political and Social Science* 9 (January 1897): 127–33.
———. "How to Figure the Extinction of a Race." *Nation* 64, no. 1657 (April 1, 1897): 246–48.
———. "The Health and Physique of the Negro American." *American Journal of Public Health* 93, no. 2 (February 2003): 272–76.
Dumenil, Lynn. *Freemasonry and American Culture, 1880–1930*. Princeton, NJ: Princeton University Press, 1984.
Erichsen, John Eric. *On Railway and Other Injuries of the Nervous System*. Philadelphia, PA: Henry C. Lea, 1867.
Evans, Brad, and Julian Reid. *Resilient Life: The Art of Living Dangerously*. Cambridge, UK: Polity, 2014. Kindle Edition.
Ewald, François. "Insurance and Risk." In *The Foucault Effect: Studies in Governmentality*. Edited by Graham Burchell, Colin Gordon, and Peter Miller, 197–210. Chicago, IL: University of Chicago Press, 1991.
Eyerman, Ron. *Is This America?: Katrina as Cultural Trauma*. Austin, TX: University of Texas Press, 2015.
Fagan, James O. *Confessions of a Railway Signalman*. Boston: Houghton Mifflin Company, 1908.

Fichtelberg, Joseph. *Risk Culture: Performance and Danger in Early America*. Ann Arbor, MI: University of Michigan Press, 2010.

Fineman, Martha Albertson. *The Autonomy Myth: A Theory of Dependency*. New York: New Press, 2004.

———. "Equality, Autonomy, and the Vulnerable Subject in Law and Politics." In *Vulnerability: Reflections on a New Ethical Foundation for Law and Politics*. Edited by Martha Albertson Fineman and Anna Grear. New York: Routledge, 2016.

———. "The Vulnerable Subject: Anchoring Equality in the Human Condition." *Yale Journal of Law and Feminism* 20 no. 1 (2008): 1–25.

Fineman, Martha Albertson, and Anna Grear, Editors. *Vulnerability: Reflections on a New Ethical Foundation for Law and Politics*. New York: Routledge, 2016.

Fisher, Philip. *Still the New World: American Literature in a Culture of Creative Destruction*. Cambridge, MA: Harvard University Press, 1999.

Fishkin, Shelley Fisher. *From Fact to Fiction: Journalism and Imaginative Writing in America*. Baltimore, MD: Johns Hopkins University Press, 1985.

Fleissner, Jennifer L. *Women, Compulsion, Modernity: The Moment of American Naturalism*. Chicago, IL: University of Chicago Press, 2004.

Foote, Stephanie, and Stephanie LeMenager. "Editors' Column." *Resilience: A Journal of the Environmental Humanities* 1, no. 1. (January 2014). Accessed September 15, 2014.

Franklin. Thomas E. *Thomas E. Franklin Portfolio*. http://www.thomasefranklin.com/#a=0&at=0&mi=2&pt=1&pi=10000&s=0&p=3

Frederickson, Kathy. "Working Out to Work Through": Dreiser in Muldoon's Body Shop of Shame. In *Theodore Dreiser and American Culture: New Readings*. Edited by Yoshinobu Hakutani. Newark, DE: University of Delaware Press, 2000.

Freedgood, Elaine. *Victorian Writing about Risk: Imagining a Safe England in a Dangerous World*. Cambridge, UK: Cambridge University Press, 2006.

Freud, Sigmund. *Moses and Monotheism*. Translated by Katherine Jones. New York: Vintage, 1939.

Friedman, Lawrence. *A History of American Law*. New York: Simon & Schuster, 1973.

Friedman, Lawrence M., and Jack Ladinsky. "Social Change and the Law of Industrial Accidents." *67 Columbia L. R.* 50 (1967).

Fyfe, Paul. "Accidents of a Novel Trade: Industrial Catastrophe, Fire Insurance, and Mary Barton." *Nineteenth-Century Literature* 65, no. 3 (December 2010): 315–47.

———. *By Accident or Design: Writing the Victorian Metropolis*. Oxford, UK: Oxford University Press, 2015.

Garrard, Greg. "Environmental Humanities: Notes Towards a Summary for Policymakers." In *The Routledge Companion to the Environmental Humanities*. Edited by Ursula Heise, John Christensen, and Michelle Niemann, 462–72. New York: Routledge Press, 2017.

Ghosh, Amitav. *The Great Derangement: Climate Change and the Unthinkable*. Chicago, IL: University of Chicago Press, 2016.

Giddens, Anthony. *The Consequences of Modernity*. New York: Polity, 2013.

Giggie, John M. "Railroads in the African American Experience: A Photographic Journey." *Journal of Southern History* 77, no. 3 (2011): 743–44.

———. "'When Jesus Handed Me a Ticket': Images of Railroad Travel and Spiritual Transformation among African Americans, 1865–1917." In *The Visual Culture of American Religions*, 249–66. Berkeley, CA: University of California Press, 2001.

Gilbert, Pamela K., Editor. *A Companion to Sensation Fiction*. Malden, MA: Wiley-Blackwell, 2011.

Gilson, Erinn. *The Ethics of Vulnerability: A Feminist Analysis of Social Life and Practice*. New York: Routledge, 2014.

Glasgow, Ellen. *Barren Ground*. New York: Doubleday, 1925.

Glenn, Brian J. "Postmodernism: The Basis of Insurance." *Risk Management and Insurance Review*, (2003) 131–43.

———. "The Shifting Rhetoric of Insurance Denial." *Law and Society Review* 34, no. 3 (2000): 779–808.

Go, Julian. "Inventing Industrial Accidents and Their Insurance: Discourse and Workers' Compensation in the United States, 1880–1910." *Social Science History* 20, no. 3 (October 1996): 401–38.

Goodman, Nan. *Shifting the Blame*. Princeton, NJ: Princeton University Press, 1998.

Goodman, Nan, and Simon Stern. Editors. *The Routledge Research Companion to Law and Humanities in Nineteenth-Century America*. New York: Routledge, 2017.

Gregg, Melissa, and Gregory J. Seigworth, Editors. *The Affect Theory Reader*. Durham, NC: Duke University Press Books, 2010.

Grossberg, Michael, and Christopher Tomlins. Editors. *The Cambridge History of Law in America*. Cambridge, UK: Cambridge University Press, 2011.

Gulf, Colorado, & Santa Fe Railway Company v. J. O. Hayter, 93 Tex. 239; 54 S.W. 944; 1900 Tex. LEXIS 133.

Habegger, Alfred. "A Well-Hidden Hand." *Novel: A Forum on Fiction* 14, no. 3 (1981): 197–212.

Hamilton, Ross. *Accident: A Philosophical and Literary History*. Chicago, IL: University of Chicago Press, 2008.

Harde, Roxanne, and Lydia Kokkola, Editors. *Eleanor H. Porter's Pollyanna: A Children's Classic at 100*. Jackson, MS: University Press of Mississippi, 2014.

Harrington, Ralph. "The Railway Accident: Trains, Trauma, and Technological Crises in Nineteenth-Century Britain." In *Traumatic Pasts: History, Psychiatry, and Trauma in the Modern Age, 1870–1930*. Edited by Mark S. Micale and Paul Lerner. London: Cambridge University Press, 2001.

Hartman, James D. *Providence Tales and the Birth of American Literature*. Baltimore, MD: Johns Hopkins University Press, 1999.

Heise, Ursula K. *Sense of Place and Sense of Planet: The Environmental Imagination of the Global*. Oxford, UK: Oxford University Press, 2008.

Heise, Ursula, Jon Christensen, and Michelle Niemann, Editors. *The Routledge Companion to the Environmental Humanities*. New York: Routledge, 2016.

Hewitt, Elizabeth. "The Vexed Story of Economic Criticism." *American Literary History* 21, no. 3 (2009): 618–32.

Higgens-Everson, R. Rudy. "From Industrial Police to Workmen's Compensation: Public Policy and Industrial Accidents in New York, 1880–1910." *Labor History* 39 no. 4 (November 1998): 365.

Hill, Marc Lamont, and Todd Brewster. *Nobody: Casualties of America's War on the Vulnerable, from Ferguson to Flint and Beyond*. New York: Atria Books, 2016.

Hiro, Molly. "How It Feels to Be without a Face: Race and the Reorientation of Sympathy in the 1890s." *Novel: A Forum on Fiction* 39, no. 2 (2006): 179–203.

Hirsch, Marianne. "Vulnerable Times." In *Vulnerability in Resistance*. Edited by Judith Butler, Zeynep Gambetti, and Leticia Sabsay. Durham, NC: Duke University Press, 2016.

Hobsbawm, Eric. *The Age of Extremes: A History of the World, 1914–1991*. New York: Pantheon Books, 1995.

Hoeller, Hildegard. "Herland and Hisland: Illness and 'Health' in the Writings of Charlotte Perkins Gilman and Theodore Dreiser." *Dreiser Studies* 34, no. 2 (Winter 2003): 24–43.

Hoffman, Frederick L. *History of the Prudential Insurance Company of America*. Newark NJ: Prudential Press, 1900.

———. *Race Traits and Tendencies of the American Negro*. New York: Macmillan, 1896.

Holden, Edward S. "Earthquakes and How to Measure Them." *Century Magazine* 24, no. 7 (1894): 749–59.

Hollibaugh, Lisa. "'The Civilized Uses of Irony': Darwinism, Calvinism, and Motherhood in Ellen Glasgow's *Barren Ground*." *The Mississippi Quarterly* 59, no. 1/2 (Winter 2006): 31–63.

Homestead, Melissa, and Pamela Washington, Editors. *E. D. E. N. Southworth: Recovering a Nineteenth-Century Popular Novelist*. Knoxville, TN: University of Tennessee Press, 2012.

Hones, Sheila. "Distant Disasters, Local Fears: Volcanoes, Earthquakes, Revolution, and Passion in *The Atlantic Monthly*, 1880–84." In *American Disasters*. Edited by Steven Biel. 180–96, New York: New York University Press, 2001.

Horowitz, Helen Lefkowitz. "Victoria Woodhull, Anthony Comstock, and Conflict Over Sex in the United States in the 1870s." *The Journal of American History* 87, no. 2 (2000): 403–34.

Horwitz, Morton. *The Transformation of American Law, 1780–1860*. Cambridge, MA: Harvard University Press, 1977.

Houser, Heather. *Ecosickness in Contemporary U.S. Fiction: Environment and Affect*. New York: Columbia University Press, 2014.

Huddock, Amy E. "Challenging the Definition of Heroism in E. D. E. N. Southworth's *The Hidden Hand*." *American Transcendental Quarterly* 9, no. 1 (1995): 5–20.

Huet, Marie-Hélène. *The Culture of Disaster*. Chicago, IL: University of Chicago Press, 2012.

Ings, Katherine Nicholson. "Blackness and the Literary Imagination: Uncovering *The Hidden Hand*." In *Passing and the Fictions of Identity*. Edited by Elaine K. Ginsberg. Durham, NC: Duke University Press, 1996.

Ip, Greg. *Foolproof: Why Safety Can Be Dangerous and How Danger Makes Us Safe*. New York: Little, Brown and Company, 2015.

James, William. "On Some Mental Effects of The Earthquake." In *Writings, 1902–1910*. New York: Library of America, 1987.

Jones, Paul Christian. "Burning Mrs. Southworth: True Womanhood and the Intertext of Ellen Glasgow's 'Virginia.'" *Southern Literary Journal* 37, no. 1 (Fall 2004): 25–40.

———. "'This Dainty Woman's Hand . . . Red with Blood': E. D. E. N. Southworth's *The Hidden Hand* as Abolitionist Narrative." *American Transcendental Quarterly* 15, no. 1 (2001): 59–80.

Jordan, David Starr, Editor. *The California Earthquake of 1906*. San Francisco, CA: A.M. Robertson, 1907.

Kalsem, Kristin. *In Contempt: Nineteenth-Century Women, Law, and Literature*. Columbus, OH: Ohio State University Press, 2012.

Kendi, Ibram X. "A History of Race and Racism in America in 24 Chapters." *The New York Times*, February 22, 2017. https://www.nytimes.com/2017/02/22/books/review/a-history-of-race-and-racism-in-america-in-24-chapters.html?_r=0

———. *Stamped from the Beginning: The Definitive History of Racist Ideas in America*. Washington, DC: Nation Books, 2016.

Kernan, Frank J. *Reminiscences of the Old Fire Laddies And Volunteer Fire Departments of New York and Brooklyn: Together with a Complete History of the Paid Departments of Both Cities*. New York: M. Crane, 1885.

Kilmer, Paulette D. "*The New York Times* Accident Stories: Sensational Coverage Warns of Consequences." In *Sensationalism: Murder, Mayhem, Mudslinging, Scandals, and Disasters in Nineteenth-Century Reporting*. Edited by David B. Sachsman and David W. Bulla. New Brunswick, NJ: Transaction Publishers, 2013.

Kirby, Lynn. *Parallel Tracks: The Railroad and the Silent Cinema*. Durham, NC: Duke University Press, 1997.

Klein, Naomi. *The Shock Doctrine: The Rise of Disaster Capitalism*. New York: Knopf, 2007.

———. *This Changes Everything: Capitalism vs. The Climate*. New York: Simon & Schuster, 2015.

Krüger, Fred, Greg Bankoff, Terry Cannon, Benedikt Orlowski, and E. Lisa F. Schipper, Editors. *Cultures and Disasters: Understanding Cultural Framings in Disaster Risk Reduction*. London, UK: Routledge, 2015.

Lacey, Mark J. *Security, Technology and Global Politics: Thinking with Virilio*. New York: Routledge Press, 2014.

Lamey, H. T. *Side Lights*. Denver, CO: McIntyre Publisher, 1906.

Landry, H. Jordan. "Of Tricks, Tropes, and Trollops: Revisions to the Seduction Novel in E. D. E. N. Southworth's *The Hidden Hand*". *Journal of the Midwest Modern Language Association* 38, no. 2 (2005): 31–44.

Laski, Gregory. "'No Reparation': Accounting for the Enduring Harms of Slavery in Stephen Crane's "The Monster." *J19: The Journal of Nineteenth-Century Americanists* 1, no. 1 (2013): 37–69.

Lee, Maurice S. *Uncertain Chances: Science, Skepticism, and Belief in Nineteenth-Century American Literature*. New York: Oxford University Press, 2013.

Leikam, Susanne. "'Transnational Tales' of Risk and Coping: Disaster Narratives in Late Nineteenth and Early Twentieth Century San Francisco." *Transnational American Studies*. Conference Proceedings of the Annual Meeting of the German Association of American Studies 2011, Regensburg. Ed. Udo Hebel. Heidelberg: Winter, 467–87.

Lelekis, Debbie. *American Literature, Lynching, and the Spectator in the Crowd: Spectacular Violence*. Lanham, MD: Lexington Books, 2015.

Levy, Jonathan. *Freaks of Fortune: The Emerging World of Capitalism and Risk in America*. Cambridge, MA: Harvard University Press, 2012.

———."The Ways of Providence: Capitalism, Risk, and Freedom." Ph.D. Dissertation. University of Chicago, 2008.

Lipartito, Kenneth. "*Prophet of Innovation: Joseph Schumpeter and Creative Destruction* by Thomas K. McCraw" (book review). *Journal of Interdisciplinary History* 39, no. 1 (Summer 2008): 151–52.

Loewenstein, Antony. *Disaster Capitalism: Making a Killing Out of Catastrophe*. New York: Verso, 2015.

Looby, Christopher. "Southworth and Seriality: *The Hidden Hand* in the *New York Ledger*." *Nineteenth-Century Literature* 59, no. 2 (2004): 179–211.

London, Jack. "The Story of an Eyewitness." *Collier's*, May 5, 1905. https://www.parks.ca.gov/?page_id=24206

Loving, Jerome. *The Last Titan: A Life of Theodore Dreiser*. Berkeley, CA: University of California Press, 2005.

Luciano, Dana. "The Gothic Meets Sensation: Charles Brockden Brown, Edgar Allen Poe, George Lippard and E. D. E. N. Southworth." 314–29. *A Companion to American Fiction: 1780–1865*. Edited by Shirley Samuels, Oxford, UK: Blackwell, 2006.

Luckhurst, Roger. *The Trauma Question*. New York: Routledge, 2008.

Luhmann, Niklas, and Nico Stehr. *Risk: A Sociological Theory*. Translated by Rhodes Barrett. New Brunswick, NJ: Aldine Transaction, 2005.

Lutes, Jean Marie. *Front-Page Girls: Women Journalists in American Culture and Fiction, 1880–1930*. Ithaca, NY: Cornell University Press, 2006.

———. "Lynching Coverage and the American Reporter-Novelist." *American Literary History* 19, no. 2 (2007): 456–81.

Lutz, Tom. *American Nervousness, 1903: An Anecdotal History*. Ithaca, NY: Cornell University Press, 1990.

Lyman, Henry M. "Nervous Disorders in America." *The Dial*, no. 2 (1881): 81–82.

Lyons, Paul. *American Pacificism: Oceania in the U.S. Imagination*. New York: Routledge, 2006.

Mackenzie, Catriona, Wendy Rogers, and Susan Dodds, Editors. *Vulnerability: New Essays in Ethics and Feminist Philosophy*. New York: Oxford University Press, 2013.

Macpherson, Sandra. *Harm's Way: Tragic Responsibility and the Novel Form*. Baltimore, MD: Johns Hopkins University Press, 2009.

Malin, Brenton J. *Feeling Mediated: A History of Media Technology and Emotion in America*. New York: New York University Press, 2014.

Mangham, Andrew, Editor. *The Cambridge Companion to Sensation Fiction*. Cambridge, UK: Cambridge University Press, 2013.

Marks, G. H. *Reminiscence and Lessons of the San Francisco Conflagration 18–21, April 1906: A Paper Read Before Members of the Birmingham Insurance Institute on February 26, 1909*. New York: Edgar C. Ruwe Co. Inc., 1909.

Marx, Leo. *The Machine in the Garden: Technology and the Pastoral Ideal in America*. New York: Oxford University Press, 1964.
Matus, Jill. "Emergent Theories of Victorian Mind Shock: From War and Railway Accident to Nerves, Electricity and Emotion." In *Neurology and Literature, 1860–1920*. Edited by Anne Stiles, 163–83. Palgrave Studies in Nineteenth-Century Writing and Culture. Palgrave Macmillan UK, 2007.
Mayou, Richard A. "Accident Neurosis Revisited [Editorial]." *British Journal of Psychiatry* 168, no. 4 (1996): 399–403.
McCoy, Marina Berzins. *Wounded Heroes: Vulnerability as a Virtue in Ancient Greek Literature and Philosophy*. Oxford, UK: Oxford University Press, 2013.
McWilliams, John C. "'Men of Color': Race, Riots, and Black Firefighters' Struggle for Equality from the AFA to the Valiants." *Journal of Social History* (Fall 2007): 105–25.
Mecklenburg, Virginia M., Robert W. Snyder, and Rebecca Zurier. *Metropolitan Lives: The Ashcan Artists and Their New York, 1897–1917*. New York: W. W. Norton & Company, 1996.
Meighen, J. F. D. "May Damages be Recovered for Physical Injuries Resulting from Fright Cases?" *The Central Law Journal* (1901): 339–52.
Mendelson, Denuta. *Interfaces of Medicine and Law*. Brookfield, VT: Ashgate, 1998.
Merchant, Carolyn. *The Columbia Guide to American Environmental History*. New York: Columbia University Press, 2005.
Meyerowitz, Joel. *Aftermath: World Trade Center Archive*. New York: Phaidon Press, 2006.
Micale, Mark S. *Hysterical Men: The Hidden History of Male Nervous Illness*. Cambridge, MA: Harvard University Press, 2008.
Miller, Ross. *American Apocalypse: The Great Fire and the Myth of Chicago*. Chicago, IL: University of Chicago Press, 1990.
Miller, Shawn E. "Desire and Materiality in Ellen Glasgow's *Barren Ground*." *Mississippi Quarterly: The Journal of Southern Cultures* 63, no. 1–2 (Winter–Spring 2010): 79–99.
Mohun, Arwen P. *Risk: Negotiating Safety in American Society*. Baltimore, MD: Johns Hopkins University Press, 2012.
Monod, David. *The Soul of Pleasure: Sentiment and Sensation in Nineteenth-Century American Mass Entertainment*. Ithaca, NY: Cornell University Press, 2016.
Moody, John. *How to Analyze Railroad Reports*. New York: Analyses Publishing, 1912.
———. *Moody's Manual of Railroads and Corporate Securities*. New York: O. C. Lewis Company, 1900.
Morris, Charles. *Decisive Events in the Story of the Great Republic: Or, Half-Hours with American History*. Pennsylvania Publishing Company, 1892.
———. *The San Francisco Calamity by Earthquake and Fire: A Complete and Accurate Account of the Fearful Disaster Which Visited the Great City and the Pacific Coast, the Reign of Panic and Lawlessness, the Plight of 300,000 Homeless People and the World-Wide Rush to the Rescue*. J. C. Winston, 1906.
———. *The Volcano's Deadly Work: From the Fall of Pompeii to the Destruction of St. Pierre . . . a Vivid and Accurate Story of the Awful Calamity Which Visited the Islands of Martinique and St. Vincent, May 8, 1902, as Told by Eye-Witnesses and by Our Special Representative, General Samuel A. McAlister*. W. E. Scull, 1902.
Morton, Timothy. *The Ecological Thought*. Cambridge, MA: Harvard University Press, 2010.
Motley, Warren. *The American Abraham: James Fenimore Cooper and the Frontier Patriarch*. Cambridge, UK: Cambridge University Press, 1987.
Murison, Justine S. *The Politics of Anxiety in Nineteenth-Century American Literature*. Cambridge, UK: Cambridge University Press, 2013.
Murphy, Sharon Ann. *Investing in Life: Insurance in Antebellum America*. Baltimore, MD: Johns Hopkins University Press, 2013.
———. "Securing Human Property: Slavery, Life Insurance, and Industrialization in the Upper South." *Journal of the Early Republic* 25, no. 4 (2005): 615–52.

Myers, Jeffrey. *Converging Stories: Race, Ecology, and Environmental Justice in American Literature*. Athens, GA: University of Georgia Press, 2005.

Naito, Jonathan Tadashi. "Cruel and Unusual Light: Electricity and Effacement in Stephen Crane's 'The Monster.'" *Arizona Quarterly: A Journal of American Literature, Culture, and Theory* 62, no. 1 (2006): 35–63.

Nancy, Jean-Luc. *After Fukushima: The Equivalence of Catastrophes*. Translated by Charlotte Mandell. New York: Fordham University Press, 2014.

Nelson, Nell. "In an Engine Car: Nell Nelson's Midnight Ride on the Washington Express." *The New York World*, Sunday January 5, 1890, 9.

"Neurasthenia, the Result of Nervous Shock, as a Ground for Damages." *Central Law Journal* 59 (1904): 83–89.

Newitz, Annalee. *Pretend We're Dead: Capitalist Monsters in American Pop Culture*. Durham, NC: Duke University Press Books, 2006.

Ngai, Sianne. *Ugly Feelings*. Cambridge, MA: Harvard University Press, 2007.

Nixon, Rob. *Slow Violence and the Environmentalism of the Poor*. Cambridge, MA: Harvard University Press, 2013.

Nobisso, Josephine. *John Blair and the Great Hinckley Fire*. Illustrated by Ted Rose. Boston: Houghton Mifflin, 2000.

Norton, Peter D. *Fighting Traffic: The Dawn of the Motor Age in the American City*. Cambridge, MA: MIT Press, 2008.

Nostwich, T. C. "Historical Commentary." In *Theodore Dreiser Journalism: Newspaper Writings, 1892–1895*. Volume I. Philadelphia, PA: University of Pennsylvania Press, 1988.

Novak, William J. *The People's Welfare: Law and Regulation in Nineteenth-Century America*. Chapel Hill, NC: University of North Carolina Press, 1996.

O'Brien, Tim. *The Things They Carried*. New York: Houghton Mifflin Harcourt, 1990.

Okker, Patricia. "'Reassuring Sounds': Minstrelsy and *The Hidden Hand*." *American Transcendental Quarterly* 12, no. 2 (1998): 133–44.

Oldfield, John. "State Politics, Railroads, and Civil Rights in South Carolina, 1883–89." *American Nineteenth Century History* 5, no. 2 (July 2004): 71–91.

Oliver and Wife v. The Town of La Valle (1875), 36 Wisc., 592; 1875 Wisc. LEXIS 13.

Oppenheim, Herbert. *Textbook of Nervous Diseases*. Edinburgh: T. N. Foulis, 1911.

Orvell, Miles. "After 9/11: Photography, the Destructive Sublime, and the Postmodern Archive." *Michigan Quarterly Review* 45, no. 2 (Spring 2006). https://quod.lib.umich.edu/cgi/t/text/text-idx?cc=mqr;c=mqr;c=mqrarchive;idno=act2080.0045.201;g=mqrg;rgn=main;view=text;xc=1

Otis, Laura Christine. *Networking: Communicating with Bodies and Machines in the Nineteenth Century*. Ann Arbor, MI: University of Michigan Press, 2011.

Packer, Jeremy. *Mobility without Mayhem: Safety, Cars, and Citizenship*. Durham, NC: Duke University Press Books, 2008.

Page, Herbert. *Injuries of the Spine and Spinal Cord and Nervous Shock*. Philadelphia, PA: Blakiston, 1885.

Palmer, Lew R. "History of the Safety Movement." *The Annals of the American Academy of Political and Social Science* 123 (1926): 9–19.

Palmer, Stephanie C. *Together by Accident: American Local Color Literature and the Middle Class*. Lanham, MD: Lexington Books, 2008.

Parker, Andrew, Austin Sarat, and Martha Merrill Umphrey, Editors. *Subjects of Responsibility: Framing Personhood in Modern Bureaucracies*. New York: Fordham University Press, 2011.

Peters, M. Sheffy. "Danger Ahead!" In *Godey's Lady's Book*. Edited by J. H. Haulenbeek, 470–47. Volume CVIII (January–June 1884). Philadelphia, PA: J. H. Haulenbeek & Co.

Pettegrew, John. *Brutes in Suits: Male Sensibility in America, 1890–1920*. Baltimore, MD: Johns Hopkins University Press, 2007.

Pizer, Donald. "Late Nineteenth Century American Literary Naturalism: A Reintroduction." *American Literary Realism* 38 (2006): 189–202.

Porter, Eleanor H. *Pollyanna*. Boston: The Page Company Publishers, 1913.

Powers, Michael. *Acts of God and Man: Ruminations on Risk and Insurance*. New York: Columbia University Press, 2011.

Pratt, Lloyd. *Archives of American Time: Literature and Modernity in the Nineteenth Century*. Philadelphia, PA: University of Pennsylvania Press, 2016.

Previts, Gary John, and Barbara Dubis Merino. *A History of Accounting in America: A Historical Interpretation of the Cultural Significance of Accounting*. New York: John Wiley & Sons Inc., 1979.

Prout, H. G. "Safety in Railroad Travel." *Scribner's Magazine* 6, no. 3 (1889): 327–51.

Purcell v. St. Paul City R. Co. (1892) 1892 48 Minn. 134, 50 N. W. Rep 1034; 1892 Minn. LEXIS 386.

Puskar, Jason. *Accident Society: Fiction, Collectivity, and the Production of Chance*. Stanford, CA: Stanford University Press, 2012.

Recuber, Timothy. *Consuming Catastrophe: Mass Culture in America's Decade of Disaster*. Philadelphia, PA: Temple University Press, 2016.

Reichman, Ravit. *The Affective Life of Law: Legal Modernism and the Literary Imagination*. Stanford, CA: Stanford Law Books, 2009.

Rhode, Deborah L. *Justice and Gender: Sex Discrimination and the Law*. Cambridge, MA: Harvard University Press, 1989.

Richter, Amy G. *Home on the Rails: Women, the Railroad, and the Rise of Public Domesticity*. Chapel Hill, NC: University of North Carolina Press, 2005.

Riggio, Thomas P. "Dreiser and the Uses of Biography." In *The Cambridge Companion to Theodore Dreiser*. Edited by Leonard Cassuto and Clare Virginia Eby. Cambridge, UK: Cambridge University Press, 2004.

Riis, Jacob A. "Heroes Who Fight Fire." *The Century Magazine*, February 1898: 483–97.

Ritzenberg, Aaron. *The Sentimental Touch: The Language of Feeling in the Age of Managerialism*. New York: Fordham University Press, 2012.

Robertson, Michael. *Stephen Crane, Journalism, and the Making of Modern American Literature*. New York: Columbia University Press, 1997.

Rogers, Donald W. *Making Capitalism Safe: Workplace Safety and Health Regulation in America, 1880–1940*. Urbana, IL: University of Illinois Press, 2009.

Rosenthal, Lecia. *Mourning Modernism: Literature, Catastrophe, and the Politics of Consolation*. New York: Fordham University Press, 2011.

Rowlandson, Thomas. *Treatise on Earthquake Dangers Causes and Palliatives*. San Francisco, CA: Dewey & Co, 1869.

Rozario, Kevin. *The Culture of Calamity: Disaster and the Making of Modern America*. Chicago, IL: University of Chicago Press, 2007.

Sachsman, David B., and David W. Bulla, Editors. *Sensationalism: Murder, Mayhem, Mudslinging, Scandals, and Disasters in Nineteenth-Century Reporting*. New Brunswick, NJ: Transaction Publishers, 2013.

Sarat, Austin, Editor. *Catastrophe: Law, Politics, and the Humanitarian Impulse*. Amherst, MA: University of Massachusetts Press, 2009.

Scharff, Virginia. *Taking the Wheel: Women and the Coming of the Motor Age*. New York: Free Press, 1991.

———. *Twenty Thousand Roads: Women, Movement, and the West*. Berkeley: University of California Press, 2002.

Schivelbusch, Wolfgang. *The Railway Journey: The Industrialization of Time and Space in the 19th Century*. Berkeley, CA: University of California Press, 1977.

Schlanger, Margo. "Injured Women before Common Law Courts, 1860–1930." *Harvard Women's Law Journal* 79 (1998): 79–140.

Schnapp, Jeffrey T. "Crash (Speed as Engine of Individuation)." *Modernism/Modernity* 6, no. 1 (January 1999): 1–49.

Schumpeter, Joseph. *Can Capitalism Survive?: Creative Destruction and the Future of the Global Economy*. New York: Harper Perennial Modern Classics, 2009.

———. *Capitalism, Socialism and Democracy*. 5th Revised edition. London, UK: Routledge, 1994.

Schweik, Susan. "Disability Politics and American Literary History: Some Suggestions." *American Literary History* 20, no. 1–2 (Spring–Summer 2008): 217–37.

———. *The Ugly Laws: Disability in Public*. New York: New York University Press, 2010.

Sears, Clare. *Arresting Dress: Cross-Dressing, Law, and Fascination in Nineteenth-Century San Francisco*. Durham, NC: Duke University Press Books, 2014.

Seiler, Cotten. *Republic of Drivers: A Cultural History of Automobility in America*. Chicago, IL: University of Chicago Press, 2008.

Seltzer, Mark. *Bodies and Machines*. New York: Routledge, 2014.

———. *Serial Killers: Death and Life in America's Wound Culture*. New York: Routledge, 1998.

Shaler, N. S. "The Floods of the Mississippi Valley." *Atlantic Monthly*, May 1883, 647.

Shockley, Evie. "The Haunted Houses of New Orleans: Gothic Homelessness and African American Experience." In *Katrina's Imprint: Race and Vulnerability in America*. Edited by Keith Wailoo, Karen M. O'Neill, Jeffrey Dowd, and Roland Anglin, 95–114. New Brunswick, NJ: Rutgers University Press, 2010.

Shrady, Nicholas. *The Last Day: Wrath, Ruin, and Reason in the Great Lisbon Earthquake of 1755*. New York: Penguin Books, 2009.

Shulman, George. "On Vulnerability as Judith Butler's Language of Politics: From *Excitable Speech* to *Precarious Life*." *Safe:* Volume 39, nos. 1&2 Spring/Summer 2011, 227–35. New York: The Feminist Press, CUNY, 2011.

Simmel, George. "The Metropolis and Mental Life." In *Simmel on Culture: Selected Writings*. Edited by David Frisby and Mike Featherstone. London, UK: Sage, 1997.

Singer, Ben. *Melodrama and Modernity*. New York: Columbia University Press, 2001.

Slotkin, Richard. *Regeneration through Violence: The Mythology of the American Frontier, 1600–1860*. Middletown, CT: Wesleyan University Press, 1973.

Smith, Kimberly K. *African American Environmental Thought: Foundations*. Lawrence, KS: University Press of Kansas, 2007.

Smith, Sidonie. *Moving Lives: Twentieth-Century Women's Travel Writing*. Minneapolis, MN: University of Minnesota Press, 2001.

Solnit, Rebecca. *A Paradise Built in Hell: The Extraordinary Communities that Arise in Disaster*. New York: Viking, 2009.

Sorrentino, Paul. *Stephen Crane: A Life of Fire*. Cambridge, MA: Harvard University Press, 2014.

Southworth. E. D. E. N. *The Hidden Hand*. New York: Oxford University Press, 1997.

———. *Ishmael: Or, in the Depths*. New York: Grosset & Dunlap, 1884.

Spofford, Harriet P. "The Black Bess." *Galaxy* 5 (1868): 517–28.

Squires, Gregory, and Chester Hartman, Editors. *There Is No Such Thing as a Natural Disaster: Race, Class, and Hurricane Katrina*. New York: Routledge, 2006.

Stallman, R. W., and E. R. Hagermann, Editors. *The New York City Sketches of Stephen Crane and Related Pieces*. New York: New York University Press, 1966.

"Statistics of Fires for 1894." *Proceedings of the Twenty-Ninth Annual Meeting of The National Board of Fire Underwriters*. New York: Styles and Cash, 1895.

Steadman, Jennifer Bernhardt. *Traveling Economies: American Women's Travel Writing*. Columbus, OH: Ohio State University Press, 2007.

Steinberg, Ted. *Acts of God: The Unnatural History of Natural Disaster in America*. New York: Oxford University Press, 2006.

Stiles, A., Editor. *Neurology and Literature, 1860–1920*. New York: Palgrave Macmillan, 2007.

Stoler, Ann Laura. *Along the Archival Grain: Epistemic Anxieties and Colonial Common Sense*. Princeton, NJ: Princeton University Press, 2009.

Streeby, Shelley. *American Sensations: Class, Empire, and the Production of Popular Culture*. Berkeley, CA: University of California Press, 2002.

Tebeau, Mark. *Eating Smoke*. Baltimore, MD: Johns Hopkins University Press, 2013.

"The Horrors of Travel." *Harper's Weekly. A Journal of Civilization* 9, no. 456 (1865): 594.

Thompson, Clive. "When Pedestrians Ruled the Streets." *Smithsonian*. Accessed May 31, 2017. http://www.smithsonianmag.com/innovation/when-pedestrians-ruled-streets-180953396/
Thomson, Rosemarie Garland. *Extraordinary Bodies*. New York: Columbia University Press, 1997.
Tibbets, Flora V. Woodward. "Neurasthenia, The Result of Nervous Shock, As A Ground for Damages." *Central Law Journal* 59 (1904): 83–86.
Travis, Jennifer. *Wounded Hearts: Masculinity, Law, and Literature in American Culture*. Chapel Hill, NC: University of North Carolina Press, 2005.
Twain, Mark. "The Great Earthquake in San Francisco." *New York Weekly Review*, November 25, 1865.
Urry, John. *Mobilities*. Cambridge, UK: Polity Press, 2007.
Virilio, Paul. *The Original Accident*. Cambridge, UK: Polity, 2007.
Vose, George L. "Safety in Railway Travel." *The North American Review* 135, no. 4 (October 1882): 374.
Wajcman, Judy. *Pressed for Time: The Acceleration of Life in Digital Capitalism*. Chicago, IL: University of Chicago Press, 2015.
Wailoo, Keith, Karen M. O'Neill, Jeffrey Dowd, and Roland Anglin, Editors. *Katrina's Imprint*. New Brunswick, NJ: Rutgers University Press, 2010.
Walker, Rafael. "The Bildungsroman after Individualism: Ellen Glasgow's Communitarian Alternative." *Genre* 49, no. 3 (December 1, 2016): 385–405.
Warren, Joyce W. *Women, Money, and the Law: Nineteenth-Century Fiction, Gender, and the Courts*. Iowa City, IA: University of Iowa Press, 2005.
Weed, Samuel Richard. "My Early Experience and Recollections of the Great Fires and the First Fire Department in San Francisco. Paper, Prepared by Request for the Annual Meeting of the Pacific Coast Underwriters' Association in San Francisco, January 14, 1908." The Churchill Collection, Kathryn and Shelby Cullom Davis Library, St. John's University.
Weinstein, Cindy. "'What Did You Mean?': Marriage in E. D. E. N. Southworth's Novels." *Legacy: A Journal of American Women Writers* 27, no. 1 (2010): 43–60.
Welke, Barbara Young. *Law and the Borders of Belonging in the Long Nineteenth Century United States*. New York: Cambridge University Press, 2010.
———. *Recasting American Liberty: Gender, Race, Law, and the Railroad Revolution, 1865–1920*. Cambridge, UK: Cambridge University Press, 2001.
Wertheimer, Eric. *Underwriting: The Poetics of Insurance in America, 1722–1872*. Stanford, CA: Stanford University Press, 2006.
Wesley, Marilyn C. *Secret Journeys: The Trope of Women's Travel in American Literature*. Albany, NY: State University of New York Press, 1998.
White, G. Edward. *Tort Law in America: An Intellectual History*. Oxford: Oxford University Press, 1980.
White, Richard. *Railroaded: The Transcontinentals and the Making of Modern America*. New York: W. W. Norton & Company, 2011.
Wiebe, Robert H. *The Search for Order: 1877–1920*. New York: Hill and Wang, 1967.
Williams, Raymond. *Keywords: Vocabulary of Culture and Society*. New York: Oxford University Press, 1985.
Williams, William Carlos. "The Young Housewife." In *The Collected Poems of William Carlos Williams: 1909–1939*. Volume 1. Edited by A. Walton Litz and Christopher MacGowan. San Francisco, CA: New Directions 1986.
Wilson, Christopher P. *Labor of Words: Literary Professionalism in the Progressive Era*. Athens, GA: University of Georgia Press, 1985.
Winchester, Simon. *A Crack in the Edge of the World: America and the Great California Earthquake of 1906*. New York: Harper, 2005.
Winseck, Dwayne R., and Robert M. Pike. *Communication and Empire: Media, Markets, and Globalization, 1860–1930*. Durham, NC: Duke University Press, 2007.
Witt, John Fabian. *The Accidental Republic: Crippled Workingmen, Destitute Widows, and the Remaking of American Law*. Cambridge, MA: Harvard University Press, 2006.

———. "From Loss of Services to Loss of Support: The Wrongful Death Statutes, the Origins of Modern Tort Law, and the Making of the Nineteenth-Century Family." *Law and Social Inquiry* (2000): 717–55.

———. "Toward A New History of American Accident Law: Classical Tort Law and the Cooperative First-Party Insurance Movement." *Harvard Law Review* 114, no. 3 (January 2001): 690.

Wolff, Megan J. "The Myth of The Actuary: Life Insurance and Frederick L. Hoffman's *Race Traits and Tendencies of The American Negro*." *Public Health Reports* 121, no. 1 (2006): 84–91.

———. "The Money Value of Risk: Life Insurance and the Transformation of American Public Health, 1896–1930." Ph.D. Dissertation. Columbia University, 2011.

Woodward, Kathleen. *Statistical Panic: Cultural Politics and Poetics of the Emotions*. Durham, NC: Duke University Press Books, 2009.

Yablon, Nick. "The Metropolitan Life in Ruins: Architectural and Fictional Speculations in New York, 1909–19." *American Quarterly* 56, no. 2 (2004): 308–47.

———. *Untimely Ruins: An Archaeology of American Urban Modernity, 1819–1919*. Chicago, IL: University of Chicago Press, 2009.

Yates, JoAnne. *Structuring the Information Age: Life Insurance and Technology in the Twentieth Century*. Baltimore, MD: Johns Hopkins University Press, 2008.

Young, Elizabeth. *Black Frankenstein: The Making of an American Metaphor*. New York: New York University Press, 2008.

Zelizer, Viviana A. *Economic Lives: How Culture Shapes the Economy*. Princeton, NJ: Princeton University Press, 2010.

Zimmerman, David A. *Panic! Markets, Crises, and Crowds in American Fiction*. Chapel Hill, NC: University of North Carolina Press, 2006.

Zimring, Carl A. *Clean and White: A History of Environmental Racism in the United States*. New York: New York University Press, 2016.

Žižek, Slavoj. *Living in the End Times*. London, UK: Verso, 2010.

Index

ability, xii, 13, 45, 73–74, 86, 127, 133; for improvement, 8, 11; of men, 52, 72, 82; of women, 31, 39, 58
accident cosmology, 33, 75
accidents, 7, 33, 39, 41n14–41n15, 84–85; in *Barren Ground*, 61–63, 65n21; in "The Black Bess," 47–48; of Day (doctor), 34–35; in Dreiser, 68–69, 79, 84–85; fear of, 46, 53, 76; industrial, 23, 75, 77; miscarriages with, 61–62; in nineteenth century, 7, 9–10, 13, 21, 23; in *Pollyanna*, 57, 60; with railroads, 23, 32, 41n14, 53–55, 68–71, 72, 75–77; in Southworth, 23, 32–33, 34–35, 37, 39
accountability, 34
accounting, 13, 79, 80, 82–83, 86, 125
adaptation, 58, 60, 74, 99, 128
advocate, for women, 26–27
The Affective Life of Law (Reichman), 56
agency, xii, 30, 44, 46, 56, 63; ecological, 14, 120; female, 12, 27, 38; political, 3, 8; vulnerability and, 9, 11
Alcott, Louisa May, 20, 30, 41n10
Aldrich, Mark, 32
An Amateur Laborer (Dreiser), 70–71, 72–73, 78–79, 85, 86
American capitalism, 98
The American Fireman, 102
American Nervousness (Beard), 74
American Pacificism (Lyons), 2
American Safety Museum, 86, 89n23
The Anatomy of a Railroad Report (Woodlock), 82
"Anne" (Davis), 55–56
archive, 33, 120, 127, 130, 132, 134n4; disaster archive, 120, 134n4; morbid archive, 120, 134n4
Atherton, Gertrude, 126
Austin, Mary Hunter, 130–133

automobility, 44, 46, 57, 58–59, 60
autonomy, 11–12, 36, 37, 55

Baldwin, James, 110
Barren Ground (Glasgow), 60, 61–63
Beard, George Miller, 74
Beck, Ulrich, 6
Benjamin, Walter, 20, 23
Bentley, Nancy, 45
Betts, Bob, 1, 2
Between the World and Me (Coates), 14
bias, of court, 25–26
Biers, Katherine, 45, 111
Black, Capitola, 12, 19, 32, 33, 36–37, 39, 40; Black, D. and, 29–30; in court, 22, 24–25; domestic security fantasy of, 27–28; gender issues of, 21, 25, 39; in Hurricane Hall, 27–28; Old Hurricane and, 19, 25, 27–29, 30, 31; slavery of, 21, 29, 40n9; vulnerability of, 21, 24–25, 39
"The Black Bess" (Spofford), 47; accident of, 47–48; engineer of, 46, 48–49, 51; engine trouble in, 46–56, 64n8; Margaret in, 47–48, 50, 51–52; metaphor of, 46; narrative of, 47–48
Black Donald, 29–30
Black Frankenstein (Young), 113
boosterature, 95
Bouk, Dan, 105–106
Bourke, Joanna, 121
Breuer, Josef, 75
Brown, Bill, 45, 68, 97
"Burned to Death" (Dreiser), 68–69
Butler, Judith, 5, 9, 52
By Accident or Design (Fyfe), 68

The California Earthquake of 1906, 130
capitalism, 99; disaster, 98, 114n7, 118, 126; industrial, 14, 70–71;

technological, 97–98
Capitalism, Socialism, and Democracy (Schumpeter), 93
capitalist modernity, 20
catastrophes, 45, 100–101, 123, 126, 129; environmental, 7, 10, 14, 15, 108, 110, 113; Hurricane Katrina, 99–100, 104; narratives of, 23, 91, 95, 96, 97, 99, 118, 120, 121; San Francisco earthquake, 126–127, 132
catastrophic imaginary, of humanity, 5
catastrophic logic, of modernity, 7, 16n15, 99
Chamallas, Martha, 35–36
Chicago Fire, 93, 95, 123
children, traffic deaths of, 59
Chopin, Kate, 3, 9, 53–55
class, 13, 48, 55, 98, 103, 106, 125; middle-class white women, 20, 32, 44
Coates, Ta-Nehisi, 14, 96–97, 109–110
Coen, Deborah R., 118
Cole, Alyson, 8, 52–53
collective precariousness, 52
collective vulnerability, 5
collisions, 33
colonists, in *The Crater*, 1–3, 4–5
"The Comet" (Du Bois), 9–10, 108–109, 110, 113
compensation, economic, 13, 104
conflagration, 112–113, 123, 129–130; in Crane's work, 33, 91–93, 94, 95, 99–101, 113n1; narratives of, 10, 33, 45, 91, 93–94, 95, 96, 99, 101, 102, 104–105, 110
constitutive vulnerability, 8
Cooper, James Fenimore, 44, 86, 119. *See also The Crater*
cosmopolitan flotsam, 125, 132
court of law, 25–26, 27; Black, Capitola, in, 22, 24–25; Day, Clara, in, 25–26; fright and shock cases with, 37; New York Supreme Court, 33–34; reasonable man standard of, 35–36
Crane, Stephen, 3, 44, 62, 97, 105, 111; conflagrations in work of, 33, 91–93, 94, 95, 99–101, 113n1. *See also* "The Monster"
crash culture, 45, 46, 69

crash lit, 12, 46, 50, 53, 58, 60
The Crater, 3, 5, 8, 10, 15n2, 119, 121; Betts in, 1, 2; colonists in, 1–3, 4–5; egalitarian principles in, 2–3; "End of Days" in, 4, 15n6; environmental and societal danger in, 2–6; exploitive racial hierarchy in, 2–3; national prophesies of insecurity in, 3–4; naval disaster in, 1; plot of, 1–2; process of refusal in, 5; San Francisco earthquake in, 10, 14–15, 119–120, 133; savages in, 2–3, 4–5; slaves in, 3; survivors in, 1–2, 4–5; violence and racial terror in, 2; Woolston in, 1–2, 4, 6, 98
creative destruction, 14, 93–94, 96, 97–100, 114n3, 118, 124
Cult of True Victimhood (Cole), 52–53
cultural climate, of earthquakes, 119
cultural imaginary, 56, 74
cultural violence, 47
culture, 6, 10, 20, 67, 75, 76; crash, 45, 46, 69; industrial, of nineteenth century, 6, 74; speed with, 11, 56
The Culture of Disaster (Huet), 121
Currier & Ives, 100, 101–103; *The American Fireman*, 101; *The Darktown Fire Brigade*, 102; *Hook and Ladder Gymnastics*, 102; "The Life of a fireman," 100; *The Life of a Fireman*, 102; *The Rescue*, 102; *Taking a Rest*, 102

"Danger Ahead!" (Peters), 50
dangers, 45–46, 51, 56, 104–105; environmental, 2–6, 99, 104, 119; of railroads, 32, 52; safety and, 21, 22–23, 32; societal, 2–6
The Darktown Fire Brigade, 102
Darkwater (Du Bois), 108–109
The Daughter of a Magnate (Spearman), 49
Davis, Rebecca Harding, 3, 9, 12, 55–56
Day (doctor), 22, 33, 34–35, 36, 39
Day, Clara, 22, 30, 35, 41n16; in court, 25–26; in Hidden House, 28, 29, 32, 36
Death Rode the Rails (Aldrich), 32
deaths, 35, 39, 44, 59

democratization, 78, 124–125, 126
The Descendant (Glasgow), 60
The Deserted Wife (Southworth), 22
destruction, 93, 121–123, 124–129; creative, 14, 93–94, 96, 97–100, 114n3, 118, 124
Dickens, Charles, 76, 88n13
disability, 103–104
disaster capitalism, 98, 114n7, 118, 126
disasters, 1, 45, 91, 95, 96, 103; environmental, 3, 6, 98, 108; narratives of, 1, 7, 13, 15, 67, 69, 97, 98, 113; natural, 94, 98, 109, 120, 121–123, 132; railroad, 51, 67, 69, 70, 75
The Discarded Daughter (Southworth), 22
domestic insecurity, 28
domesticity, 49–50
domestic paternalism, 27
domestic violence, 20, 25
Dreiser, Theodore, xii, 3, 62, 78, 80, 86, 94–95; as journalist, 9, 13, 67, 87n4; railroad accidents and, 68–71, 72, 77; as railroad laborer, 70, 72–74, 88n11; in sanatorium, 71–72; Teddy relating to, 33, 71, 74, 79, 80, 81–82, 83–86, 87; on traumatic neurasthenia, 11, 70, 71, 72–73, 76. See also *An Amateur Laborer*; "The Mighty Burke"; "The Mighty Rourke"
Dublin, Louis I., 105
Du Bois, W. E. B., 9–10, 14, 96–97, 105, 107–110, 111, 113

Earthquake Commission, 130
Earthquake Observers (Coen), 118
earthquakes, 117–119, 119, 121, 130; in *The Crater*, 10, 14–15, 119–120, 133. See also San Francisco earthquake
"Earthquakes and How to Measure Them" (Holden), 117, 120
Eating Smoke (Tebeau), 94
ecological agency, 14, 120
ecological hazard, 13–14
ecological risk, 14
ecological thought, 109
economic compensation, 13, 104

economic progress, 14, 96
economic structure, of insurance companies, 105
economic vulnerability, 126
egalitarian principles, in *The Crater*, 2–3
emotional security, 21, 34
empowerment, 24
"End of Days," in *The Crater*, 4, 15n6
engineer, in "The Black Bess," 46, 48–49, 51
engine trouble, in "The Black Bess," 46–56, 64n8
environmental catastrophes, 7, 10, 14, 15, 108, 110, 113
environmental crisis, 7, 14
environmental dangers, 2–6, 99, 104, 119
environmental hazards, 10
environmental humanities, 9, 14–15
Erichsen, John Eric, 75
Ewald, François, 45, 105, 115n18

fear, 5, 31, 37, 87, 93, 119, 132; of accidents, 46, 53, 76; racial, 3, 30, 52, 106, 113
Fear (Bourke), 121
felt reports, 14, 118, 119, 121, 126, 128–131, 132–133
female agency, 12, 27, 38
female protagonists, of Southworth, 27
Fighting Traffic (Norton), 59
The Financier (Dreiser), 77
Fineman, Martha Albertson, 8–9, 11
"The Fire" (Dreiser), 94–95
firefighters, 94–96, 104, 111, 114n10; heroism of, 96, 100–103, 113; racism of, 102–103; volunteer, 102
The Fire Next Time (Baldwin), 110
fires: destruction of, 93–94; Great Chicago Fire, 93, 95, 123; in "The Monster," 103–104, 111; narratives of, 91–93; safety relating to, 104–105
fragility, 5, 16n9, 36, 52
Franklin, Benjamin, 101
Frantic Panoramas (Bentley), 45
Freemasons, 2, 78, 79–80, 83–84, 85
Freud, Sigmund, 75–76, 88n15
fright and shock, 75; court cases relating to, 37; in *The Hidden Hand*,

36–39; miscarriages caused by, 37–38, 41n21; physical injuries with, 37; vulnerabilities relating to, 38
Fyfe, Paul, 68

Gambetti, Zeynap, 9
gender, 21, 25, 36, 39, 46
gendered social relations, 53–55
The Genius (Dreiser), 78
Geographical Survey, 117–118
geographic mobility, 44
Geological Society, U.S., 118
Giddens, Anthony, 6
Gilded Age, 7
Glad game, 57, 58
Glasgow, Ellen, 3, 38, 60–63, 65n21
Glenn, Brian, 106
Godey's Lady's Book, 31, 50
gothic homelessness, 104, 106

harm, 35–36, 37, 50, 52–53, 56, 75, 77; capacity for, 11–12, 48; potential, 45, 85, 86; vulnerability to, 5, 7, 21, 34, 40
Harm's Way (Macpherson), 56
hazards, 10, 13–14, 21, 48, 60
heroes, firefighters as, 100–103
"Heroes Who Fight Fire" (Riis), 94, 101
heroism, 24, 51, 93, 95, 120, 124, 126; of firefighters, 96, 100–103, 113; legal, 11, 23, 27
The Hidden Hand (Southworth), 11, 19; accidents and collisions in, 33; Day, Clara, in, 25–26; fright and shock in, 36–39; human sensorium in, 21; legal proceedings in, 21–23, 26–27; physical and emotional security in, 21, 34; race and gender politics in, 21; safety and danger in, 21, 22–23, 32. *See also* Capitola Black
Hidden House, 25, 27, 28, 29, 32
Hoffman, Frederick L., 106–108
Holden, Edward S., 117–118, 120, 133n1
Home on the Rails (Richter), 31, 49
"Honor's Fortune" (Alcott), 30
hostile machine culture, 20
How Our Days Became Numbered (Bouk), 105–106

How the Other Half Lives (Riis), 94–95, 95
How to Analyze Railroad Reports (Moody), 82
"How to Figure the Extinction of a Race" (Du Bois), 107
Huet, Marie-Hélène, 121
humanities, environmental, 9, 14–15
humanity, 5, 36, 94, 104, 121
human sensorium, 20–21, 23, 35
human vulnerability, 11, 24, 34, 91, 119–120, 124
Hurricane Hall, 19, 27–29
Hurricane Katrina, 99–100, 104, 120
Hurricane Maria, 99

imagined community, 55
individualism, liberal, 9
industrial accidents, 23, 75, 77
industrial capitalism, 14, 70–71
industrial culture, of nineteenth century, 6, 74
industrialization, 61, 77
industrial progress, 74, 77
industrial technology, in nineteenth century, 20
injuries, 13, 37, 52, 55, 56, 73
insecurity, 3–4, 27, 28
insurance companies, 104–105, 108, 115n16; economic structure of, 105; life evaluation with, 105, 109, 115n28; racist practices of, 106–108, 109, 115n22, 115n24; risk management of, 6–7, 16n14, 23, 106; San Francisco earthquake relating to, 127–130
insurance underwriting, fantasy of, 103
interdependence, 36, 40, 46, 103, 110, 111, 133
Interstate Commerce Commission, 83
invulnerability, 8, 9
"The Irish Section Foreman Who Taught Me How to Live" (Dreiser), 78
Ishmael, 23–24, 26–27, 36, 38
Ishmael (Southworth), 11, 23, 24

James, William, 120–121, 131
"jaywalker," 60, 61, 65n19

Jimmie, in "The Monster," 84, 96, 103, 110, 113
Johnson, Henry, 96, 97, 103–104, 106, 110–111, 112–113
journalist, Dreiser as, 9, 13, 67, 87n4
juridical subjecthood, 22

Kerber, Linda, 35–36
Klein, Naomi, 98, 114n8, 118

Lamey, H. T., 128–129
Land of Little Rain (Austin), 130
language: of agency, 56; of vulnerabilities, 7, 16n18, 46, 56, 125–126
law: failure of, 27–32; public court of, 27; tort, 22–23, 34–35, 38, 41n17, 75
legal issues: in *The Hidden Hand*, 21–23, 26–27; in *Ishmael*, 23–24; in nineteenth-century literature, 22
legal paternalism, 12, 24, 27, 33, 38
Le Noir, Gabriel, 25–26, 29, 30, 34–35, 39
liberal individualism, 9
Life of an American Fireman (Porter, Edwin), 102, 111
literary conventions, of sensation, 24
literary imagination, of nineteenth century, 6
litigiousness, 23
London, Jack, 3, 44, 124–126
The Lost Heiress (Southworth), 22
Luciano, Dana, 20
Luckhurst, Roger, 75
Lutes, Jean, 67, 87n2
Lynde, Francis, 49
Lyons, Paul, 2

Macpherson, Sandra, 56
"Maggie" (Crane), 97
manhood, 13, 79–80, 83, 86, 89n20
Margaret, in "The Black Bess," 47–48, 50, 51–52
Marks, G. H., 127
masculinity, 3, 8, 44, 71, 73, 81, 100–101; privileges of, 52, 72, 82; whiteness and, 3, 8, 13, 85, 96, 101, 102, 103, 110
mastery, 9, 13, 15, 100, 119, 132, 133

The Material Unconscious (Brown), 45
Metropolitan Life Insurance Company, 105, 108
middle-class white women, 20, 32, 44
"Midnight Ride" (Nelson), 50
"The Mighty Burke" (Dreiser), 71, 73–74, 76, 77–80, 83–84, 85–86; Teddy in, 71, 74, 80, 81–82, 87
"The Mighty Rourke" (Dreiser), 71, 73–74, 80–82, 83–86; Teddy as accountant in, 33, 79, 83–86
miscarriages, 37–38, 41n21, 61–62
Mitchell, S. Weir, 72
mobility, 44, 52, 55
modernity, 7, 56, 61; capitalist, 20; catastrophic logic of, 7, 16n15, 99; technological, 45–46, 52
modern societies, risk management of, 6–7
The Money Value of Man (Dublin), 105
"The Monster" (Crane), 9, 13–14, 91, 101; fire in, 103–104, 111; Jimmie in, 84, 96, 103, 110, 113; Johnson in, 96, 97, 103–104, 106, 110–111, 112–113; Trescott in, 103–104, 106, 113
Moody's Investors Service, 82
Moody's Manual of Railroads and Corporation Securities (Moody), 82
Moses and Monotheism (Freud), 76
Muldoon, William, 71–72, 77, 78, 81
myths, 9, 11–12

National Board of Fire Underwriters, 93
national prophesies, of insecurity, 3–4
National Safety Council, 86
"The Nation Roused Against Motor Killings," 59
natural disasters, 94, 98, 109, 120, 121–123, 132
nature, 62, 68, 73, 74, 82, 103, 113; of harms, 52, 124; mastery over, 14, 75, 91, 100, 112, 119, 132–133; state of, 3, 4–5
Nelson, Nell, 3, 12, 50–51
neurasthenia, 11, 48, 70, 71, 72–73, 76, 88n7; Dreiser and, 71, 77, 88n7
"Neurasthenia, The Result of Nervous Shock, As a Ground for Damages,"

76
newspaper role, 67–68
New York Central Railroad, 70, 72, 78, 82
New York Supreme Court, 33–34
nineteenth century: accidents in, 7, 9–10, 13, 21, 23; industrial culture of, 6, 74; industrial technology in, 20; technological innovations of, 6; transformation during, 13; vulnerable subjects during, 27; women plaintiffs in, 33–36
nineteenth-century American literature: imagination of, 6; legal issues in, 22; sentimental, 20; women fiction in, 19–20
nineteenth century sensorium, 23
Nixon, Rob, 10
Norton, Peter D., 59, 86

Oakley, Dorinda, 60–63
office technicalia, 79, 82, 83
Old Hurricane, 19, 22, 25, 27–29, 30–31, 34, 36
Oliver and WIFE v. The Town of La Valle Wisconsin, 37
On Railway and Other Injuries of the Nervous System (Erichsen), 75
"On Some Mental Effects of the Earthquake" (James), 121
"The Open Boat" (Crane), 97
otherness, 14, 97, 106, 119
outlaw texts, 22

paternalism, 8; domestic, 27; legal, 12, 24, 27, 33, 38
patriarchy, 22, 33, 63, 65n23
pedestrians, 59–60
personhood, 21, 23, 36, 37, 38
Peters, M. Sheffy, 12, 50
physical injuries, with fright and shock, 37
physical security, 21, 34
The Pioneers, 3
plaintiffs, women as, 33–36
political agency, 3, 8
Pollyanna (Porter, Eleanor): adaptation of, 58–59; car accident in, 57, 60; critics of, 58; as young orphan,

57–59
Porter, Edwin, 111
Porter, Eleanor, 57–59, 60
Precarious Life (Butler), 5, 9
precariousness, 8, 14, 51, 52, 97, 109, 132
precarity, 5, 10, 109
Pressed for Time (Wajcman), 11, 49
progress, 11, 31, 56, 98, 100, 102; of colony, Crater, 1, 2; discourse on, 7, 58, 132; economic, 14, 96; industrial, 74, 77; scientific, 5
Prout, H. G., 49–50
Prudential Life Insurance Company, 106–107
Purcell v. St. Paul City R. Co., 38

racial fear, 3, 30, 52, 106, 113
racial hierarchy, 2–3
racial terror, 2
racial violence, 10, 69
racial vulnerability, 14
racism, 109; of firefighters, 102–103; during Hurricane Katrina, 99; of insurance companies, 106–108, 109, 115n22, 115n24
"The Railroad and the People" (Dreiser), 77
railroad laborer, Dreiser as, 70, 72–74, 88n11
railroads, 31; accidents with, 23, 32, 41n14, 53–55, 68–71, 72, 75–77; accounting with, 13, 79, 80, 82–83, 86, 125; dangers of, 32, 52; industry of, 32; shock and trauma relating to, 75; technological violence with, 32
railway brain, 76
The Railway Journey (Schivelbusch), 49
reasonable man standard, of courts, 35–36
"The Record of Accident," 69
Reichman, Ravit, 56
Reminiscence and Lessons of the San Francisco Conflagration (Marks), 127
Reminiscences of the Old New York Fire Laddies, 101
resilience, xii, 58, 60, 70, 73
resistance, 8, 9, 22, 58, 63, 87
responsive state, 9, 11

Richter, Amy, G., 31, 49
rights, of women, 12, 27
Riis, Jacob A., 94–96, 99
risk: chance, accident and, 7; culture of, 6; ecological, 14; exposure to, 98; perceptions of, 7; technologies of, 7
risk management, 46; insurance relating to, 6–7, 16n14, 23, 106; of modern societies, 6–7
risk society, 45–46, 56, 58, 64n6
A Romance in Transit (Lynde), 49
Rowlandson, Thomas, 123–124
Rozario, Kevin, 7

Sabsay, Leticia, 9
safety, 21, 22–23, 29, 32, 104–105
"Safety in Railroad Travel" (Prout), 49
San Francisco earthquake: cosmopolitan flotsam with, 125, 132; destruction by, 121–129; evidence collection of, 120, 134n3; insurance claims relating to, 127–130; narratives of, 119–120, 121–130; seismology shaped by, 117–118, 121, 130; urban development after, 123
San Francisco Underwriter's Association, 126
savages, in *The Crater*, 2–3, 4–5
"Saving lives at a tenement-house fire," 92, 93
Schivelbusch, Wolfgang, 49, 62
Schumpeter, Joseph, 14, 93–94, 97–98, 118
scientific progress, 5
scientific racism, 105–108. *See also* Frederick L. Hoffman; Nathan Shaler
security, 21, 27–28, 34
seismology, 117–118, 121, 130
self-made man, 8
self-mastery, 13, 60
sensation novel, 19–20, 32, 36
sensations, 121; of fright and shock, 36; literary conventions of, 24
sentiment, 19
sentimental literature, 20
September 11, 2001, 5, 95, 101, 114n11, 120
sexual violence, 20, 25, 69

Shaler, Nathan, 4–5, 16n8
shock. *See* fright and shock
The Shock Doctrine (Klein), 98
Shockley, Evie, 103
Side Lights (Lamey), 128–129
Sister Carrie, 77
The Sisters-in-Law (Atherton), 126
"Sixteen Dead" (Dreiser), 69
slavery, 3, 21, 23, 29, 40n9, 105, 109, 116n31
slow violence, 10
social justice, 8, 109
societal danger, 2–6
Sorrentino, Paul, 96
Southworth, E. D. E. N.: female protagonists of, 27; *The Hidden Hand* by, 11, 19, 21–23; *Ishmael* by, 11; serialization of, 36
"Southworth's Reimagining of the Married Women's Property Reforms" (Stockton), 22
Souvenir of the Destruction of San Francisco by Earthquake and Fire as seen through the Camera, 124
Spearman, Frank, 49
spectacles, 10, 110–111; of disaster, 25, 45, 46, 97, 99, 119, 120, 123, 124
speed, 39, 52, 54, 63, 94, 112; of culture, 11, 56; with technology, 6, 20, 44; transportation relating to, 46, 49, 51, 59
Spofford, Harriet P., 9, 12, 46
statistical management, of earthquakes, 119
Stockton, Elizabeth, 22, 27
"Story of an Eyewitness" (London), 124
"The Story of an Hour" (Chopin), 53–55
structural violence, 10
Studies on Hysteria (Freud and Breuer), 75
survivors, in *The Crater*, 1–2, 4–5

Tebeau, Marc, 94
technical innovations, 11, 17n25
technological and managerial culture, 10
technological capitalism, 97–98

technological dangers, 56
technological disaster, 45
technological innovations, 6, 45, 56
technological modernity, 45–46, 52
technological society, 6, 11
technological violence, 13, 44, 46, 56, 69; impact of, 12, 32, 52, 63
technologies, 6, 7, 9, 20, 44
threat horizon, 5–6
"The Toil of the Laborer" (Dreiser), 73–74, 77, 78
tort law, 22–23, 34–35, 38, 41n17, 75
transformation, during nineteenth century, 13
transportation, speed with, 46, 49, 51, 59
trans-spatial and trans-temporal threats, 5–6
trauma, xii, 53, 54, 75, 76, 131
The Trauma Question (Luckhurst), 75
Treatise on Earthquake Dangers, Causes and Palliatives (Rowlandson), 123
"The Tremblor" (Austin), 130–131
Trescott (doctor) in, "The Monster," 103–104, 106, 113
Tuscarora Hose Company Number Six, 111
Twain, Mark, 120–121
Twelve Men (Dreiser), 71, 78, 80–81

Union Fire Company, 101
universal vulnerability, 10
urban development, after San Francisco earthquake, 123

value, 3, 35, 45, 56, 83, 117, 125; cultural, 36, 113; human, 103–104, 105–109; in insurance, 105
victimhood, 10, 12, 52–53, 54, 63
victimization, vulnerabilities and, 36
violence, 2, 29; cultural, 47; domestic, 20, 25; racial, 10, 69; sexual, 20, 25, 69; slow, 10; structural, 10; technological, 12, 13, 32, 44, 46, 52, 56, 69; vulnerability relating to, 36
Virilio, Paul, 5, 56, 124
Virtual Modernism (Biers), 45, 111
"The Vital Statistics of the Negro" (Hoffman), 106–107

volunteerism, 101
vulnerabilities, 4, 15, 17n19, 52, 78, 81, 133; agency and, 9, 11; of Black, C., 21, 24–25, 39; collective, 5; concept of, 7–8; constitutive, 8; with earthquakes, 118–119; economic, 126; fright and shock relating to, 38; to harm, 5, 7, 21, 34, 40; human, 11, 24, 34, 119–120, 124; with Hurricane Katrina, 99; invulnerability and, 8, 9; language of, 7, 16n18, 46, 60, 125–126; meanings of, 8; negative associations with, 8; racial, 14; universal, 10; victimization and, 36; violence relating to, 36
Vulnerability in Resistance (Butler, Gambetti, Sabsay), 9
vulnerable subjects, during nineteenth century, 27

Wajcman, Judy, 11, 49
Warner, Susan, 57
Warren, Joyce, 33–34
Wertheimer, Eric, 103, 115n16
The Wheel of Life (Glasgow), 60
"When Every One is Panic Stricken/A Realistic Pen Picture of a Fire/In a Tenement" (Crane), 91–93, 94, 95, 101, 113n1
The Wide Wide World (Warner), 57
Williams, William Carlos, 43–45, 63, 64n1
women, 12, 19; ability of, 31, 39, 58; advocate for, 26–27; middle-class white, 20, 32, 44; physical and emotional security of, 21, 34; as plaintiffs, 33–36; rights of, 12, 27; whiteness and, 20, 32, 34, 44, 46, 51, 108
Women, Money, and The Law (Warren), 33–34
"Women, Mothers, and the Law of Fright" (Chamallas and Kerber), 35–36
Woodlock, Thomas, 82
Woolston, Mark, 1–2, 4, 6, 98, 121
wound culture, 67, 75, 76
wounds, 56
writers, women as, 12

Young, Elizabeth, 113

"The Young Housewife" (Williams), 43–44, 64n1

About the Author

Jennifer Travis is associate professor of English at St. John's University in New York City. She is the author of *Wounded Hearts: Masculinity, Law, and Literature in American Culture,* and the co-editor with Milette Shamir of *Boys Don't Cry: Rethinking Masculinity and Emotion in the U.S.* Her current work includes a forthcoming collection of essays, edited with Jessica DeSpain, *Teaching Nineteenth-Century American Literature in the Digital Age* (University of Illinois Press, Topics in the Digital Humanities) and an archival project with art historian Susan Rosenberg, which repurposes historical insurance materials in the Kathryn and Shelby Cullom Davis Library for a humanities audience. Her work has appeared in such journals as *American Literary History, Legacy,* and *Arizona Quarterly,* among others, and she is the recipient of fellowships from the American Association of University Women, The Humanities Institute at the University of Connecticut, and research grants for archival work from the Newberry Library, the Huntington Library, and the Gilder Lehrman Institute of American History.

www.ingramcontent.com/pod-product-compliance
Lightning Source LLC
Chambersburg PA
CBHW052049300426
44117CB00012B/2037